Fade to Black and White

Perspectives on a Multiracial America series
Joe R. Feagin, Texas A&M University, series editor

The racial composition of the United States is rapidly changing. Books in the series will explore various aspects of the coming multiracial society, one in which European-Americans are no longer the majority and where issues of white-on-black racism have been joined by many other challenges to white dominance.

Titles:

Melanie Bush, *Breaking the Code of Good Intentions*

Amir Mavasti and Karyn McKinney, *Middle Eastern Lives in America*

Richard Rees, *Shades of Difference: A History of Ethnicity in America*

Katheryn Russell-Brown, *Protecting Our Own: Race, Crime, and African Americans*

Elizabeth M. Aranda, *Emotional Bridges to Puerto Rico: Migration, Return Migration, and the Struggles of Incorporation*

Victoria Kaplan, *Structural Inequality: Black Architects in the United States*

Angela J. Hattery, David G. Embrick, and Earl Smith, *Globalization and America: Race, Human Rights, and Inequality*

Pamela Anne Quiroz, *Adoption in a Color-Blind Society*

Adia Harvey Wingfield, *Doing Business with Beauty: Black Women, Hair Salons, and the Racial Enclave Economy*

Erica Chito Childs, *Fade to Black and White: Interracial Images in Popular Culture*

Jessie Daniels, *Cyber Racism: White Supremacy Online and the New Attack on Civil Rights*

Fade to Black and White

Interracial Images in Popular Culture

Erica Chito Childs

ROWMAN & LITTLEFIELD PUBLISHERS, INC.
Lanham • Boulder • New York • Toronto • Plymouth, UK

ROWMAN & LITTLEFIELD PUBLISHERS, INC.

Published in the United States of America
by Rowman & Littlefield Publishers, Inc.
A wholly owned subsidary of The Rowman & Littlefield Publishing Group, Inc.
4501 Forbes Boulevard, Suite 200, Lanham, Maryland 20706
www.rowmanlittlefield.com

Estover Road
Plymouth PL6 7PY
United Kingdom

British Library Cataloguing in Publication Information Available

Library of Congress Cataloging-in-Publication Data

Childs, Erica Chito, 1971-
  Fade to black and white : interracial images in popular culture / Erica Chito Childs.
    p. cm.
  Includes index.
  ISBN-13: 978-0-7425-6079-6 (cloth : alk. paper)
  ISBN-10: 0-7425-6079-1 (cloth : alk. paper)
  ISBN-13: 978-0-7425-6080-2 (paper : alk. paper)
  ISBN-10: 0-7425-6080-5 (paper : alk. paper)
  ISBN-13: 978-0-7425-6541-8 (electronic)
  ISBN-10: 0-7425-6541-6 (electronic)
  1. Interracial marriage--United States--History. 2. Interracial marriage in mass media.
3. Sex in mass media. 4. Popular culture--United States. 5. Racism--United States. 6.
Race awareness--United States. 7. United States--Race relations. I. Title.
  E185.62.C54 2008
  305.800973--dc22

                                                      2008009692

Printed in the United States of America

♾ ™ The paper used in this publication meets the minimum requirements of
American National Standard for Information Sciences—Permanence of Paper for
Printed Library Materials, ANSI/NISO Z39.48-1992.

For Jada and Christopher, in the hope that you will one day be surrounded by images that reflect your beauty, intelligence, and the content of your character

Contents

~

Acknowledgments

This book has been part of a long journey of research that began with my first book *Navigating Interracial Borders*. After reading a draft of that first book, Eduardo Bonilla Silva encouraged me that there was a second book on the media examples right before me, and while I didn't believe him at first, I pursued the idea. Joe Feagin saw what Eduardo had seen and supported the project from its beginning stages. Without the support of both of them, this book would have never materialized. In particular, Joe Feagin helped me reframe my analysis within not only a cultural framework but also the structural framework of racism. A long list of friends and colleagues also offered valuable insight on all or part of the book, most notably France Winndance Twine, Jeanne Flavin, Heather Dalmage, Joane Nagel, David Brunsma, and Stephanie Laudone. All of my colleagues at Hunter College have been supportive of this research, and generous funding was provided by the Hunter College/NSF funded Gender Equity Project and a PSC-CUNY research grant. Hunter College students have provided great examples, and a number of students have worked in various capacities on this project such as Carolyn Ly and Ming Shi. At Roman & Littlefield, Alan McClare, Sarah Stanton, and Elaine McGarraugh have been instrumental in bringing the project to fruition. As always, this book could not have been completed without Christopher and Jada who have watched this project from the beginning, as 5- and 7-year olds who couldn't really understand how watching television and movies could be work, to the final stages of editing where now, as 8- and 10-year olds, they question the interracial images they see on their favorite shows.

INTRODUCTION

~

Fade to Black and White

Miscegenation tales of violation, tragedy, and capture; amalgamation stories of sacrifice, salvation, loss, and redemption; and utopian fairy tales in which love conquers all, sometimes literally. From *The Birth of a Nation* to *Jungle Fever*, the O. J. Simpson trial to the Duke lacrosse team media spectacles, interracial sex has been represented in a myriad of ways, conjuring up multiple images of sex, race, and taboo. Still interracial sex and marriage represent a transgression of symbolic racial borders and provide a space for groups to express and play out their ideas and prejudices about race and sex that are integral to understanding the ways in which sexuality is racialized and discourses on race are imbued with sexual meanings. Envy and desire of racial Others is as much a part of racism as fear and hatred. Since interracial couples exist on the color line within society, the ideas and beliefs about these unions are a lens through which we can understand contemporary race relations. While traditional studies of interracial couples have continually sought to explain the "phenomenon" of interracial unions—explaining how and why they came together, how they compare to same-race couples, or at best documenting the experiences of these couples—I argue that we should not interrogate the couples, but rather we should turn our critical eye on the processes that have created the images and ideas that construct couples as interracial in the first place.

Why Study Interracial Images?

This book offers a provocative and innovative look at interracial sexuality and marriage through the racial discourses and images used in popular culture and the media. The ways that interracial sex are depicted through images and discourse in popular culture and the media provide not only a lens into the contemporary views on interracial sex and marriage in society but also the larger racial hierarchy. These images (and the lack of depictions) both shape and are shaped by contemporary attitudes about race and sex in the United States today. Only in a society where race is given primary importance do we even have couples socially constructed as interracial. Still, news reports play up the idea that the numbers of interracial couples are growing, even skyrocketing, and present these unions as so common that interracial relationships barely raise an eyebrow anymore, especially given that Americans have elected Barack Obama, the first black biracial president. Yet according to the latest U.S. Census data in 2000, 94.1 percent of all marriages were between people of the same race, with only 0.6 percent of all marriages between blacks and whites and 0.9 percent of marriages between white men and Asian women. Media attention usually focuses on black-white relationships, even though these unions remain least common, while Asian-white intermarriage is most common, especially between white men and Asian women. If Latinos are separated and counted as a distinct group, interracial marriages between white men and Latinas account for 1.6 percent of all marriages, followed by 1.3 percent of all marriages being between white women and Latino men.[1] Interracial marriages remain a small percentage of all marriages, though media reports may tell us otherwise. Despite the relatively low number of interracial marriages, interracial sex and marriage remains an important issue to study for what it tells us about the roles of race, gender, and sexuality in contemporary society. While several recent works have explored this issue from legal, sociohistorical, and sociological perspectives, these works at best briefly address popular culture/media images and influences.[2] Yet I argue that we can learn as much, if not more, from looking at the ways interracial sex and marriage are described, discussed, depicted, and imagined as we can from interviewing couples identified as interracial or from surveying communities about their attitudes on interracial mating. Also, those studies that do explore media and cultural representations of interracial sexuality have tended to focus on one type, such as black-white couples or white-Asian couples[3] with virtually no discussion of the representations of interracial romance of Latinos, whereas my analysis looks at varied racial combinations, examining the different meanings and context based on the race and gender of those individuals involved.

Beyond the importance of looking at the issue of interracial sex and marriage, the relevance of studying popular culture and the media is clear in the growing number of works that use this approach to explore issues of race, gender, and sexuality.[4] The mass media, including popular culture, is a legitimate source of data for research that contributes to our understanding of not only popular culture but also our collective beliefs, values, and social institutions.[5] Media, in all its varied forms, can have a normalizing regulatory function, yet it is also a place where meanings and practices are constructed, negotiated, and consumed.[6] Popular cultural forms such as television, film, or music "play a crucial role in this ongoing meaning-making process,"[7] especially given that many in the United States live in racially homogeneous areas and social networks are still largely monoracial. As Hernán Vera and Andrew M. Gordon argue,

> the movies, along with many other products of popular culture, such as television and music, provide us with the elements we use in our everyday life to think with and to function in an increasingly complex world. We live in the bubble of our stock of knowledge, that collection of ways of thinking, feeling, and acting we share with other members of our society . . . we live using sincere fictions, those mental templates we use to relate to others. (2003, 185)

Since cultural representations "draw upon and operate on the basis of a kind of generalized societal common sense and the terms of society and people's social location in it,"[8] these mass media representations of interracial sex and relationships are part of the ways the interracial couples' relationships and everyday experiences are "racialized," meaning that the relationship takes on or is given a racial meaning within the context of American society.[9] As Patricia White argues:

> Cinema is public fantasy that engages spectators' particular, private scripts of desire and identification. Equally at stake in spectatorship are the way organized images and sounds psychically imprint us and the way they mediate social identities and histories. (1999, xv)

In essence, the ways that interracial couples are socially constructed within media and popular culture mirrors the social construction of race and racial groups in society.

Therefore, I explore the cultural images and sociopolitical discourses on interracial couplings that are produced and reproduced in prime-time television, mainstream American films, popular music, media coverage of high-profile events, and the Internet. Methodologically, cultural analysis of film, television, and media is complex for a number of reasons. Given the complex dynamics operating in mass media and the varied social locations of the viewers, there are multiple readings on any given text. Films, television, and other media forms are "sites of constant ideological struggle," where a hegemonic work is produced and then negotiated by the audience.[10] As Stuart Hall argues, film creates meaning, yet the meanings attached to these images are not "wholly determined by the producer and simply accepted by a passive audience."[11] People invest very different meanings in the images they see, so it is impossible to know how the varied audience receives the representation, though it can be argued that there is a dominant ideology or "dominant gaze" that is produced. In other words, the audience is encouraged to empathize and identify with the images as natural, universal, and beyond challenge.[12] The issue is not only about who creates the images but also who is the intended audience, and given the marketing mind-set of all media, there is a certain demographic or possibly multiple demographics being pursued. The reception of any text such as film is a dynamic and dialectical process, where the viewer can accept or reject the dominant ideology that is produced. As media scholars have pointed out, spectators, particularly spectators of color, may read the representation as a "dominant narrative" that reinforces stereotypes, or they may construct an "alternative narrative" that alters or rejects the stereotypes.[13] Regardless of the interpretation, popular culture and media (re)produces racialized images and discourses on interracial relationships, where interracial love can represent a multiracial utopia, a spiral into chaos and squalor, or a temporary exotic diversion off the beaten path.

Looking at these mediums, there are many questions to be answered. What does "interracial couple" mean, and how do the meanings attached to these unions differ based on the race and gender of those involved? Who produces these meanings, and what purpose do they serve? As Foucault (1990) argues—in his broad historical framework on the relationship between power/knowledge and sexuality—it is necessary to question what is the meaning or significance of the discourse against interracial sexuality, "what reciprocal effects of power and knowledge they ensure . . . and what conjunction and what force relationships make their utilization necessary."[14] In other words, if interracial sexuality is constructed as deviant, it is important to consider, Whom does it benefit and why is it still significant? Also, the meanings of *interracial* vary greatly depending on whether we are looking at a black man with a white woman (often the first image that comes to mind for most when the word *interracial* is used) or a white man with an Asian woman. And what does *interracial couple* mean when looking at Latinas/os? Was singer/actress Jennifer Lopez's relationship with the African American music mogul Sean

"P. Diddy" Combs an interracial relationship, or was her relationship with the white actor Ben Affleck interracial? Given the fluidity of identity among Latinos in the United States and the difficulties of racial designations, what does the idea of an interracial couple mean, if anything, when talking about Latinos?[15] When an interracial union is shown, is it a ploy to attract non-white audiences to an otherwise all-white production, or is it still geared primarily toward whites, as a way to symbolically indulge in erotic, taboo, interracial sexual fantasies?[16] And how does this change when we are talking about lesbian and gay interracial couples, which are rarely visible on television or mainstream film? The ways these images are received and how they are then used in racial communities' discourses can differ greatly.

While some of these questions may seem to have a simple answer, upon closer look, the images produced about interracial couples are markedly complex and offer a lens through which to understand whiteness, blackness, and otherness in relation to each other as well as the larger state of race relations. Films and other media forms can appear to espouse rather liberal attitudes toward race, while maintaining a rigid hierarchy regarding interracial relations. These images and depictions of interracial couples reveal the underlying beliefs about interracial unions that are prevalent within communities—and are understood as not only a reflection of dominant beliefs but also a powerful influence on what people believe. Coverage of incidents involving interracial sex also illustrates the different ways these stories are presented, understood, and received. So it is important to consider how many interracial couples will be tolerated, and more importantly, what story lines, images, and representations will be accepted and embraced. These representations of interracial sex and couples are not simply abstract ideas but have emerged out of everyday realities and experiences; they are an integral part of racial ideology, "a substantive set of ideas and notions defending white power and privilege as meritorious and natural and accenting the alleged superiority of whites and the inferiority of those who are racially oppressed."[17] While we may have different views on what constitutes interracial and there are multiple interpretations possible, the movies, television, and the media provide us with ways of understanding who interracial couples are and what these unions represent.

Framing the Images

To show how these images and discourses not only reflect popular attitudes about different groups but also contribute to securing different racial positions in society, I rely on theories of structural racism and critical perspectives on popular cultural images. In reviewing America's history, an integral part of the racist framework has been the stories that are told in communities, in the media, and in popular culture to rationalize and legitimize white oppression of blacks and other racial minorities. Certain stories have been told about interracial relations, while other stories were silenced or ignored. And these stories continue to be predominantly controlled by a small group of white, elite men. The importance of the powerful white media elite who own and control the images cannot be overemphasized, though as Feagin (2006) documents, many mainstream scholars discuss these issues "in ways that remove the dominant white agents of discrimination largely from view."[18] Using both a cultural and structural analysis, I will introduce the recurring themes in representations of interracial sex and relationships in television, film, media coverage of high-profile incidents and other forms of popular culture such as music and sports. While news reports and even some academic scholars may trumpet the increased number of interracial couples in television and film as a signal of increased acceptance—not unlike early assimilationist theory that saw intermarriage as a sign of a racial or ethnic group's acceptance into society—I argue that these representations do more to solidify ideas of interracial relationships as deviant, detrimental, outside the norm, or only possible with an exceptional person of color to highlight the mass of unexceptional people of color, who often are portrayed as vehemently opposed to interracial unions.[19] These representations are part of the institutionalized system of racism and discrimination and embody the principles of inequality and oppression in very specific ways, and for very specific purposes. The varied representations can be discussed in three main conceptual frames of what stories can be told: (1) interracial relationships are deviant, especially if it includes a white woman; (2) the interracial relationships are used to privilege, protect, and illustrate the power of whiteness, particularly white men; and (3) interracial relationships are used to perpetuate racist attitudes and practice while denying race matters.

First Frame: Constructing Interracial Relationships as Problems

When images of interracial trysts do emerge, they tend to be deviant, ranging from temporary hookups, absurd pairings, dangerous encounters, relationships in a remote or distant land, or symbolic of a spiral into disorder and chaos. The contemporary patterns of representing interracial relationships as problematic or ignoring them altogether are part of "the treatment of human sexuality in American society . . . a curious combination of censorship and excessive visibility, of embarrassed silences and talk-show babble."[20] More importantly, interracial representations reflect how we think about race and sex in America, since the stories that are told are the ones that we are familiar with and want to cling to.

Still in media and popular culture, despite popular reports by various news outlets, interracial relationships remain largely invisible and are not featured. By not showing these relationships, these unions remain outside the norm.[21] Throughout the various media forms, I will document the relative invisibility of interracial relationships. This invisibility takes the form of interracial pairings cast opposite each other without any romance or even altering stories to exclude romance if the characters are of different races. This invisibility also extends to the media, who tend to ignore stories in which interracial couples are persecuted. Or even more frequently, incidents where black women have been sexually assaulted or raped by white men are largely ignored or presented as beyond belief.[22] The reasons behind the lack of depictions of interracial couples will also be addressed, particularly in terms of the ways the producers, directors, and writers discuss their casting choices and story lines.

The majority of interracial stories we see and hear on television, film, and in the news—especially if it involves a white woman—are removed from, or in some way exist outside of, mainstream society. This pattern of deviance is significant given that these representations do not appear out of nowhere, are created by a handful of persons, and are part of the larger racial ideologies and structure of society.[23] I include a variety of types of representations found in news reports, television, and film depictions under the umbrella of deviance. In film and television representations, interracial trysts are used for comedy or an obstacle in the main plot through temporary hookups or absurd pairings. Interracial pairings are also used to supply an exotic twist or to heighten the intrigue through dangerous encounters, relationships in a remote or distant land, or spirals into disorder and chaos. While news media usually ignore any stories about interracial couples other than a few celebratory pieces on color-blind love, a media spectacle erupts when there are allegations of sexual assault, rape, and murder in which a white woman is the victim and a man of color is the accused, especially in comparison to the lack of attention to black women as victims. Representations of interracial relations and the decisions that are made about what can be told and what is "unspeakable" reveal the ideas, practices, and prerogatives of the dominant group—whites, and more specifically, white men.

Second Frame:
Privileging, Protecting, and Empowering Whiteness

While this book focuses on the representations of interracial relationships, the images and discourses surrounding these unions are mainly about defining what whiteness is and what it should not be. As emerges in the first frame of deviance, interracial relationships are used to create certain ideas about other racial groups, their position in society, and the reasons why these unions don't and shouldn't happen, particularly for white women. This second frame of representations involves the tendency to use interracial relationships to highlight the goodness of white society, white people, or a specific white individual, particularly white men.

This occurs through a variety of strategies, including having the white man save the woman of color and often her whole community. It also takes the form of depicting the person of color as an exception who is different from others in that individual's community, thereby worthy of being with a white person; and/or presenting communities of color as racist and unaccepting of whites and interracial relationships. These representations are not new ideas but reformulations of ideas that are learned and passed down from families and through the media: "another type of intergenerational reproduction and transmission of cultural understandings that sustains systemic racism involves the perpetuation of critical racial images and stereotypes by such cultural institutions as the mass media, which have mostly been controlled generation after generation by whites in power."[24] This should not be surprising given that white men control most media outlets, in terms of the creation, production, and promotion of media. Whoever creates the images and "controls the language in which issues are discussed controls the issues,"[25] and most U.S. mainstream popular culture and media representations still operate from a white perspective.[26] Furthermore, "the public domain is one where white masculinity guards its power most zealously."[27] While new spaces of inclusion for blacks, Latinos, and Asians have opened, the ability or desire to provide alternative representations of interracial relationships is limited, and still mainstream films produced by black or minority filmmakers are owned, censored, or at least influenced by whites in terms of the final project that is produced.

Third Frame:
The Simultaneous Perpetuation and Denial of Racism

The two frames—representations of interracial trysts as either deviant and removed from mainstream (white) society, or heroic stories of whiteness—

serve to reinforce specific messages about contemporary race relations. Interracial couples are also used as the poster child for the claims that America has become color-blind. In media and popular culture, such as print and television commercials, "there's an America that's full of neighborhoods where black and white kids play softball together, where biracial families email photos online and where Asians and blacks dance in the same nightclub."[28] Yet, as Darnell Hunt argues,

> [I]n a time when the U.S. population is diversifying at a dizzying rate, when popular accounts of race present it as an anachronistic concern, when color-blind ideology shapes much of our public policy, and when affirmation of cultural hybridity and multiple subjectivities is all the rage, blackness remains a curious, palpable presence in our land. (2005, 1)

Nowhere is this clearer than when interracial sex or even the possibility of it is introduced, even if only in film or music. By making more noticeable portrayals of interracial relationships that tell particular stories, race can be simultaneously affirmed and denied. As Patricia Hill Collins argues, the irony of color-blind arguments that maintain race no longer matters is that they depend on having some visible diversity in order to claim we are color-blind: it would problematize the color-blind argument if all media were all-white because that would seem racially exclusive. Therefore, not showing interracial unions ever would be problematic because it would serve as "evidence" that whites opposed these unions. Yet the interracial representations need to put forth very particular images of color that are safely contained, as I outline above, in terms of either making these unions deviant or pushing a story that privileges whites. Therefore, the third theme focuses on how these representations seek to deny white racism and construct communities of color as "racist" while still perpetuating ideas of racial difference.

Looking at the patterns of representations, these interracial stories put forth messages about race, racism, and race relations. Film, television, media accounts, and even the Internet can be read and analyzed as *texts* that reveal not only dominant beliefs about interracial couplings but also America's racial hierarchy. Interracial stories are more than entertaining images; rather, these interracial images function to serve the white hegemony in making interracial relationships deviant by projecting stereotypes and racial biases as "reality."[29] Stories about interracial unions problematize these relationships while denying that race matters and attempt to protect whiteness by constructing persons and communities of color as the problem. This is done in a number of different ways, such as portraying racism—and more specifically white opposition to interracial unions—as something that happened in the past, through media accounts of historical events or films set in past decades. In contemporary stories, an individual racist white person or small group of extreme racists may be portrayed, but whites as a group are not depicted as racist or opposed to interracial relationships. Instead, the problems with interracial relationships are either presented as based in the relationship or the white characters oppose the relationship for other supposedly nonrace-related reasons. Also, it is increasingly more common for individuals, families, and communities of color to be portrayed as the ones who oppose interracial unions. At the same time, from the comfort of their own living room television, home computer, or neighborhood movie theater, white audiences can consume images of racial Others and interracial sex visually without actually having to experience it, secure in the knowledge that race does not matter and therefore they are not racist.

Outline of the Book

While I have divided the ideas into chapters loosely based around the media form, the themes and stories travel and emerge sometimes in every chapter. Just as particular media spectacles or images may emerge in different media arenas, so the different parts of the story are hashed out in each chapter. In chapter 1, I provide an overview of the historical conditions of the different racial groups in terms of how whites constructed ideologies and enacted treatment based on concerns over interracial sexuality, tying this to the emergence of early media images of the different groups. Chapter 2 includes an in-depth analysis of television depictions of interracial unions, beginning with a brief historical discussion. For television images, prime-time shows that have included an interracial couple since 1995 are analyzed in depth and categorized by the dominant themes that emerge in the representations.[30] In chapters 3 and 4, I provide an analysis of a selection of mainstream contemporary (1990s–present) films whose story lines involve an interracial couple, dividing it up by how white men with women of color are portrayed and how men of color are portrayed with white women, and to a lesser extent with woman of a race other than their own. While my search of films was exhaustive, my analysis does not include all films with an interracial couple; the films that are discussed were chosen because of their high profile and mass marketing.[31] Also, any films that did not fit the patterns were noted. Chapters 5 and 6 look at media and certain forms of popular culture and the different representations and receptions that exist. In chapter 5, media coverage of interracial events is explored through a brief discussion of major media stories involving individuals of a different race. I also juxtapose media coverage of the rape allegations and pretrial motions against the black Los Angeles Laker basketball player Kobe Bryant and the white Duke University lacrosse team to explore media accounts of interracial sex and the gendered and racialized coverage. Chapter 6 tackles the intersecting media worlds often described as multiracial—focusing on hip-hop music, sports, and popular culture geared toward youth—to see if different representations exist or are emerging in these areas.

Through these interracial images and stories, we see how race, sex, and a myriad of issues are imagined and lived in contemporary America. By looking at these media worlds through these varied chapters, not only do we experience how interracial couples are understood and represented but also examine the contemporary discourses and worldviews on the issues of race, gender, class, and sexuality that are encompassed in these representations. Since popular media forms are arguably one of the most influential sources of racial ideology, it is important to critically analyze the dominant images put forth and to ask the question, What do or would "suitable representations" look like?[32] Do the contemporary depictions of interracial couples signal a trend toward greater acceptance, therefore improving race relations, or do the depictions simply reproduce certain images and ideas about these unions and the racial hierarchy? Is the contemporary trend of increasing depictions of interracial couples something new, or is it simply a repackaging of old ideas in a new fashion? When the high-profile media case ends or the movie screen fades to black and white, what interracial image are we left with?

Notes

1. Looking at interracial marriage rates is complicated because there is a difference if you consider Latinos, who can be of any race. The Census estimates that about 19 percent of all interracial marriages are between blacks and whites. In 2000, 1.9 percent of all opposite-sex cohabitations were between blacks and whites. Rachel Sullivan, Long Island University, provided these Census statistics.

2. Chito Childs 2005; Dalmage 2000; Kennedy 2002; Moran 2001; Romano 2002; Root 2001.

3. For an excellent analysis of white-Asian interracial sexuality in selected films before 1990, see Gina Marchetti, *Romance and the "Yellow Peril": Race, Sex, and Discursive Strategies in Hollywood Fiction* (Berkeley: University of California Press, 1993); also Gary Hoppenstand, "Yellow Devil Doctors and Opium Dens: A Survey of the Yellow Peril Stereotypes in Mass Media Entertainment," in *The Popular Culture Reader*, 3rd edition, eds. Christopher D. Geist and Jack Nachbar (Bowling Green, OH: Bowling Green University Popular Press, 1983), 171–85.

4. Patricia Hill Collins's *Black Sexual Politics* (Routledge, 2004) incorporates discussion of popular culture and the important role it plays in black communities, especially in connection to norms of race, gender, and sexuality. Scholars such as Herman Gray and Darnell Hunt have documented the production and reception of images of African Americans in television, film, and other popular culture forms, while Clara Rodriguez has written about the representations of Latinos in film and media, arguing that it is important to consider these representations since "film critics and researchers alike give scant voice to the presence of Latinos." There have been a number of recent books that look specifically at popular culture and media, such as Linda Williams's *Playing the Race Card: Melodramas of Black and White from Uncle Tom to O. J. Simpson* (Princeton, 2001), which explores how representations of race revolve around certain stories or "melodramas" about black and white, and Hernán Vera and Andrew M. Gordon's *Screen Saviors: Hollywood Fictions of Whiteness* (Lanham, MD: Rowman & Littlefield, 2003), which documents the patterns of representing white men as saviors in film.

5. Ferguson and Golding 1997; Miller and McHoul 1998.

6. Herman Gray discussed these ideas at the American Sociological Association meetings in 2005.

7. Hunt 2005, 2.

8. Gray 2004 [1995], 9.

9. Omi and Winant 1994. Feagin (2006, 7) notes that "racial formation theory assesses well and insightfully the critical importance of racial ideology but not so much the historical foundation and systemic character of contemporary racial oppression."

10. Marchetti 1993, 283.

11. Hall 1981; Marchetti 1993, 283.

12. Russell 1995, 57; see also Crenshaw and Peller 1993; Delgado 1995.

13. See Manthia Diawara, "Black Spectatorship: Problems of Identification and Resistance," *Screen* 29, 4 (Autumn 1988): 66–79. For a discussion of these issues of representation and reading of lesbian depictions see Patricia White, *Uninvited: Classical Hollywood Cinema and Lesbian Representability* (Bloomington: Indiana University Press, 1999).

14. Foucault 1990, 102.

15. In my earlier work on black-white couples, I was always being told by white neighbors in Rhode Island to look in Central Falls because there are "lots of interracial couples." Yet these "interracial couples" in Central Falls (one would need only to check the Census data that show that the majority of the residents are Latino) are actually Latino individuals of different hues and colors but from the same ethnic background, primarily Puerto Rican.

16. Gina Marchetti makes this argument in her work *Romance and the "Yellow Peril": Race, Sex, and Discursive Strategies in Hollywood Fiction*, where she documents that the numerous films, especially in the mid-1900s, that featured Asian-white couplings on the silver screen were not geared toward Asians or Asian Americans since

they represented such a small percentage of the American population, so she argues these images were for whites, as "signifiers of racial otherness to avoid the far more immediate racial tensions between blacks and whites or the ambivalent mixture of guilt and hatred toward Native Americans and Hispanics." See pages 1 and 6.

17. See Joe Feagin, *Systemic Racism: A Theory of Oppression* (New York: Routledge, 2006), 28. Feagin argues that in America, there is systemic racism, which "encompasses a broad range of racialized dimensions," including racist framing and racist ideology, which would include the representations of interracial sex and relationships that I cover in this book.

18. Feagin 2006, 4–5.

19. Scholars such as Derrick Bell, Patricia Hill Collins (2004), and Joe Feagin (2006) have argued that whites make changes that give the illusion of equality, which makes it harder to show the racism that still permeates society while maintaining the power and privilege. See Derrick Bell, *Silent Covenants: Brown v. Board of Education and the Unfulfilled Hopes for Racial Reform* (New York: Oxford University Press, 2004) and Patricia Hill Collins, *Black Sexual Politics: African Americans, Gender, and the New Racism* (New York: Routledge, 2004).

20. Hill Collins 2004, 36.

21. It is widely argued that racial and ethnic minorities, as well as gays and lesbians, are underrepresented on television and in film or negatively stereotyped. Darnell Hunt, Herman Gray, and others document the lack of positive representation of African Americans and the overrepresentation of negative depictions. Clara Rodriguez stresses the importance of giving voice to the role of Latinos in media and popular culture, because media critics and researchers too often ignore Latinos.

22. In 2007, a young black woman was held captive, tortured, sexually assaulted, forced to eat feces, and raped by a group of six white men and women, but it received minimal media attention.

23. As Vera and Gordon note, film and television are "part of a project, part of something that wants to be brought into being" (2003, 85).

24. Feagin 2006, 45.

25. Joe Feagin and Hernán Vera, *White Racism*, page 118. They make this argument in relation to the "Willie" Horton case, in which Republicans during the 1988 presidential race used this case in which a black man raped a white woman while on a prison furlough. They essentially renamed him "Willie," since in court documents and according to the man himself he had always been called William.

26. "The contemporary media industry . . . is controlled by a handful of multinational media conglomerates whose market power overrides virtually all other forces in shaping the programming choices that confront viewers." Darnell Hunt, "Making Sense of Blackness on Television," *Channeling Blackness: Studies on Television and Race in America* (Oxford: Oxford University Press, 2005), 16. While I originally planned to devote a portion of the book to the images created by and for nonwhite audiences and how interracial relationships are portrayed between racial groups other than whites, there were relatively few depictions in mainstream American films and

television. Yet throughout the book, whether interracial relationships are depicted differently by black filmmakers or in films geared toward Latino or African American audiences will be explored.

27. John Fiske, "Hearing Anita Hill (and Viewing Bill Cosby)," in Darnell Hunt, "Making Sense of Blackness on Television," *Channeling Blackness: Studies on Television and Race in America* (Oxford: Oxford University Press, 2005), 121.

28. Erin Texeira, "Multiracial Scenes Now Common in TV Ads," February 15, 2005. Accessed at www.msnbc.msn.com/id/6975669.

29. In *Seeing Films Politically*, Mas'ud Zavarzadeh (1991, vi) notes "that both momentous and trivial films fulfill this hegemonic function . . . the distortive messages conveyed in so-called minor or trivial films have a far greater effect on popular culture precisely because of their insignificant nature; they create 'the space in which the daily is negotiated; it is the space that is represented as *real*.'" Other scholars have argued that films offer sincere fictions of white saviors that "attempt to efface the memory of the origins of white privilege and to deny its continuing existence and its appalling results" (Vera and Gordon 2003, 15).

30. I will examine different forms of media, using a theoretical, nonrandom sampling method based on grounded theory. While the frequency of interracial relationships portrayed will be noted, given the scope of the project to give a comprehensive overview of contemporary representations of interracial sexuality, it is necessary to use a grounded approach where patterns emerge, and the collective meanings can be discussed and examples can be given. In each section, the analysis is similar, with the emphasis placed on how the couple is characterized, what role "race" plays within the story line, what are the dominant images of interracial unions, and what meanings are attached to these unions. Also, the different dynamics depending on the race and gender of the couple will be noted. After identifying and providing documentation of patterns that exist in the representations of interracial sex and couples, the underlying ideologies and the historical and contemporary conditions they are tied to will be clearer.

31. See www.imdb.com; www.cinemedia.com; www.afionline.org; moviebox office.about.com.

32. Herman Gray (2004 [1995]) uses the term *suitable representations* in regard to depictions of blackness; see also Gooding-Williams 1993.

CHAPTER ONE

~

Historical Realities and Media Representations of Race and Sexuality

Popular culture and media representations of interracial sexuality and relationships have to be interrogated against the backdrop of the historical practices and socially constructed ideologies about interracial intimacy, especially in terms of the specific beliefs and practices involving different groups. Constructing race is a collective process and practice, which produces "a distinctive set of meanings."[1] In particular, race and sex mix together in many ways to create distinct ideologies about all groups: the "clash of sexualities was an important feature in the development of ideologies that defined each group and the construction of ethnic boundaries that divided them."[2] Interracial sexuality was forbidden through public discourse and laws, especially between white women and all nonwhite men. For white men, having sex with women of any race was acceptable at least as long as it was not public. Yet based on the different histories of the various racial and ethnic groups, distinctly different images of interracial sexuality were produced depending on the race and gender of those involved. Women and men were racialized differently, and racial groups were constructed in different ways that justified their treatment and position in society. Most importantly, whiteness was constructed through this exclusion and oppression of other groups, especially African Americans.[3]

White Europeans built America from the very beginning upon the exploitation of people of color to ensure the economic and social power, status, and wealth of whites. "White-generated and white-maintained oppression is far more than a matter of individual bigotry, for it has been from the beginning a material, social and ideological reality."[4] While white Europeans colonized America and built the nation on top of Native Americans, with the enslavement of black Africans, and through the exploitation and/or exclusion of Asians, Latinos, and Others, this new nation was also constructed through ideologies, including sexualized beliefs about different groups. The issue of power can never be overemphasized in terms of who has the ability and access to create the images, determine the discourses that prevail, and ultimately construct the framework in which we live and watch. People of color "have been the objects of representation rather than its subjects and creators because racism often determines who gets access to the means of representation in the first place . . . the question of power at issue in the ability to make and wield representations."[5] The ideas constructed about different racial groups have more to do with constructing the identity of those who are creating the images than those the images are created about.[6] As Lipsitz argues, there is "a possessive investment in whiteness,"[7] and whites help maintain their dominant position by constructing and strengthening ideas about whiteness, often through this construction of otherness. This still happens in contemporary media and popular culture depictions where what white means is told and shown through depictions of nonwhites.

While the varied and different histories of racial and ethnic groups have been well documented by other scholars, here I will briefly explore the mosaic of contemporary images that come out of the changing realities of race for different groups, connecting the separate yet intertwined representations and realities. These images we see in film, television, and news media are mirrors, created to reflect and influence social behavior in much the same way that laws and policies are created, and in America it is largely a white male elite that produces these images as well as the realities. In what follows I will briefly present the images, attitudes, and behaviors associated with the different racial groups, particularly as they relate to interracial relationships. The role whites, and more specifically white elites, had and still have in creating, cultivating, and enforcing ideas of racial superiority and the racial hierarchy will be reviewed.

Imagining the Other

Native American Indians

Early accounts of white Europeans document the way sexuality was an integral part of how indigenous peoples were racialized, and their subsequent treatment. As early as 1504, Amerigo Vespucci wrote "[f]or their women, being very lustful, cause the private parts of their husbands to swell up to such a huge size that they appear deformed and disgusting."[8] Vespucci further described how these "lustful" women "when they had the opportunity of copulating with Christians, urged by excessive lust, they defiled and prostituted themselves," blaming interracial sexual encounters on the indigenous women.[9] The idea of indigenous peoples as different and less civilized included these ideas about deviant and excessive sexual practices that were contrasted against the white European Christian explorers and settlers. Early discourses about "Indians" warned of the dangers through captivity narratives, where white men were killed and white women raped. While there were more instances of white men impregnating or marrying "Indian" women popularized in tales of Pocahontas, the dangers of white-indigenous relations were clearly outlined. "The big, dark Indian was pictured simultaneously as a thrill and a sexual threat to white women and consequently a competitive sexual threat to white men."[10] By constructing indigenous peoples as dangerous—physically, morally, and sexually—the white colonizers could justify their removal and slaughter. To discourage whites from engaging in relationships with "Indians," during the 1600s and 1700s discourses were also developed about whites who lived with or slept with indigenous peoples—that they were untrustworthy and morally corrupt. Yet there were conflicting views on white-indigenous marriages: some scholars argued that these unions were a "shame and disgrace," while others suggested that white men who married "Indian" women but remained firmly grounded in white settlements with little or no contact with her peoples were more accepted than those who lived amongst the indigenous people.[11] Still, if these marriages did occur and were tolerated or recognized favorably, it was almost exclusively between a white man and an indigenous woman. By the 1900s, as native peoples were massacred or stripped of their lands and confined to reservations, the perceived sexual danger they presented faded. As Joane Nagel argues:

> Real Indians were to be relegated to history, and the imagined Indian was transformed in whites' minds, if not in native realities, from a hypersexualized savage into a tamed domestic put in service to the American national project. America could now use this new, improved, safely resexualized, and thus truly noble savage to refashion its own image of itself.[12]

The stories that continue to be told about Native Americans romanticize whites' relationships with native tribes and peoples, such as Disney's *Pocahontas* or stories of white men incorporated into a tribe such as *Dances with Wolves*.

African Americans

Just as the Americas and its indigenous peoples were imagined as savagely sexual and sexually different, Africa and its people had been racialized and sexualized in the writings of white Europeans, who described large genitalia, "lustful" behaviors, and deviant practices on their travels to Africa.[13] Similar discourses accompanied the interactions between white Europeans and enslaved Africans in America. In the early days of the colonies such as Virginia, there were both white indentured servants and enslaved Africans "who occupied a common social space—a terrain of racial liminality that had not yet developed rigid caste lines . . . shar(ing) a condition of class exploitation and abuse."[14] Initially religion was used to differentiate groups, with the English colonists identified as Christians and Africans characterized as heathens. Yet as Africans were more frequently converted to Christianity, the law became "no negro or Indian, though baptized and free, should be allowed to purchase Christians."[15]

Whites inscribed racial difference, with whiteness defined as free, civilized, and superior against blackness, which was defined as savage, inferior, and destined to be enslaved. Whites both feared and desired blackness, projecting what they feared about themselves onto blackness. Therefore whiteness was equated with civilization and purity. Accompanying these ideologies emerged a discourse against white-black interracial intimacy, which was further used to construct racial boundaries.[16] Interracial sex was constructed as deviant within the institution of slavery, and from the beginning it was primarily aimed at preventing black African male slaves from engaging in sexual relations with white women. It has been well documented how whites created these ideas about black people to justify their enslavement.[17] In order to ensure that sexual relations between the races did not occur, those who engaged in interracial sex were formally and informally punished through fines, whippings, banishment, and/or imprisonment. Countless laws were passed, and a racist discourse was constructed that portrayed black bodies as degenerate, excessive, and animalistic in contrast to the desexualized and civilized ideal of white bodies.[18] For example, the 1691 Virginia law banned "the abominable and spurious issue" of interracial unions. Violators were punished with banishment, and any white woman who gave birth to a child from such a union would relinquish the child into thirty years of servitude.[19] Laws such as these played a major role in the construction of racial groups and set the standards for race relations, demonstrating how "law constructs race in a complex manner through both coercion and ideology, with legal actors as both conscious and unwitting participants."[20]

While black men were killed or physically brutalized for being in close proximity to a white woman, white men routinely physically and sexually abused black women. At the same time, black men were construed as sexual savages and black women were portrayed as promiscuous and immoral.[21] The image of black women and black femininity was also being devalued by white Eurocentric standards of beauty and femininity,[22] intensified by the lack of power that women, particularly black women, have in a patriarchal system relative to men. "The sexual slander of Africans directed attention away from the true scandal of whites' savage sexual treatment of blacks,"[23] such as the frequent abuse and lynching of black men for allegedly raping or desiring sexual relations with white women, as well as the widespread rape and sexual abuse of black women by white men.[24] The painful history of miscegenation, the rape of black women both during and after slavery, and the brutality inflicted upon black men by whites over the accusation of interracial sexuality has been well documented, often drawing on personal histories.[25] As Du Bois writes: "The red stain of bastardy, which two centuries of systematic legal defilement of Negro women had stamped upon his race, meant not only the loss of ancient African chastity, but also the hereditary weight of a mass of corruption from white adulterers threatening almost the obliteration of the Negro home."[26] Prominent white leaders such as Benjamin Franklin sought to protect what Franklin described as "the lovely White" by constructing black sexuality as dangerous, deviant, and unacceptable. For example, Thomas Jefferson described black men as preferring white women because of her "flowing hair" and "more elegant symmetry of form," arguing that the emancipation of blacks brought with it the possibility of racial mixture "staining the blood of his master,"[27] yet it is well-documented that he had a relationship with Sally Hemings, a slave. Furthermore, there are numerous cases documented where interracial marriage occurred between white slave owners and black slave women, such as the case of Robert Lumpkin, who left his slave jail and auction house to his wife, Mary Lumpkin, a black woman and former slave.[28] This illustrates the complicated and contradictory connection between race and sexuality, highlighting the simultaneous white fear and desire of blackness. Still once constructed the ideologies that were used to prevent, explain, justify, and cover up the sexual exploitation, rape, and lynching of black men and women during slavery[29] did not disappear with the end of slavery. In contrast, the need to oppress blacks actually increased after emancipation, and the increased white fear of blacks was linked to interracial sexuality and preventing miscegenation. As Valerie Smith argues, mobs of whites frequently raped black women in order to restrict the progress of black communities as a whole and black men in particular . . . especially during the period from Reconstruction through World War II, accusations of interracial rape were used to legitimate lynching, a form of random, mob violence connected routinely to the alleged rape of a white woman by a black man, even when no evidence of sexual assault existed.[30]

In the 1800s, throughout states from Illinois to New York to Wisconsin, white lawmakers (and their white communities) argued to restrict black migration and deny political and civil rights to blacks in order to prevent blacks "from marry(ing) our sisters and daughters."[31] Whites sought to keep blacks away from their families and children, especially in neighborhoods and schools, as evidenced in these examples:

> Whites petitioned the Indiana Senate to establish segregated schools. The committee on education agreed that the Negro race was inferior and that the admission of Negro children "into our public schools would ultimately tend to bring about that feeling which favour their amalgamation with our own people." When Massachusetts prohibited racial discrimination in the public schools, a northern newspaper cried: "Now the blood of the Winthrops, the Otises, the Lymans, the Endicotts, and the Eliots, is in a fair way to be amalgamated with the Sambos, the Catos, and the Pompeys. The North is to be Africanized."[32]

Interracial relationships and biracial children threatened whites' sense of group position and the existence of mutually exclusive "racial categories" on which it is based. Therefore, to strengthen this sense of group membership, crossing racial boundaries continued to be constructed as "deviant" by the white group. Interracial sex and marriage could not be labeled deviant without first constructing a white identity that was in opposition to blacks; the underlying basis for interracial sexuality as deviant being the claim that blacks and whites are biologically and culturally different.[33] Since courts had the authority to determine who was white, judges utilized varying definitions and "evidence" to determine an individual's race, producing and giving meaning to white and nonwhite identities in the process. "The law serves not only to reflect but to solidify social prejudice, making law a prime instrument in the construction and reinforcement of racial subordination."[34]

An important aspect of this is the construction of "whiteness" as property, translating a sense of racial superiority into a right that all whites could be assured would be upheld by the courts and the larger society. Within this long and complex history of "race relations," marriage rules and laws (informal and formal) can be seen as extensions of the white construction of race and political supremacy. As Max Weber argued, the legal prohibitions against intermarriage and "the sense of horror at any kind of sexual relationships between the two races . . . are socially determined" and "result from the tendency . . . to monopolise social power and status" based on racial differences.[35]

Throughout the 1900s, restricting black rights and movement was tied to the fear of black bodies merging with white bodies, or at least black men coming in contact with white women. "In light of the traditional merger of the political, the social, and the sexual within American culture, the concept of the 'Negro Problem' manifested itself as a white concern that blacks in search of citizenship must also desire to invade all other aspects of white life, including the white home."[36] In fact, "the threat of blacks' voting, working, buying property, and thereby inevitably achieving full American citizenship must be reimagined as, and thus contained by, the threat of black rape."[37] Reflecting these views, the Mann Act of 1910 was passed which "prohibited the importation and interstate transportation of women for immoral purposes," singling out the threat of native black and immigrant men as traffickers of white women for prostitution and elicit sex.[38] Similarly, Hollywood's Motion Picture Production Code, also called the Hays Code, which was written in 1930 and adopted by the movie industry in 1934 through 1968, included a proposition that outlined the opposition to interracial relations, "Miscegenation (sex relationship between the white and black races) is forbidden," and it was also applied to other groups such as Latinos.[39]

At this same time, "race, popular culture, and the white imagination were forged in nineteenth and early twentieth century popular forms of minstrelsy, film and literature."[40] From the early works of Shakespeare's *Othello*, which explores the dangers of interracial love between a Moor and a white Venetian noblewoman, there is a simultaneous fear and desire of blackness that could be read and seen in literary and theatrical works. Images from popular nineteenth-century novels such as *An Imperative Duty* by William Dean Howells portrayed "the white hero Dr. Olney (who) is drawn to the octoroon-in-hiding Rhoda Algate because of the threat of her submerged Africanity . . . blackness becomes an alluring 'deformity' . . . her 'imperceptible' otherness generates a sexual excitement that at once defies and affirms the laws of American racial custom."[41] Black women were portrayed as either dark-skinned, sexless mammies, oversexed Jezebels, or tragic mistresses, with the last two options reserved for light-skinned women.

The threat of black men in popular culture has also been well documented.[42] The earliest American films such as D. W. Griffith's *Birth of a*

Nation (1915) focused on the threat of black men as sexual predators of innocent white women. The movie ends with a black leader Silas Lynch trying to sexually assault Elsie Stoneman, a white congressman's daughter, while in a separate scene the heroically depicted Ku Klux Klan kill a black soldier when he attempts to rape a white southern aristocrat's daughter who jumps off a cliff to her death rather than be raped. Griffith even stated one of the goals of the film was "to create a feeling of abhorrence in white people, especially white women, against colored men."[43] At the time, the National Association for the Advancement of Colored People (NAACP) opposed the film with the argument that "whites would be mistakenly led to believe that blacks were not deserving of integration into white society."[44] These images were used to construct blacks in certain ways for the purpose of keeping them subordinated and also to influence whites, especially white women, from interacting with black men. As time progressed and major changes occurred, including the civil rights movement of the 1960s, African Americans achieved legal and political gains, with corresponding changes in popular culture depictions. For example, Sidney Poitier achieved great success as an African American male actor, with one of his more famous roles being that of the black fiancé of a young white woman in *Guess Who's Coming to Dinner* (1967). While African Americans receive the most representations in film and television of any minority group, the ideologies constructed have not been abandoned or completely altered. As Feagin argues,

> Perhaps the white focus on and obsession with black Americans historically and the frequently extreme character of white rationalizations of antiblack oppression, are linked to the fact that white Americans as a group have for centuries oppressed a group of people who are often, in reality, their unacknowledged kin. (2006, 15)

Despite the different histories of Native Americans and African Americans in the United States, a common thread exists where whiteness is constructed through ideas of native and black people as fundamentally different and inferior in all realms, not the least being sexually.

The Yellow Peril

Asian Americans, like Native Americans and African Americans, were racially sexualized before they even arrived on the shores of America.[45] Scholars such as Ronald Takaki and Gina Marchetti have traced the idea of Asians as dangerous to the West's fear of the "East" as early as medieval Europe's fear of Genghis Khan. Shortly after Chinese men began arriving in large numbers in the mid-1800s in the West to work, whites described Chinese men as "heathen, morally inferior, savage, childlike, and lustful" while "Chinese women were condemned as a 'depraved class,' their immortality associated with a physical appearance 'but a slight removal from the African race.'"[46] Immigration practices and laws were intricately tied to these constructions of Asian men and women. Since Asian immigration was largely used as a tool for cheap labor recruitment of Asian males, who were viewed as "temporary individual units of labor rather than as members of family groups," the immigration of Asian women was restricted.[47] For example, in 1875, Congress passed the Page Law that forbade the entry of Chinese and other "Mongolian" prostitutes, and later laws in 1903, 1907, and 1917 allowed for the deportation of Chinese women suspected of prostitution and defined Asian women as sexual objects. Given that prostitution was widespread at this time, Chinese women were singled out based on the white racist fear that they would bring in "especially virulent strains of venereal diseases, introduce opium addiction, and entice young white boys to a life of sin."[48] Furthermore, these restrictions also served to desexualize Asian men, as they were denied the ability to have families, constructed as asexual and nonmasculine, and the Asian American population was minimized.[49]

While being characterized as asexual and feminine, given the lack of available Asian women for Asian men to marry, Asian men were also constructed as a potential threat to white women. Therefore antimiscegenation laws were enacted against interracial marriage in general and there were even specific laws that forbade Asian-white intermarriage, such as California's 1880 statute, which prohibited marriage between a white person and a "negro, mulatto, or Mongolian." At the 1878 California Constitutional Convention, a white lawmaker had argued, "Were the Chinese to amalgamate at all with our people, it would be the lowest, most vile, and degraded of our race, and the result of that amalgamation would be a hybrid of the most despicable, a mongrel of the most detestable that has ever afflicted the earth."[50] The legal exclusion of Asians through various immigration acts affected Asian American communities until the eventual abolishment of "national origins" as a basis for quotas with immigration in 1965. Asian men were unable to start families because immigration laws banned the immigration of most Asian women, and antimiscegenation laws prohibited men of color from marrying white women. Despite the structural factors preventing Asian men from marrying, Asians were also constructed as the "yellow peril," posing a threat from military invasion, business monopolization through foreign trade, competition for labor positions, and miscegenation with whites. In particular, whites produced ideologies that characterized Asian men as unmasculine and sexually deviant, eunuchs, and rapists. Early images of Asians on-screen further expanded these ideas. Edward Said's work on *Orientalism* has been used by media scholars studying Asian images, arguing "Hollywood narrative[s] . . . create a mythic image of Asia that empowers the West and rationalizes Euroamerican authority over the Asian other (with) romance and sexuality provid(ing) the metaphoric justification for this domination."[51] Asian men were depicted as demasculinized and desexualized, such as the character of Charlie Chan or the evil enemy of the white man, Dr. Fu Manchu, who wanted to take over the West yet was still depicted as feminine, wearing a long dress, long fingernails, and homosexual desires.[52] Whereas Asian men are depicted as the opposite of desirable masculinity, Asian women are racialized and sexualized as the hyperfeminine, sensuous, promiscuous, and untrustworthy exotic Other. The most common images were the "castrating Dragon Lady who, while puffing on her foot-long cigarette holder, could poison a man as easily as she could seduce him"[53] or a submissive "Lotus Blossom . . . modest, tittering behind her delicate ivory hand, eyes downcast, always walking ten steps behind her man, and, best of all, devot[ing] body and soul to serve him."[54] These images of the Dragon Lady draw from the beliefs about Asian women as dangerous prostitutes during the time of the late 1800s to early 1900s, and the Lotus Blossom images include the characterizations both on-screen and in real life of "the China Doll, the Geisha Girl, the Korean War Bride or the Vietnamese prostitute—many of whom are the spoils of the last three wars fought in Asia."[55] During the Vietnam War, American GIs had sexual encounters, both consensual and forced, with Asian women in "rest and recreation" destinations such as Bangkok, Saigon, and other locales.[56] Films also showed Asian women seducing white men such as the *Lady of the Tropics* (1939), *Love Is a Many-Splendored Thing* (1955), *The Japanese War Bride* (1952), *Sayonara* (1957), and *The World of Suzie Wong* (1960), as well as the Madame Butterfly stories where white men engage in a relationship with an Asian woman in the context of a war, such as *The Toll of the Sea* (1922) set in China, *China Gate* (1957) set in Vietnam, and the original *Madame Butterfly* set in Japan.[57] These liaisons reinforced the long-standing images of Asian women; as Lynn Thiesmeyer argues, "the western image of the Asian female, the Asian body, and Asian sexuality has been reproduced, yet scarcely updated for centuries . . . these women have become metaphors for adventure, cultural difference, and sexual subservience."[58]

Less often, Asian men were portrayed as a sexual danger to white women, as in the 1916 *Petria* movie, which focused on a group of Japanese who invade the United States and attempt to rape a white woman. Gina Marchetti documents the films that depict Asian-white interracial relationships, such as Cecil B. DeMille's *The Cheat* (1915), which tells the story of a Japanese merchant who tries to seduce a married white woman with money in ex-change for sex at the beginning of World War I and D. W. Griffith's *Broken Blossoms* (1919), about a young white girl who is desired by a Chinese mer-chant and is eventually killed by her abusive father when he thinks she has been with the Chinese man. In 1933, there was also a popular film, *The Bitter Tea of General Yen*, about a white woman (played by the famous white actress Barbara Stanwyck) who travels to China to marry a missionary but ends up being taken to the house of a Chinese General Yen (played by a Scandina-vian actor); he desires her and she has ambivalent feelings, highlighted in a dream sequence.[59] Still, Asian men rarely play the lead in American films, and when they do, they are action characters who practice martial arts with little attention paid to personal lives, such as the roles embodied by Jackie Chan and Jet Li. In these images of Asian Americans, we see how sexuality is linked to notions of racial identity and is used to illuminate who should be an American and who Americans (read "whites") should be with. "Build-ing nations and national identities involves inspecting and controlling the sexuality of citizens and condemning the sexuality of noncitizens and those considered outside the sexual boundaries of the nation."[60]

Enter Latinos

Through the histories of Asian Americans, African Americans, and Native Americans, nonwhites are clearly marked as "Other," whether desired, feared, or some combination of the two. Latinos were also socially constructed in similar ways, yet it varied greatly based on the time period, country of origin, and socioeconomic status. As white Americans "conquered" the West, many white Americans settled in Mexico, as white Americans like Stephen Austin urged Americans in 1835 to claim Texas from Mexico through war, which he characterized as between "'mongrel-Spanish-Indian and negro race' and 'civi-lization and the Anglo-American race.'"[61] Texas was annexed to the United States, and the Mexican-American War ensued shortly after. While Mexicans were seen as less civilized and inferior, Mexican women were incorporated into the white doctrine of manifest destiny and imagined as sexually available for white men. Some white men married Mexican women without much formal or informal opposition. Takaki cites a poem written during the war, "The Spanish maid, with eye of fire . . . awaits our Yankee chivalry whose purer blood and valiant arms, are fit to clasp her budding charms,"[62] illustrating the early idea about Mexican women as Latina spitfires. The rationalization of manifest des-tiny, in which the United States imagined itself as destined to take over lands west and south, referred to the expansion of land but could just as easily refer to the principles guiding white men's conquest of other women.

Throughout the 1900s, Latino immigration occurred in waves with Puerto Ricans arriving in large numbers beginning in the 1950s and Cuban migration increasing in the 1960s as a result of the Fidel Castro takeover. This increase in the numbers of Latino groups was particularly noticeable after the 1965 Immigration Act signed by President Lyndon Johnson, which prompted Latino immigration. Like the changing Latino population demographics, Clara Rodriguez (2004) documents how Latino actors and actresses experienced different periods of heightened visibility and invisibility as well as periods of passing (Latino stars assuming Anglo names and not mentioning their Latino roots) and strategic emphasis on being Latino when it was what Hollywood desired. The early screen images of Latinos reflected the ambivalent and ambiguous place of Latinos in the United States. Latinos were consistently constructed as the Other but the stereotypes ranged from the Latin Lover for men and the Latina spitfire or exotica for women to other more menacing caricatures of aliens and gangsters, depending on the social context of the film as well as the political and economic climate of the period. In the early 1900s Rudolph Valentino was a leading romantic man in films who played opposite white actresses, along with Latin women such as Dolores Del Rio and Lupe Velez who also enjoyed fame, often paired against white men.[63] Yet the allure of the Latin Lover, both male and female, could easily turn into "the Latino gigolo and Latina Vamp" and "always just beneath the surface of the romantic Latin image were the older, more negative nineteenth-century stereotypes of the vicious 'greaser with a knife' and the 'greaser girl of easy virtue.'"[64] Through the 1950s, it was not uncommon for Latina/os, particularly women who looked "European," to marry white Anglos, while in the same period it was rare to see any unions of whites with blacks, Asians, or Native Americans on screen.[65] Still, the Latino character was often a supporting role, such as the "other" woman in films such as the John Wayne classic High Noon (1952), which featured the Mexican film star Katy Jurado as the lover of Wayne's character until he finds true love with the white blonde played by Grace Kelly.

Romances between whites and Latinas were depicted in various plays/films such as the 1961 top-grossing West Side Story, which told the story of a dangerous love between a white young man and a Latina young woman from opposite sides of a neighborhood turf war. Their relationship was portrayed as dangerous and doomed, while the Puerto Rican youths were depicted as foreigners who have come to make problems for the white boys. The characterization of Latinos as foreigners, or "aliens" who do not belong,[66] became common in response to the growing numbers of Latinos who came to the United States after the 1950s. Another film, Giant (1956), starring Rock

Hudson and James Dean, also featured a relationship between a white man and Mexican woman, yet the relationship lasted because the wealthy white man was able to "save" his wife from discrimination and mistreatment. As the Latino population grew, the images and representations reflected changing understandings and growing concerns over immigration, while keeping in the framework established earlier. Even more recently, there are distinctly different representations of Latinos that are often ethnically and racially ambiguous. What emerges is that Latinos/as who act accordingly to white standards and align themselves with whites will fare well, yet the mass of "foreign" dangerous and usually darker-skinned Latinos will not be welcome or will be relegated to subordinate positions. This contradiction in images of Latinas/os clearly emerged in popular culture, reflecting white views on Latino Americans and immigrants in which Latino men could be ultimate lovers or dangerous gangsters, while the Latina women could be sexy spitfire vixens or, less often, chaste Catholic virgins, which is played up in *West Side Story*. During earlier periods, Rodriguez notes that the choices for Latino actors were to "either Europeanize their images or play up the stereotypes,"[67] which still could be argued about contemporary representations.

Interracial Meanings and Whiteness

While the histories and specific stereotypes of Native Americans, Asian Americans, African Americans, and Latinos may vary, these racialized and sexualized representations serve the same purpose. "History has presented us with the *idea* of race; it has presented us with an irresistible *social representation* or naturalized mental framework that works to order the way we see the world before us."[68] By constructing nonwhite sexuality as deviant, whites remain the norm by which others are judged. "Whiteness represents the cultural norm the implicit standard from which blackness deviates,"[69] and Latinos, Asians, all nonwhite Others fall somewhere in between. In particular, the white man's strength and dominance is maintained against the beliefs about men of color as asexual (particularly Asian men), or sexual savages. Furthermore, white women remain the ideal embodiment of womanhood in comparison to hypersexual, sexually promiscuous African American, Asian, and Latino women, and it justifies the sexual exploitation of the women by white men. The pattern of representing and constructing nonwhite sexuality as deviant and dangerous served a purpose of justifying the treatment of blacks, Latinos, Native people, and Asians, whether it was attacks, lynching, or laws to prevent members of the group from entering the United States or having full rights. As Richard Dyer (1998) argues, "the fear of one's own body, of how one controls it and relates to it and the fear of not being able to control other bodies, those bodies whose exploitation is so fundamental to capitalist economy are both at the heart of whiteness." If color is the opposite of whiteness, and it is constructed as threatening and deviant, then whiteness as a project demands protection from an invasion from color, or invades first, justifying the invasion and safe containment.

By looking at the narratives of interracial rape, sex, and unions together, we see the similarities in the purpose they serve, as well as the contradictory ideas about men of color—the Uncle Tom or black beast, the Latin Lover or greasy gangster, the sneaky Asian eunuch or devious ruler—and women of color—the mammy or the Jezebel, the Latina spitfire or exotic maid, the Dragon Lady or the Lotus Blossom. The historical realities, the way history is retold, as well as who and how contemporary stories are told, is part of what Gramsci described as the way those in power "establish a certain 'definition of reality' which is accepted by those over whom hegemony is exercised."[70] While slavery and legalized segregation have disappeared, these representations and ideologies of the intersections of race and sex are an integral part of contemporary racial oppression, or what Feagin (2006) terms systemic racism, "the racist framing, racist ideology, stereotyped attitudes, racist emotions, discriminatory habits and actions and extensive racist institutions developed over centuries by whites" which permeates all of society.[71]

Contemporary representations of interracial sex are based on the ideologies that were created to justify historical conditions and reflect contemporary debates over racial identity, racial locations, nationalism, and citizenship. The problem lies not in the images but in the social conditions that underlie, inform, and accompany these images that contribute to the subjugation and degradation of certain races and ethnicities. As we see from looking at historical and contemporary practices, interracial relationships are problematized, especially if it includes a white woman. Also laws, practices, and attitudes surrounding interracial relationships, particularly preventing these unions, have been used to privilege, protect, and illustrate the power of whiteness, particularly for white men. At the same time, interracial relationships are used to perpetuate racist attitudes and practice while denying race matters. The connection between the treatment of racial and ethnic groups in society and their treatment in the media reveals patterns that we can use as a framework for understanding the interracial images I will explore in the following chapters.

Notes

1. Stuart Hall, "The Whites of Their Eyes: Racist Ideologies and the Media," in *Silver Linings: Some Strategies for the Eighties*, eds. George Bridges and Rosalind Brunt (London: Lawrence and Wishart, Ltd., 1981).

2. Joane Nagel, *Race, Ethnicity, and Sexuality: Intimate Intersections, Forbidden Frontiers* (New York: Oxford University Press, 2003), 83.

3. See Roediger 1994, Ignatiev 1995, and Hale 1998.

4. Joe R. Feagin, *Systemic Racism: A Theory of Oppression* (New York: Routledge, 2006), xiii.

5. See Kobena Mercer, "Skin Head Sex Thing: Racial Difference and the Homoerotic Imaginary," *Competing Glances* 16 (Spring 1992): 17. The discussion of Robert Mapplethorpe's photographs of black men is illuminating for its analysis of the tension between who creates the images, who consumes the images, and how this affects/is affected by these dynamics of the different races, genders, and sexual locations of the viewer/viewed.

6. Scholars such as Edward Said in *Orientalism* make this argument about how ideas constructed by whites about the East and the Orient are more about constructing whiteness and the West.

7. George Lipsitz, *The Possessive Investment in Whiteness: How White People from Identity Politics* (Philadelphia: Temple University Press, 1998), 118.

8. As quoted in Nagel 2003, 64. See also Robert F. Berkhofer Jr., *The White Man's Indian: Images of the American Indian from Columbus to the Present* (New York: Alfred A. Knopf, 1978), 8–9.

9. Nagel 2003, 66.

10. June Namias, *White Captives: Gender and Ethnicity on the America Frontier* (Chapel Hill: University of North Carolina Press, 1993), 109 as cited in Nagel 2003, 72.

11. See John D'Emilio and Estelle B. Freedman, *Intimate Matters: A History of Sexuality in America* (New York: Harper and Row, 1998); Nagel 2003; and Ann Marie Plane, *Colonial Intimacies: Indian Marriage in Early New England* (Ithaca, NY: Cornell University Press, 2000).

12. Nagel 2003, 78.

13. See Winthrop Jordan, *White over Black: American Attitudes toward the Negro, 1550–1812* (Chapel Hill: University of North Carolina Press, 1968); Anne McClintock, *Imperial Leather: Race, Gender, and Sexuality in the Colonial Contest* (New York: Routledge, 1995).

14. Ronald Takaki, *A Different Mirror: A History of Multicultural America* (Boston: Little, Brown and Company, 1993), 55.

15. Takaki 1993, 59 citing William W. Hening, *The Statutes at Large: Being a Collection of All the Laws of Virginia from the First Session of the Legislature in 1619*, Volume 2 (Richmond, VA: George Cochran, 1822), 260, 281.

16. Bennett [1962] 1984; Gaspar and Hine 1996; Jordan 1974; Lyman 1997; Mumford 1997; Takaki 1993.

17. Bennett [1962] 1984 and Jordan 1968.

18. Frankenberg 1993, 75; Lyman 1997, 99.

19. Takaki 1993, 67 citing Hening, *Statutes* Volume 3, 86–87.

20. See Ian Haney López, *White By Law: The Legal Construction of Race*, page 13.

21. Collins 2000; Crenshaw 1993; Hooks 1981, 1992, 1996, 2000; Williams 1991, 1995.

22. Davis 1981; Essed 1991; Morrison 1972.

23. Nagel 2003, 97.

24. For a discussion see Davis 1981; Gaspar and Hine 1996; Giddings 1984; Ware 1992; and Wells 1969.

25. See Collins 2000; Davis 1981; Hooks 1981, 1996, 2000; Smith 1998; Williams 1991, 1995, 1998; Wing and Merchan 1995. Other works address the issue of interracial unions as well as the images of black and interracial sexuality, many of these in the field of literary and cultural criticism such as Baldwin 1955; Dyson 1997; Ellison 1952; Gates 1988; Hooks 1992, 1996; Hutchinson 1996; Mercer 1994; Morrison 1992; West 1993, 1994.

26. See Du Bois [1903] 1989, 9, and other examples from many black writers who discuss their personal family histories and the legacy of miscegenation: Patricia Williams (1995) recounts how her grandmother who was a slave bore children by her white slave master (who used her for sexual practice and eventually gave her to his future wife).

27. Takaki 1993, 75 citing Thomas Jefferson, *Notes on the State of Virginia* (Richmond, VA: J. W. Randolph, 1853), 157–58.

28. See David Zucchino. "With Unearthing of Infamous Jail, Richmond Confronts its Slave Past." *Los Angeles Times*, December 18, 2008.

29. See Davis 1981 and Giddings 1984.

30. See 272–73 in Valerie Smith, "Split Affinities: The Case of Interracial Rape."

31. Takaki 1993, 109 citing Alexis de Tocqueville, *Democracy in America*, Volume 1 (New York: Library of America, 1945 [originally published in 1835], 373; Eugene H. Berwanger, *The Frontier against Slavery: Western Anti-Negro Prejudice and the Slavery Extension Controversy* (Urbana: University of Illinois Press, 1967), 20, 36.

32. Takaki 1993, 110 citing Leon Litwack, *North of Slavery: The Negro in the Free States, 1790–1860* (Chicago: University of Chicago Press, 1961), 234; and Emma Lou Thornbrough, *The Negro in Indiana: A Study of a Minority* (1957), 163.

33. See Frankenberg 1993.

34. See Haney López 1996, 192 and also Bell 1995.

35. See Weber [1922] 1977, 360.

36. See Sandra Gunning, "Re-membering Blackness after Reconstruction: Race, Rape and Political Desire in the Work of Thomas Dixon, Jr.," 21.

37. See Gunning, "Re-membering Blackness after Reconstruction: Race, Rape, and Political Desire in the Work of Thomas Dixon, Jr.," chapter 1, 32.

38. See Eithne Luibheid, *Entry Denied: Controlling Sexuality at the Border* (Minneapolis: University of Minnesota Press, 2002), 13, which has an excellent discussion

of how fears about immigrant sexuality contributed to the laws and actions involving immigration and immigrant groups in the United States.

39. See Carlos E. Cortés, "Who Is Maria? What Is Juan? Dilemmas of Analyzing the Chicano Image in U.S. Feature Films," *Chicanos and Film: Representation and Resistance*, ed. Chon A. Noriega (Minneapolis: University of Minnesota Press, 1992), 83; also Patricia White, *Uninvited: Classical Hollywood Cinema and Lesbian Respectability* (Bloomington: Indiana University Press, 1999), who points us to other excellent sources on the complicated history of the Production Code, such as Gregory D. Black, *Hollywood Censored: Morality Codes, Catholics, and the Movies* (New York: Cambridge University Press, 1996).

40. Herman Gray 2004 [1995], 14. See also Clyde Taylor 1996, Toni Morrison 1992, and David Roediger 1991

41. See Gunning, "Re-membering Blackness After Reconstruction: Race, Rape and Political Desire in the Work of Thomas Dixon, Jr.," 20.

42. See Carby 1993; Entman 1990; Guerrero 1993; Mercer 1994; Wiegman 1991.

43. See Vera and Gordon 2003, 20.

44. Darnell Hunt, "Making Sense of Blackness on Television," *Channeling Blackness: Studies on Television and Race in America* (Oxford: Oxford University Press, 2005), 12.

45. Asians can often serve as a buffer between whites and other racial/ethnic minorities such as blacks and Latinos, as is currently debated by race scholars such as Bonilla-Silva, who argues that there is a Latinamericanization of race relations in which a group of honorary whites emerges between whites and nonwhites. See also Kim 1999 and Kawaii 2005 who discuss how Asians are located between blacks and whites, in a racial triangulation pattern

46. Takaki 1993, 205; see also Dan Caldwell, "The Negroization of the Chinese Stereotype in California," *Southern California Quarterly*, Vol. 53 (June 1971): 123–31 as well as original newspaper reports such as *San Francisco Alta*, June 4, 1853; *New York Times*, December 26, 1873.

47. See Espiritu 2000, 9–10.

48. See Chan 1991, 138; Espiritu 2000.

49. See Espiritu 2000; Goellnicht 1992; Lyman 1968.

50. Takaki 1993, 205; see also Megumi Dick Osumi, "Asians and California's Anti-Miscegenation Laws," in Nobuya Tsuchida, ed., *Asian and Pacific American Experiences: Women's Perspectives* (Minneapolis: University of Minnesaota Press 1982), 2, 6.

51. Marchetti 1993, 6, referencing Edward Said, *Orientalism* (New York: Vintage Books, 1979).

52. See Chin and Chan 1972; Espiritu 2000; Hoppenstand 1983; Wang 1988.

53. See Espiritu 2000; Marchetti 1993.

54. See Ling 1990, 11; Espiritu 2000.

55. See Espiritu 2000, 94; Tajima 1989, 309.

56. Nagel 2003, 30.

57. See Marchetti 1993 for detailed analyses of these films; for a discussion of the 1991 mainstream film *Showdown in Little Tokyo* see Thomas Nakayama, "Show/Down Time: 'Race,' Gender, Sexuality, and Popular Culture," *Critical Studies in Mass Communication* 11 (1994): 162–79.

58. See page 81 in Lynn Thiesmeyer, "The West's 'Comfort Women' and the Discourses of Seduction," in Shirley G. Lim, Larry E. Smith, and Wimal Dissanayake, eds., *Transnational Asia Pacific: Gender, Culture, and the Public Sphere* (Urbana: University of Illinois Press, 2003).

59. See also *Bridge to the Sun* (1961).

60. Nagel 2003, 166.

61. Takaki 1993, 174.

62. Takaki 1993, 176–77, citing William M'Carty, *National Songs, Ballads, and Other Patriotic Poetry* (Philadelphia, Published by William M'Carty 1846), 45; see also Reginald Horsman, *Race and Manifest Destiny: The Origins of American Racial Anglo-Saxonism* (Cambridge, MA: Harvard University Press 1981), 233.

63. While Valentino is actually Italian, he was considered and often referred to as Latin at that time.

64. See Antonio Rios-Bustamante, "Latino Participation in the Hollywood Film Industry, 1911–1945," page 21, where it is also documented how Dolores del Rio turned down a part in 1931 where she would have played a "cantina girl" who betrays her "Mexican bandit" boyfriend for a white American airline pilot, but a lesser-known actress Lupe Velez took it. See also Clara Rodriguez, *Heroes, Lovers, and Others: The Story of Latinos in Hollywood* (Washington, DC: Smithsonian, 2004).

65. Rodriguez 2004, 145.

66. Rodriguez 2004.

67. Rodriguez 2004, 110–11.

68. Hunt 2005, 3.

69. Hunt 2005, 4.

70. See page 173 in Chantal Mouffe, "Hegemony and the Integral State in Gramsci: Towards a New Concept of Politics," in George Bridges and Rosalind Brunt, eds., *Silver Linings: Some Strategies for the Eighties* (London: Lawrence and Wishart Ltd, 1987.)

71. Feagin 2006, xii.

CHAPTER TWO

~

The Prime-Time Color Line: Interracial Couples and Television

"Love is no longer color-coded on TV," reads the headline of a December 2005 *USA Today* article, heralding the more frequent depictions of interracial couples on the most watched shows like *ER*, *Lost*, and *Grey's Anatomy* and applauding the color-blind approach to depicting interracial couples as "race being neither an issue nor much of plot point."[1] While interracial couples are cropping up in story lines more frequently, exactly what these representations mean, and what messages they send, is debatable. Television provides us with a way of understanding, viewing, and knowing interracial relationships, or more accurately it offers us a discourse complete with images about the meanings of interracial relationships.[2] Since television is part of our popular knowledge and social life, "it serves as social space for the mediated encounters that distinguish the lived experience of today from those of old, as a place for us to vicariously sample our fondest desires or our most dreaded fears, as a comfort zone from which we can identify with our heroes or affirm our differences from undesirable Others."[3] Do the growing numbers of interracial couples on television signify that "we have arrived at the idealized American landscape of racial equality and color-blindness," or do these depictions overwhelmingly reproduce our long-standing notions about the deviant nature of interracial sex and the location of these relationships in the margins of society?[4]

This chapter explores the depictions of interracial couples and the relative invisibility/scripted visibility of interracial relationships on prime-time television.[5] After a brief history of the first interracial couples on television, contemporary television will be discussed in depth, highlighting how contemporary representations still overwhelmingly ignore interracial couples, rendering these unions invisible or problematizing interracial relationships as part of a deviant world. Furthermore, the stories that are produced for television privilege whiteness, present particular images of people of color as either dangerous or exceptions, and deny racism while promoting color blindness, fitting into the patterns of representations put forth in the introduction.

History of Television and Interracial Sex

The introduction of television revolutionized popular culture and allowed representations to come into people's homes in a way that had not been possible before. Yet the representations on television were based on the images dominant in popular thought. From the beginning, "blackness has been profoundly present on popular television, usually at the service of whiteness,"[6] while Latinos and Asians have been markedly less visible. One of the earliest interracial couples on television appeared from 1951 to 1956 on *I Love Lucy*, starring the Cuban-born Desi Arnaz and his real-life white wife Lucille Ball. Initially "the white television executives who were to back the show opposed casting a 'Latin' as the husband of an 'All-American girl'" because they said "the public would not go for it."[7] It was only after the couple traveled the United States performing their comedy routine with huge success did the television executives change their mind. Other early interracial couples appeared on shows such as *Gunsmoke* (1955–1975) and *How the West Was Won* (1978–1979), which depicted white men with Asian women. Yet in 1957, ABC canceled a popular weekly musical variety show with Alan Freed when a black singer, Frankie Lemon, danced with a white woman, highlighting the particularly problematic pairing of a white woman with a black man. Eleven years later in 1968, *Star Trek* aired what is widely regarded as the first black-white interracial kiss on television between William Shatner's character, Captain Kirk, a white man, and a black woman, Lieutenant Uhura, when the two were forced to kiss against their will by a galactic enemy.[8]

Since then, television programming has undergone many shifts.[9] In the early 1970s and early 1980s, diversity in families and households became more common with shows such as *The Jeffersons*, *Benson*, *Webster*, *Diff'rent Strokes*, and *Gimme a Break!*, yet these shows usually contained alternative family structures such as transracial adoption, single parent families, or black caretakers/assistants as part of a white family.[10] One of the earliest black-white relationships occurred on *The Jeffersons* (1975–1985) between Helen Willis, an African American woman, and her white husband, Tom

Willis. The Willis couple encompassed elements of the three patterns of deviance, privileging whiteness and putting forth certain ideologies of race. For example, the interracial union was used as a source of comedy and the butt of many of George Jefferson's jokes, including the idea that Helen was unattractive. Helen was clearly the boss of the relationship, perpetuating the Sapphire image of black women as emasculating and domineering. This interracial relationship was less threatening considering the history of interracial sex, where white men with black women was swept under the rug as compared to the strong, often violent, reaction to black men with white women, while not challenging the image of black women as aggressive. Also, the source of opposition to the interracial relationship was situated in the black community through George's comments rather than the opposition and discrimination that existed in white society.

Through the 1980s, as black characters became central in a number of prime-time shows, interracial relationships still remained rare on the small screen. In 1989, black actor Robert Guillaume co-created and starred in a comedy on ABC where his character becomes involved with a white secretary, but it was canceled after the premiere, which Guillaume "blamed part of the rejection on viewers who could not get past the premise."[11] The late 1980s sitcom *Night Court* had a side story line involving an interracial marriage between the African American court clerk Mac Robinson, who was a Vietnam War veteran, and Quon Le, a Vietnamese woman. Yet their relationship was used for comedic effect with situations based on their cultural differences, as their marriage was originally a ploy to give her citizenship and get her out of a house of prostitution, reinforcing common stereotypes.

By the 1990s, the shows that did feature racial minorities usually focused on black worlds where "African Americans face the same experiences, situations, and conflicts as whites except for the fact that they remain separate but equal."[12] In these shows, the lack of interracial relationships were presented as a result of (or blamed on) the choices of African Americans to live segregated, such as one episode of the hit sitcom *The Fresh Prince of Bel-Air*, when Will's mother is angry that her sister is marrying a white man. One of the only shows to feature an interracial couple was a short-lived show *True Colors*, an "Interracial Brady Bunch" with a black man with children marrying a white woman with children, yet the show did not last amidst low ratings, audience complaints, and even threats.

Contemporary television still has trouble dealing with the intersections of race, gender, and sexuality, particularly when it involves how relationships outside the same-race, opposite-sex norm are handled. For example, the NAACP still characterizes minority representation on commercial network television as dismal in terms of character depictions and role development for blacks, Latinos, and Asians.[13] Even when shows feature black or interracial casts, they are still usually controlled by white producers and head writers, even if there are black and other minority writers on the team. In 2000, white men accounted for 80 percent of television directors, and women (mostly white) accounted for 11 percent. Furthermore, less than 10 percent of employed television writers are persons of color.[14] This white control of television production is significant because "racial control has a direct bearing on racial content" given that individuals "develop show concepts that resonate with their own experiences or fantasies."[15] Much of prime-time television on the major networks is segregated with shows featuring primarily white casts, or predominantly black casts, as well as "a requisite number of black and multiracial relationships and friendships collected on the periphery of the action."[16] Yet simply having a multiracial cast and increasing the number of interracial relationships that are shown to a more diverse audience does not necessarily signal that meanings of these representations have improved. Television scholars have argued the importance of interrogating the representations even if they appear to be "positive" representations.[17] In what follows, I will outline how interracial relationships are depicted on contemporary television and what uses or purposes these representations serve.

Patterns of Contemporary Representations

Given the segregated nature of television shows, it is not surprising that interracial relationships are not common on TV.[18] Yet the media consistently heralds the growing number of interracial couples on television, based mostly on what they describe as the "color-blind" portrayals of interracial couples. Looking at the contemporary representations, there may be a trend to present interracial couples without mentioning race but that does not mean that these representations do not carry familiar racial messages. In what follows, I will show how television depictions of interracial unions are problematized, either through rendering them impossible/invisible or deviant. Furthermore, interracial relationships on the small screen emphasize positive portrayals of whites and a few exceptional people of color, while rewriting racial realities by denying white racism, promoting color blindness and projecting people of color as the ones who are racist.

Invisibility, Disappearing Acts, and Temporary Distractions

Interracial couples and multiracial families, in particular, are overwhelmingly absent or invisible on prime-time television. Interracial relationships do not occur, almost develop yet never materialize, and/or shows featuring interracial relationships are canceled. There are very few examples of married interracial couples, and even less examples of interracial couples raising biracial children on prime-time television. While black-white interracial couplings or possibilities are not common, there are even less depictions of Asian or Latino interracial pairings, especially considering there are so few Asian or Latino characters on television.

Shows that feature an interracial relationship often tend to be short-lived. Every September at the start of the new season, a number of shows are canceled soon after premiering, and often these canceled shows include an interracial relationship or possibility.[19] For example, in the 2004–2005 season, *TV Guide* described the short-lived show *Kevin Hill* as "the taming of an alpha male . . . charming, sexy . . . this one's a winner," where Kevin, an African American man, dated many women, including a white woman or two, yet it was quickly canceled.[20] In the same 2004–2005 season, the widely promoted NBC show *LAX* featured Heather Locklear and Blair Underwood as cutthroat rival codirectors of the Los Angeles airport who seem to have once been intimate.[21] When interviewed, Locklear said, "There will always be [sexual] tension, but I don't think we'll ever see that," which was accurate because the show was canceled shortly into the season.[22]

Beyond not showing interracial couples, another strategy of invisibility is to have an interracial union that happened in the past. This pretense of past interracial love that never materializes again was used on the popular crime drama *CSI*, where Warrick Brown, a black man, and Catherine Willows, a white woman, were involved romantically in the past, but nothing happens other than Catherine's disappointed look when Warrick announces he got married.[23] In the 2005 hit series *Grey's Anatomy*, the main character Meredith Grey's mother, a former top neurosurgeon hospitalized with Alzheimer's, had an extramarital affair twenty years before with the current chief of surgery, an African American man. The chief stayed married, but the affair destroyed Meredith's parents' marriage, and yet the chief still visits her in the nursing home until she died in the 2006–2007 season. By placing the relationship in the past, the show can claim to be racially progressive while not having to deal with actually presenting an interracial relationship.

Similarly, numerous shows have begun an interracial romance only to fizzle it out before it even had a chance to sizzle.[24] For example, on ABC's *Once and Again* in the 1999–2000 season, a teenage romance began between the lead character's white daughter, Grace Manning, and her black classmate, Jared. The executive producer Ed Zwick said "it seemed plausible" to have Grace date interracially after singer/songwriter Jackson Browne said, "Grace looked like someone who would be involved with someone of a mixed race."[25] Zwick also said the romance would explore their racial differ-ences, yet the relationship was not developed and the audience learned the relationship ended with a flippant comment by Grace that teen romances don't last.[26] Temporary relationships often occur with a guest appearance where the relationship is designed to last a few episodes at best. For example, on ABC's legal drama *Boston Legal*, the black actress Kerry Washington guest starred for six episodes and engaged in a brief relationship with the white attorney Alan Shore, who routinely romances different women every week. NBC's hit comedy *Will and Grace* used interracial possibilities, but it is already within the wacky environment of Will, a gay man, and Grace, his heterosexual roommate, who have a classic television relationship in which the audience wants them together but they can't be.[27] Ultimately both Will and Grace end up with white partners when the show ended in 2006. Other shows like *Friends* were exclusively white for years, and when it did "diver-sify" with interracial relationships, it did so in very particular ways. Ross was engaged to an Asian woman, yet the relationship was short-lived as Ross was really "meant to be" with Rachel.[28] Some shows like *ER* have featured a string of short-lived interracial affairs ranging from one-night stands to unions that lasted a few episodes, most of which are mentioned in this chapter. During the 2005–2006 season, the hit series *Desperate Housewives* included a side story line about a relationship between Danielle, the white teenage daughter of one of the four main "housewives," and Matthew, the teenage son of the only black family on the street. The relationship is initially a tool to move another story line about Matthew's mentally ill brother, and Danielle and Matthew's relationship is implied but rarely shown. It all ends when Danielle runs away from home with Matthew, who we learn had killed someone years earlier and is consequently shot and killed by the police. The relationship was overtly sexual, deviant, and ultimately disastrously deadly. While it may be initially exciting to begin an interracial relationship on screen, it seems much more difficult to develop the relationship.

One of the longest running interracial relationships that never fully developed was on *Judging Amy* (1999–2005),[29] which focused on the white character Amy Gray, a divorced mother and juvenile court judge in Hart-ford, Connecticut. While she goes through a string of flawed relationships with white men, Bruce Van Exel, her African American court services officer, is her faithful sidekick, always there to offer an ear, shoulder, or spiritual support. Bruce is presented as the perfect partner, if he wasn't black. When *Judging Amy* first began in 1999, executive producer Barbara Hall said,

I think I can safely say they're not going to be a couple. But if the show's on the air a really long time, obviously stuff has to occur, not just sexual tension, but mutual respect for one another. There's a push and pull of getting together as friends and then pulling back. We're going to keep going with that kind of dynamic because Bruce is a really enigmatic character.[30]

Though by 2001, Hall stated that the chemistry between the two actors was so strong that it could not be ignored, yet she stated that they would not deal with race in the relationship.[31]

Besides not actually engaging in an intimate dating relationship, the representations of the two characters symbolized their distance and differences. Amy's position as Bruce's superior serves as a proxy for race in why they cannot be together, with their occupational statuses preventing it yet closely mirroring their racial statuses. Amy is clearly in a position of power and in essence Bruce belongs to her, as Amy consistently tells Bruce what she wants him to do, what they are going to do, and makes decision for him, which occasionally angers Bruce. Bruce always refers to her as "Judge Amy," and he consistently pulls away from her attempts to become closer to him through conversation. Amy and Bruce kiss twice, once in Amy's dream and once when he is temporarily not working for her because of a felony charge for a fight he got into. After their kiss, he is reinstated at his job, thereby making any further contact impossible. By having Bruce be the one to pull away from Amy and to explicitly state he is committed to dating within his race (which will be discussed later), Amy and Bruce's relationship or the possibility of it can exist in a safe space, where the audience can fantasize about it without fearing it will actually happen. Like many great television shows, two characters are kept apart for different reasons, and it seems in *Judging Amy*, their different positions, both occupationally and racially, are a barrier too much to cross.[32]

This relative invisibility and hesitancy to delve into interracial relationships for any more than a few episodes can be read as part of the representations of interracial couples as deviant or outside the norm, thereby rendering it unshowable. Not surprisingly, representations of interracial families are even less common. There are relatively few examples of multiracial families, interracial couples raising children, or even biracial children on television. On two popular shows, *ER* and *Grey's Anatomy*, women involved in interracial relationships became pregnant but quickly miscarried the babies. In both instances, the relationships between the white Dr. John Carter and black AIDS worker Makemba on *ER* and the black Dr. Preston Burke and the Asian American intern Cristina Yang on *Grey's Anatomy* began as sexual encounters, but the pregnancy (and in Burke/Yang's case the miscarriage) brought them together. Also on *ER*, an Asian American intern Jing-Mei Chen becomes pregnant from a one-night stand with a black male ICU nurse.[33] Episodes later, she is pregnant, at which time she tells him she is giving up the baby for adoption, so there was no development of a relationship nor do we even see the sexual encounter.

On television, the possibility of biracial children and multiracial families is presented in surprising, comical, or negative ways. On *Desperate Housewives*, Gabrielle and Carlos, the only Latino couple, convince their Asian live-in housekeeper to carry their child.[34] She agrees to be artificially inseminated with their child, and things get even more complicated because Carlos sleeps with her while she is pregnant, yet when she gives birth the baby is black. Issues of interracial sex and racialized ideas are placed within Gabrielle and Carlos's relationship, rather than the white families of *Desperate Housewives*. Could we picture producers having one of the white couples ask their Asian housekeeper to carry their baby only to have her give birth to a black child? Later we find out that the clinic accidentally implanted the embryo from a black couple, not Gabrielle and Carlos's fertilized embryo, leaving them childless, with no discussion of what happened to the baby.[35] Even when producers such as *Judging Amy* executive producer Barbara Hall attempt to, in her words, "make the public face up to the fact that we all now have to find a way to deal with interracial matters and biracial children,"[36] she chose to do this through an accidental transracial adoption. Instead, Amy's white brother and his wife are adopting a baby from a young white woman, but when she gives birth the baby has brown skin and black, curly hair. When looking at the baby, the brother keeps saying how surprised he is that the baby is "b-b-b-big" when obviously he means black.[37] Yet in subsequent episodes, the baby's race is never addressed or considered. The 2006 hit drama series *Heroes* about people with extraordinary superpowers is one of the only shows to feature an interracial couple who have a biracial child together. Yet this multiracial family consists of a white stripper, her estranged ex-convict black husband, and their biracial son, who all have some type of supernatural powers. They no longer live together, and it reinforces many negative stereotypes.

One of the few notable exceptions occurs on the HBO series *Six Feet Under* with the story line involving a cohabiting committed gay couple, Keith Charles, a black police officer, and David Fisher, a white funeral-home owner, who struggle in their quest to be together and have children.[38] They temporarily care for Keith's niece, yet later try to find a surrogate mother to carry their child, which doesn't work out. They finally adopt two African American brothers. Keith and Charles engage in discussions of race, gender, sexuality, and confront many of the issues involving surrogate parenting, adoption by gay couples, and multiracial families, yet this type of representation is rare.

Patterns of Deviance: Comedy, Shock, Crime, and Difference

When interracial relationships are portrayed on television, these representations are most often found in side story lines. These relationships are almost exclusively depicted as comical misadventures, play on perceptions of difference for shock value, introduced as part of a criminal case, or used as symbolic of the different worlds that are being portrayed, highlighting that racially matched characters are the norm.

Putting characters of different races together has been used for comedic or shock value, where the two are clearly mismatched and the undesirability of the minority nonwhite character is emphasized.[39] On the half-hour NBC comedy My Name Is Earl, the lead character Earl, a white man, is always getting into difficult situations trying to fix his bad "karma" for things he has done wrong in the past, including his ex-wife who has run off with a black man named Darnell. The interracial relationship makes for many laughs because Joy would rather be with a doo-rag, wife-beater-clad Darnell than Earl. The fun of interracial relationships was further highlighted in an episode where Joy was afraid of how her father would react to Darnell being black, only to find out that her father loves to sleep with black women, which puts forth the problematic idea that equates sex with acceptance. The executive producer/creator minimizes the role of race, stating that the characters fit the situation and "they're calling it like they see it and talking like real people talk."[40] This is one of the shows that the USA Today article referenced in the beginning of the chapter cites as an example of the "irreverent humor" that illustrates television is color-blind.[41] Yet rather than color-blind, these depictions play on the absurdity of matching people of different races, particularly in these examples when the black characters are also portrayed as physically unappealing and of a lower socioeconomic class status.

Representing interracial relationships as absurd for laughs and using the story to establish the show as "cutting edge" is a common strategy for presenting interracial relationships. For example, Kirstie Alley's short-lived Showtime comedy Fat Actress was developed to tackle the avoidance of Hollywood to portray larger women and plays on the idea that black men prefer larger women. In the episode, the white male television executives all discuss how fat and unattractive she is, yet the black television executive

Max Cooper is attracted to her, so she invites him over. Their date quickly moves to the bedroom, where she comments on his large penis as she unbuttons his pants, yet his enthusiasm about her "juicy" body is comical to her rather than attractive.[42] Using interracial sex to push boundaries is widely recognized, as Dana Wade, the president of advertising agency Spike DDB, clearly expressed, asserting that for television ads, "certain brands might use interracial couples to convey a hip image" adding that "the whole personae of the brand is kind of risky, or on the edge."[43] Ironically these "hip" and "cutting edge" depictions are actually just barely repackaged stereotypes, such as *Fat Actress*'s depiction of well-endowed black men who desire any white women, even those deemed "fat and unattractive" by white men.[44] As Douglas Kellner argues, "difference sells," yet the presentation must be constantly adjusted to fit the contemporary discourses on race.[45] By showing interracial relationships yet parodying them at the same time, the shows can maximize their audience without alienating others.

Among the small numbers of shows with predominantly black casts (and black audiences), interracial dating is also played for laughs, yet in different ways. On shows such as *Girlfriends*, *The Hughleys*, and *One on One*, the comedy is based on the problems that come for black people who date interracially and what it says about the black person's identity and even the identity of white people who date interracially. In one episode of the show *Moesha*, an African American teen is accused by her friends of thinking she is "too good for the hood" when she dates a white boy. Despite the more serious tone of the episode, the UPN network decided to promote the show by showing what he described as "wacky, nonsensical clips . . . that were totally unrelated to the story line." *Moesha*'s television producer, Ralph Farquhar, recounted how the studio executives told him presenting the issue as serious was not what they were interested in, which he viewed as an inability to handle interracial relationships.

Not surprisingly, reality show producers have also used racial difference for comedy and shock value to heighten interest, while playing on stereotypes. The recent popularity of prime-time reality programming and the subsequent overload of reality television shows has not completely ignored interracial couples, especially in their quest for drama. Interracial stories may be appealing to show without mentioning race, and in particular by showing interracial possibilities that promote the *idea* that society is color-blind while affirming the problems with crossing the color-blind color line. Reality daytime talk show hosts such as Jerry Springer, Ricki Lake, Montel Williams, and Maury Povich have never shied away from interracial relationships, routinely bringing out young white women who are trying to identify their baby's daddy and have one or more black men to test.[46] Yet on dating shows, it was the norm to only feature same-race couples, such as on the shows of the 1980s and early 1990s like *Love Connection, The Dating Game,* and *The Newlywed Game.* The new batch of reality dating and marriage shows do dabble in diversity, but most times nonwhite contestants who are included in "the initial pools for shows like *The Bachelor* are customarily given a one week courtesy rose before being dumped the following week.[47] It's so common that the reality show satire *Joe Schmo 2* parodied it their second season in a first-week racial elimination ceremony called *Black-out.*"[48] On prime-time network television, the show *Wife Swap* featured an interracial couple in a January 2005 episode, described as "the mother of an interracial family trades with the mother of a traditional family." The interracial family consists of an unmarried white mother, black father, and biracial children, who have a messy house, meditate, and are vegans, while the other white, Italian family consists of a married white mother, white father, and kids, who have an incredibly clean house and are "traditional." When the white Italian mother Paulette first gets to the house, she sees pictures of black people and remarks, "I don't know if it is a black family and that concerns me, because me being white." She blames her uncomfortableness on the black family and never even considers the possibility that this may be a multiracial family. The show highlights the differences and explicitly defines the white family as traditional, emphasizing the "nontraditional" aspects of the other family through not only being an interracial family but also through their meditation, spiritual beliefs, and veganism.

Interracial relationships are also depicted as shadowed in deviance and danger in criminal justice and legal and medical dramas such as *House, Law & Order, CSI,* and *Cold Case.* For example, the medical drama *House* featured an episode "Fools for Love," in which an interracial couple, Jeremy, a white man, and Tracy, a black woman, are admitted to the hospital after being seriously injured in a hostage situation. Based on the trademark medical investigation of the lead doctor House, it is discovered that the couple have a rare genetic condition, which they share because they are actually half brother and sister (they were neighbors and Jeremy's white father had an affair with Tracy's black mother). This revelation is even more shocking given their perceived racial difference, and the implication that these two should not be together is clear. While race is not mentioned, their previously unknown shared parentage and rare genetic disorder serve as a proxy for race in why they should not be together. In the 2008–2009 season, *House* features an interracial relationship between the black doctor Eric Foreman and a white doctor Olivia. Yet once again, the relationship begins in deviance: Olivia is a bisexual woman who is potentially dying from Huntington's disease and they become involved because she is in his clinical medical trial. Their relationship is forbidden by the lead doctor House and has led Foreman to risk his medical career trying to save her.

On the various *Law & Order* shows, an interracial sexual encounter or relationship is occasionally featured, though most often the audience does not see the relationship but rather the interracial relationship emerges out of the criminal investigation. As discussed earlier, racial difference and the interracial relationship can be used for heightened surprise or intrigue, playing on the assumption of same-race relationships. Given that the premise of the show is that a crime has occurred, the context of the relationship is usually deviant and reinforces stereotypes.[49] For example, on *Law & Order: Special Victims Unit* "Criminal," a white college student, Rebecca, is found raped and murdered in a park. The first suspect is a black homeless man, yet attention soon turns to her professor, Javier Vega, also a black man. All evidence points to Professor Vega, and the jury does not believe his account that they were lovers and he is convicted. The police soon figure out that a fellow white student, Kyle, killed Rebecca and framed Vega because of jealousy over Vega and Rebecca's relationship. While ultimately the black man was not the murdering rapist, the myth of the black rapist underlies the story line, in which two black men are suspected and ultimately the white man used the believability of the black man's guilt as his protection. Another example that is characteristic of interracial plot lines on the *Law & Order* series is a *SVU* episode "Debt," where a Chinese American single mother of two children disappears. She had been involved in an Asian-owned Internet matchmaking service where white men could arrange to marry an Asian woman. Initially the detectives pursue the white man she had been connected with, but they soon realize that she was trying to raise the money she needed to pay off a powerful Asian man in Chinatown to bring her daughter from China. The Chinese people in Chinatown are portrayed as illegal immigrants, Asian women are portrayed as working in laundries, sweatshops, and looking for white men to marry, and Asian men are portrayed as responsible for extorting money for illegal immigrants and exploiting Asian women as prostitutes. Also, it is the white detective who personally ensures that the case is solved and risks his life and career to bring down the Asian man before he can kill the missing woman's daughter. On television, as exemplified on *Law & Order* and *House*, the interracial union serves to simultaneously glorify whiteness by making white police officers, doctors, and lawyers the heroes or "saviors" and problematizing interracial relationships, which end in murder and devastation whether it is depicted as racial, racially motivated, or not.

Beyond comedy, shock, and crime, interracial relationships are also presented as outside the norm by beginning or existing in a different social world. On shows like *ER* and *Friends*, main characters left for foreign lands only to return with new partners of a different race, such as *ER*'s white Dr. Carter, who went on a humanitarian mission to Africa and returned with a pregnant black fiancé, and *Friends'* white character Ross, who went on a paleontology dig and returned with an Asian girlfriend. The drama *Heroes* features a number of different interracial possibilities as part of interrelated stories about individuals with superhuman powers. Yet the relationships center around racial stereotypes, with Niki, a white stripper, and her estranged black husband who is an ex-convict, as well as a love triangle between Isaac, a Latino drug addict, Simone, a black woman, and Peter, a white male nurse. On the hit drama *Lost*, which centers around the survivors of a plane crash on a deserted island, there have been a few interracial relationships including Sayid, a former member of the Iraqi militia, and Shannon, a white American blond woman, which did not last. Introducing a partner of another race on *Lost* was also used to surprise the audience. When the survivors from the front of the plane found out that there were also survivors from the back of the plane on another part of the island, Rose, a black woman, was waiting to be reunited with her husband Bernard, who had been at the back of the plane. When Bernard appears, there is a moment of confusion because he is a white man. Hurley, one of the other survivors, commented, "So Rose's husband's white. Didn't see that one coming," echoing everyone's expectation of a black man. The producers acknowledged the need to address the race difference, as executive producer Carlton Cuse explained, "We thought everyone's expectation would be for her to have a black husband. We wanted to confound everyone's expectation. Everyone would be looking for the 50-year-old black guy."[50] The actress L. Scott Caldwell, who plays Rose, also commented that it would have been unrealistic not to address the racial difference, "because the idea of an interracial relationship still matters somewhere to somebody, it is ultimately much better to explore it than ignore it."[51] The example of Rose and Bernard shows how interracial relationships become acceptable to show when they are removed from realistic situations and everyday life, serve to bring suspense or surprise, or are presented in a way that does not threaten, such as a fifty-something white man with a fifty-something black woman, safer by the gender combination, age, and remote locale. It seems interracial relationships may be more appealing when they happen in alternate worlds like *Lost*'s mysterious deserted island, *Heroes'* world of superpowers, or when characters on shows leave their everyday worlds, further symbolizing that these unions are not the norm.[52]

Patterns of Representations: Good Desirable Whites, Exceptional People of Color, and Others

Intricately wrapped in the representations of interracial unions are the ways that whiteness, blackness, and racial Others are represented. When interracial relationships occur, if it is not shadowed in a world of deviance, the

person of color involved is presented as an exceptional person, usually removed from their racial community, and the "goodness" of the white person
is explicitly confirmed through the relationship.

When interracial relationships are shown on television, it is most commonly between a white man and woman of color. The representation of a
woman of color dating a string of white men, sometimes at the same time and
often to the exclusion of men of her own race, appears throughout a number
of shows. On a show like *ER*, which is celebrated for its racially diverse cast,
there are characters who only engage in interracial relationships, such as Dr.
Neela Rasgotra, an Indian medical student from Britain who has a number of
interracial flirtations and relationships, actually never having a relationship
with an Asian American/Indian man.[53] Despite low rates of intermarriage
between white men and black women, this pairing appears most frequently.[54]
For example, on the hit show *Friends*, the two white male characters of Joey
and Ross simultaneously dated Charlie, a beautiful black female paleontolo-
gist. This pattern of representation of an African American woman who is
only involved with wealthy white men is also found on the UPN's *Girlfriends*.
The show revolves around the lives of four African American women, all
best friends, and one of the four women almost exclusively dates white men,
preferably ones with money.[55] While race is addressed, supposedly from the
perspective of black people, a white man produces the show.[56] Similarly,
Nip/Tuck, a popular prime-time cable network show on FX, featured a multi-
episode guest appearance by the African American actress Sanaa Lathan,
who played a woman torn between her "rich tycoon husband and the plastic
surgeon Christian Troy treating him," both of whom are white.[57] The actress,
Sanaa Lathan, described the relationships,

> I have so much respect for [*Nip/Tuck* creator] Ryan Murphy, because my
> character could have been any race. But race never came into it, and I love
> that.[58]

Race may not have been addressed, but given the small number of depictions
of black women on television, this representation of a black woman romantically involved with not one but two rich white men undoubtedly fuels
racialized and gendered stereotypes. These images of black women chasing
wealthy or powerful (sometimes older) white men support the long-standing
beliefs about black women and plays into white male fantasies where these
black women are sexually attracted and available only to white men.[59] While
the black women depicted tend to be very successful and very attractive like
most women on television, they are disconnected from black communities,

and their beauty is often based on white standards with light skin and long, straight hair. While "the uncontrolled sexuality of the Black woman may not loom as large in white fear as her male counterpart, it is still always there, serving as an alibi for the white male use of the Black woman as his sexual property."[60]

One of the most visible, "successful" interracial relationships on prime-time occurred in the 2003–2004 season of ER. Dr. John Carter, one of the regular ER doctors, returns from a humanitarian mission in the African Congo with Makemba, who is pregnant with his child and described as "a beautiful native AIDS worker." While we only see briefly how their relationship developed in the Congo through a few flashbacks, the pregnancy both highlights the sexual nature of the relationship and links these two otherwise opposite individuals into a relationship.[61]

The geography of their relationship is also very symbolic. While they meet in a war-torn African country, their relationship brings them back to Carter's home in the United States, yet she does not feel comfortable in Chicago and leaves to go back to Africa for a few weeks, where the distance between them geographically further serves to symbolize the "difference" between them. The ER producers address racial difference in a few different ways in Dr. Carter and Kem's relationship. When they talk about their baby, Carter says, "nature likes ethnic diversity" and Kem replies laughing, "we should make him marry a Latino or an Asian." Yet these discussions of race are very superficial and focus on the celebration of multiracialism. While their relationship withstands the problems they are encountering, Kem returns to Chicago, only to lose the baby, and immediately returns to Africa. The next episodes focus on how Carter is coping with the loss of his son and his pain, clearly situating the audience as aligned with Carter while Kem is someplace else, the Other. Carter and Kem's interracial relationship is shown as two "star-crossed lovers" from different worlds who engage in a wildly exciting and romantic love but are plagued by obstacles. After episodes apart, Carter flies to Paris where Kem is tending her sick mother, again placing their relationship in a geographically different location. The audience learns that Kem has a white mother and was actually raised in Paris, as she described the difficulties of being "a novelty . . . a very white mother, black father, (and her) a brown girl" which is why she moved to Africa. Carter says he will "give it all up for her" to move to Africa, but she doesn't want him to. In the language we see how Kem could try his world presumably because it was white and civilized, but for Carter to move with her would be too much of a sacrifice, which symbolizes the lesser value of Africa and the worth of Carter's life, especially given his recent tenure and promotion. For Carter and Kem to be together he must give up his established life and as he says, "start over," which he ultimately does. Interracial love requires sacrifice and may only be possible outside of one's community and world. This idea of white man as missionary or savior who becomes involved with a woman of color—usually a light-skinned, biracial, and exotic woman—and leaves his former life behind is one of the most common representations that exists, as I will highlight later in chapter 3 with movies like *Bulworth* and *Monster's Ball*.

Similarly, when a black man is paired opposite a white woman on prime-time television, there is a very specific type of character that is depicted, such as the characters of Bruce Van Exel (*Judging Amy*), Preston Burke (*Grey's Anatomy*), and Peter Benton (*ER*). For example, on *Judging Amy*, even though Amy and Bruce never enter into an actual intimate dating relationship, Bruce is exceptional as a conservative voice of reason as Amy's literal left-hand man. It is safe to place him with a white woman, even safer after he voiced his opposition to dating white women, and the opposition to interracial dating was simultaneously placed on minority communities through the character of Bruce and a Latino character Ignacio. Ironically on *Judging Amy*, the producer Barbara Hall had criticized what she saw as the way "a lot of the African American characters are 'whited up' by the time they get on television," yet it can be argued that she does something similar with Bruce. Bruce is Amy's perfect partner, yet "safe" because he is removed from the black community, unlikely to acknowledge racial problems, does not believe in interracial dating (though it seems he might make an exception for Amy), and safely constructed as Amy's confidant. On *Grey's Anatomy*, the top surgeon Preston Burke, who is involved with an Asian American medical intern Cristina Yang, is presented as having "transcended . . . racial origin and, in so doing, have become normal."[62] The creator/executive producer Shonda Rhimes espouses a color-blind approach, stating that they simply "cast(ing) whoever we thought was best for the part."[63] This fits into the pattern of presenting some black characters as "just ordinary people" as part of a color-blind ideology that pretends race no longer matters. Yet the idea of difference is clearly portrayed through Burke's character who is stoic, very serious, conservative, trustworthy, and professional while Yang is portrayed as cutthroat competitive, unemotional, and disorganized. In one scene where Burke and Yang are in a fight because she was hesitant to move in with him, Burke quietly, yet assertively, tells her, "I am Preston Burke. I am a widely regarded thorasic surgeon . . . and most important I am a good person . . . I cook . . . ," and then describing her he says, "You are a slob. . . . You are a slovenly angry. . . . guarded stubborn person." This scene clearly shows and even has him state—just in case the audience didn't notice—he is exceptional and she is lucky to have him, thereby justifying the interracial union and simultaneously making Yang an undesirable mate, so who cares that she is with a black man?[64] The racialized message is still received yet in a color-blind package like contemporary racism and promotes an assimilationist perspective that encourages the view that race does not matter.[65]

On *ER*, Dr. Peter Benton is a difficult person who had a string of problematic relationships, with Jeannie, a married African American hospital worker who eventually found out she was HIV positive from her husband, and with Carla, a working-class African American hairdresser, who he has a child with. After this string of misses, he developed a brief relationship with a white British doctor, Elizabeth Corday, and she helps change him into a more pleasant person.[66] Through Benton's interaction with Corday, he loosens up, and she even gets him drunk after he states he never drinks. While he had always been portrayed as very serious, conservative, brilliant, and upwardly mobile, especially in relation to his family, through his relationship with her he is happy, silly, and even sensitive. The relationship between Benton and Corday, while not discussed in racial terms, plays on the differences between the two and the transformation of Benton. In many ways, through the interracial relationship we see how "blackness is . . . a condition from which black people can be liberated . . . escaped from the shackles of his racial origins."[67] Still, both deny their relationship at different points. At Benton's son baptism, he says he doesn't have a white girlfriend when asked by his family while his nephew says, "Daddy (Benton's brother-in-law) said he heard Grandma turning over in her grave," clearly marking Benton's black family as opposed to interracial relationships. Yet the relationship also causes problems for Corday in terms of her career. Her white male supervisor wants to date her and feels her relationship with Benton will upset him, yet it is not addressed in racial terms but rather just a situation of romantic interest and jealousy. Benton is potentially capable of being with a white woman because he is removed from blackness in terms of family and stereotypical behavior, and he improved even more when with a white woman, in contrast to failed relationships with black women. While Alex Kingston, who played Corday, described the relationship as having "transcended race,"[68] the actor Eriq La Salle saw it differently as he expressed his very public outrage and demanded the on-screen successful interracial relationship end given the unsuccessful relationships he had with black women.[69] The relationship ended with Corday becoming involved with the white doctor Mark Greene and Benton eventually becoming involved with a black doctor.

The "tamed black man" character becomes even more apparent in contrast to other black male characterizations, such as *ER*'s Dr. Gregg Pratt, an African

American doctor who dates many women yet never a white woman. Through the course of a number of scenes, Dr. Pratt is more likely to be accused of trying to inappropriately touch a white woman than date her.[70] He is also linked sexually to a Chinese American doctor Jing-Mei, which helps to not only solidify his reputation as a womanizer but also characterize her as sexually available.[71] It is clear that Pratt's character is much different than the "tamed black men" characters like Bruce, Benton, and Burke, like Bill Cosby, who become less threatening, even nonthreatening, as an exception to the mass of black men; therefore, these men can coexist within white society, "containable within family values."[72] Their presence as an "economically and socially successful representatives of middle- and upper-class black America (and) apparent acceptance of majority culture common sense" reaffirms the "myth of assimilation."[73]

While there are few examples of Latinos on television, Latina/o characters in interracial relationships are often depicted ambiguously with little discussion or mention of their ethnicity or race, in essence also exceptions particularly because they are removed from Latina/o communities. On *Grey's Anatomy*, one of the supporting characters, Dr. Callie Torres, was dating and married a white intern in the 2007 season. While her ethnicity or identity as a Latina is never discussed directly, she is clearly shown to be different than the other white women, in terms of her behavior (more like one of the guys) and her appearance (larger frame and less feminine). In later seasons, Callie's husband divorces her and she becomes involved in a relationship with a white woman, further highlighting her "deviant" sexuality. Another example is the Latino actor Jimmy Smits, who played Senator Matt Santos, who ran for president on the 2005–2006 season of *The West Wing*. He is married to a blond white woman, and the way his ethnicity/race is portrayed is through his family more than his own character. This pattern is clear by looking at the television roles Smits has played where his racial/ethnic background was rarely mentioned, such as Victor Sifuentes on the 1980s hit drama *L.A. Law*, who was often linked to a fellow white attorney and more recently, Detective Bobby Simone on *NYPD Blue*, who was also involved with a fellow white woman detective. Yet these relationships were not presented as interracial. The fluidity of Smits's characters illustrates how race and ethnicity is socially constructed and the differing levels of acceptance of race mixing depending on who is involved. Smit's characters on *NYPD Blue* and *The West Wing* are raceless and portrayed with only traces of ethnicity, thereby more able to cross over and be paired with white women.[74]

When a man or woman of color is paired with a white person for any sustained period of time as a central story line, they are almost always an exceptional being. As George Lipsitz argues, "On television, black people who do not belong on *The Cosby Show* belong on *Cops*." In terms of interracial relationships on television, when black and Latino men are involved, they

tend to be criminal suspects and working-class buffoons such as on *Law &
Order* and *My Name Is Earl*, which emphasize deviance and undesirability,
or incredibly handsome supersurgeons and professionals like on *ER*, *Grey's
Anatomy*, and *Judging Amy*, who live detached from communities of color.

Rewriting Race through Interracial Relationships

While these patterns of depictions undoubtedly reproduce racial hierarchies
and reinforce racial stereotypes, a number of television show producers
maintain that they have adopted a color-blind strategy, which they argue
transcends race.[75] For example, on the popular *Ally McBeal* show, the executive producer argued,

> We are a consciously color-blind show. In the history of the show, we have never
> addressed race. The reason is simple. In my naive dream, I wish that the world
> could be like this. Since Ally lives in a fanciful and whimsical world, there is not
> going to be any racial differences or tensions. All people are under one sun.[76]

On the show for a short time, Ally dates Greg Butters, a successful black doctor, and they spend time together at a mostly white after-work hangout of the
firm. The producer David Kelley stated, "Greg and Ally . . . will have their
ups and downs. But their problems will be organic to the couples and to being
men and women."[77] Yet Ally and Greg's time together never developed into
a serious relationship. Also, being set in Boston, this color-blind approach
allows the producers such as Kelley to ignore the unpleasantness of Boston's
still segregated realities with noted racial problems.

Denying that race matters is a common strategy on a number of shows
such as *The New Adventures of Old Christine*, which features a divorced white
woman with a child in a private school where she becomes interested in a
black teacher, Mr. Harris. Their attraction is highlighted with a passionate
embrace, yet they cannot date because of a school policy that forbids dating
between teachers and parents. Race is never discussed other than in flippant
comments about the black teacher like "Who knew diversity could be so
gorgeous?" The creator Kari Lizer, like *Ally McBeal*'s producer David Kelley,
stated,

> It's shocking to see how segregated comedies are. . . . I don't see (race) entering
> their personal relationship. It's not a factor and there are enough factors for
> them to deal with. It's not a fresh area and I would love it to be a non-issue.[78]

While opposition to interracial relationships is not discussed as a possible
barrier to their relationship, making their relationship forbidden for other
reasons such as school policy serves similar purposes. They date briefly with

Mr. Harris appearing in only eight episodes over two seasons (2006–2008), before he leaves and Christine returns to white men.[79]

The producers of ER also adopt the idea that color does not matter, at least when it comes to some relationships. Referring to a relationship between Neela, an Indian doctor, and Michael, a black doctor, the executive producer David Zabel states, "Honestly, we really don't even talk about it or consider that it's an interracial couple. The romance is meant to 'sweep viewers away, making them forget about race.'" The actress, Parminder Nagra, who plays Neela, makes a similar argument:

> (It) would be more of an issue if ER suddenly cast an Indian man for her to love. . . . why wouldn't these two people get together . . . it's important to have this on screen . . . we know racism exists. Let's show people getting on. Let's be positive about it.[80]

Yet despite these positive voices of support, their relationship was short-lived, and immediately after they get married, Michael voluntarily returns to the Iraq War and is killed.

While television producers will discuss their color-blind approach, other more pervasive racial strategies exist, yet are not acknowledged. For example, Aaron Sorkin, the white producer/creator of the critically acclaimed show The West Wing, discussed how the show received hate mail when the president's white daughter, Zoey Bartlet, begins a relationship with black presidential aide Charlie Young:[81]

> Frankly, the most surprising thing . . . is that these people were watching our show and not WWF Smackdown . . . in my world, such (romances) are not particularly noteworthy. Having said that, I created an extreme case to remind us that it's not completely irrelevant.[82]

According to Sorkin, racism is something found among a certain group who watch the WWF wrestling show, presumably less educated and of a lower socioeconomic status than those who watch The West Wing. The extreme case of racism he is referring to is the cliffhanger episode where skinheads shoot at the president and his aides because of the interracial relationship between the president's daughter Zoey and Charlie. Thomas Schlamme, The West Wing's executive producer, discussed how depicting interracial couples on television is indicative that "the taboo has started to diminish," yet Schlamme said they (he and executive producers Aaron Sorkin and John Wells) were more interested in exploring the political implications of having the president's daughter date interracially. Schlamme adds, "It makes for good drama. And we can also look at the drama of hate in this country. The racial aspect is not at the center."[83] Ironically Schlamme disconnects racism from the hate that he portrays and acts as if race is not a factor. Sorkin also discussed, "I feel like the best contribution I can make as a writer toward these things is by ignoring them . . . we were getting into science-fiction," because he believes interracial relationships are widely accepted.[84] Yet he further contradicts himself when he argues that he didn't want to focus on race, stating, "I never really thought I was going to tackle interracial relationships or blow the lid off anything." Yet if it is so acceptable and common, why don't the shows they produce have more interracial couples featured?

Shows like *The West Wing, ER, My Name Is Earl, Judging Amy,* and others promote the idea that racism exists only among white extremists, a few bad whites, or communities of color, often using an interracial relationship as the way to show this. For example, on *Judging Amy,* a white male court worker objected to Amy and Bruce's close relationship and falsely filed a charge of sexual impropriety against them. When the court administrator called them in to discuss these allegations, Amy reacts angrily, accusing racism and sexism, while Bruce wants to allow them to be disciplined without fighting. Even when one or two whites are shown as racist or discriminatory, there are always good and just white people who fight for what is right often more than their black counterparts, like Amy. On *ER,* when the white Dr. Carter takes Kem with him to meet his father at a board meeting for the foundation trust he oversees, Carter's father looks disturbed that Kem is there, and he is even more distressed, along with the other white board members, when Carter announces that the foundation will now devote its resources to social issues such as hunger and homelessness rather than art and cultural affairs. After the meeting, Carter's father accuses him of disappearing around the world and coming back as "an avenging angel . . . with a pregnant African girl." Carter's father is presented as one disconnected voice of opposition and racial prejudice, while the audience is aligned with Carter, who has been transformed by Kem, reminiscent of the noble savage/exotic Other representation discussed earlier. Similarly, on *ER* there is an older white male administrative assistant who routinely espouses racist and sexist comments,[85] like referring to Carter's African girlfriend as "he's got African love on the line . . . Kenya love nest." The predominantly white television producers prefer to present intolerance and racism as the case of one individual, yet "white generated and white maintained oppression"[86] occur not through isolated incidents but through a structure of racism where it is comical for a white man to espouse discriminatory remarks.

While denying white racism exists in anything more than a few marginalized individuals and maintaining the color blindness of the white individuals, television producers often strategically place opposition to interracial relationships with the characters of color. Shows like *The Jeffersons*, *Night Court*, *City of Angels*, *The Hughleys*, *ER*, and *Judging Amy* have all showcased opposition to interracial relationships among individuals and families of color. On *ER* the black doctor Greg Pratt tries to sabotage a white doctor's blind date with an African American woman. When the attractive black woman shows up, Pratt tries to embarrass the white doctor by mentioning his three nipples but this only serves to make her like him more, as she reveals that she has six toes. This depiction highlights the idea that race does not matter, instead emphasizing the similarities between the white doctor and the black woman because of their anatomical oddities. On *Judging Amy*, Amy's mother Maxine Gray, a sixty-something social worker, dates a Latino gardener, Ignacio,[87] though his Latino identity is rarely addressed. Yet when his daughter dates a white man, he expresses opposition and says he wants his daughter to know her "culture" and have "racial pride." Amy discusses his opposition with her black colleague Bruce, expecting that he will think Ignacio is wrong like they do, but he tells her that "honoring my race informs my personal life."[88] Beyond placing opposition with the black and Latino characters, Bruce's opposition to interracial relationships also serves as a clear obstacle to any possible relationship.[89]

Latino and black characters become the voices of opposition to interracial unions, implying their views are racist and exclusionary, while the white characters are presented as open-minded and accepting. For example, on *Judging Amy*, the white characters devote their lives to fighting social injustices, including Amy, the juvenile court judge, her mother Maxine, the radical social worker, her brother and his wife, who adopt a biracial child, and her other brother who at one point teaches writing to prisoners. These characterizations serve to release whites from any responsibility for racism or opposition to interracial relationships. This fits in with the safe color-blind model where the black or minority character is removed from his or her racial community, happily living among all whites, and most likely to be the one who has the problem with interracial relationships. A color-blind approach to interracial relationships does not make us forget race, but rather we simply interpret the interaction within the existing understandings of race. In these relationships and the lives of the African American, Latina, and Asian characters, race is rarely addressed and the relationships are never put forth as long-term but rather distractions on the way to real love or for comic effect. Furthermore, as we have seen when interracial relationships are introduced, it rarely lasts for more than a few episodes and the issue of race or racial difference is rarely addressed, or as mentioned earlier, it is presented as an individual issue. When opposition to interracial unions is addressed, it tends to be depicted as a problem of one racist white individual or group, or more commonly as a problem for black and minority communities. It also creates a safe space to represent black characters such as Bruce Van Exel and Greg Pratt because they do not desire relationships with white women and oppose interracial relationships. Thereby "color is safely contained," whether it be outside of white intimate realms of family and marriage, or if the person of color is allowed in, their "color" must be contained outside of their worlds, such as the black man who is removed from his family and community and adopts what is put forth as "white" values.[90]

Conclusion

While we are seeing more depictions of interracial relationships on the small screen, these depictions are still few and far between, and when depicted these relationships present particular images and serve specific purposes. Television dabbles in interracial unions, yet they rarely materialize, and when they do, the relationship is often impossible for other reasons, such as work or school policies that forbid it or that the person really belongs with someone else. In representations of interracial intimacy, the individuals, couples, and relationships are presented in a certain number of ways that either represent the danger/deviance of interracial relationships or the minimal acceptability of the relationships because it is short-term or with an exceptional person of color. Regardless of whether interracial couples are shown or ignored, certain images and discourses are conveyed. For example, Asian men are rarely seen on prime-time television, and when they are shown, the representations fall within classic stereotypes, such as the 2006–2007 season of *Beauty and the Geek*, where three nerdy Asian brothers vie for the attention of mostly white "beauties." Coupled with the tendency to pair Asian women exclusively with white men on shows like *Ally McBeal*, *ER*, and *Friends* spin-off *Joey*, these representations reflect a dominant narrative about whiteness where Asian women choose white America over their own culture and men, reinforcing the idea of Asian men as undesirable and desexualized, and are reflected beyond the small screen in high rates of intermarriage between white men and Asian American women.[91] Regardless of the racial makeup, interracial relationships particularly between whites and blacks are either alienating (not even shown),[92] taboo and shown as problematic, or a fantasy, a fetish that allows the viewer (and possibly used to attract more viewers) to dabble in difference, living vicariously through the TV characters, yet still existing as marginal story lines rather than centered.[93] Multiracialism and consuming color as exotic may be tolerated, even purposefully marketed,[94] yet this fits in with the historical pattern where whites have been simultaneously appalled and intrigued, offended and attracted to racial Others sexually, while monitoring, disciplining, and indulging. As Stuart Hall argued, "there's nothing that global postmodernism loves better than a certain kind of difference: a touch of ethnicity, a taste of the exotic . . . 'a bit of the other.'"[95]

The particular patterns of representations reflect the stories we know and the stories we want to continue to see.[96] Journalists like Ann Oldenburg and Carmen Van Kerchove, codirector of New Demographic, a diversity training company, argue, "the more people see positive and normal representations, that will lessen the fear and taboo,"[97] referring to many of the television relationships discussed here, but I argue that these representations are not normalizing interracial relationships or lessening the novelty. While the growing numbers of interracial couples on television have been used to argue that America has become a color-blind, multiracial utopia, instead I argue these depictions overwhelmingly reproduce our long-standing notions about the deviant nature of interracial sex and the location of these relationships in the margins of society.[98] Just because race is not discussed does not mean it does not exist, rather in its deliberate denial it can be ever more present. As Henry Giroux argues about the sexually suggestive interracial Benetton clothing advertisements, these depictions do not increase racial tolerance and awareness, because they are "decontextualiz[ed], dehistoriciz[ed], and recontextualiz[ed]" and reproduce the dominant social relations rather than challenge them. Therefore, couples and relationships can still be racialized, even deviantized without even having to mention race. More importantly, these images enter our homes weekly, even nightly, which makes "these representations of difference" believable, knowable, and familiar.[99]

These representations include racialized comments and symbolic images of difference, while promoting the notion of color blindness by placing outright opposition and racial prejudice as existing with an extreme racist group or bigoted individual. The representations of whites as a group remain positive, particularly in relation to characters of color. The problem of race is squarely placed with people of color, and the idea that all groups can be equally prejudice is common without the acknowledgment of white racism. Race and gender issues are also often tied together with gender trumping race, in terms of the characters addressing the sexist comments or behavior but not recognizing or addressing racism or racist comments.[100] Furthermore, the black, Latino, or Asian characters who do engage in interracial relationships are presented as immersed in white communities and "race-less." We are in an era of exceptions, and on television, minority characters like The West Wing's Matthew Santos, ER's Makemba, or Grey's Anatomy's Preston Burke who do date or marry interracially are presented as exceptional exceptions that are separated from communities of color, and even their own families.[101] Other more dangerous interracial possibilities are still taboo. Did *Kevin Hill*, which featured the black actor Taye Diggs as a charismatic and sexual lawyer, and *LAX*, which paired the white Heather Locklear with the black actor Blair Underwood with sexual tension and attraction, fail to attract large network audiences because both portrayed confident, assertive, overtly sexual black men who, unlike the tamed black men on *ER*, *Grey's Anatomy*, and *Judging Amy*, did not have a problem romancing white women?

The interracial relationships we see on television do not challenge racial boundaries but rather happen securely in the constructed borders, such as a black woman in an all-white world or an interracial nonwhite relationship. The fantasy of interracial relationships cannot be bogged down with the unpleasantness of racism, inequality, and discrimination, so it erases these structural and institutional realities that shape everyday social interaction. Interracial relationships may be popping up more frequently on television, but they do more to reinforce the current racial situation rather than challenge us to move beyond it. Still, in contemporary television the fascination with interracial sexuality may be more acceptable than the reality. Since "economically, culturally, and politically, popular television remains firmly in white control,"[102] interracial images on television allow white people to satisfy their attraction/fascination with illusions of interracial sex in a safe space, so they watch it without being contaminated by it, and better yet can say, "I am hip. . . . I am not a racist. . . . I watch interracial couples on TV."

Notes

1. Ann Oldenburg, "Love Is No Longer Color-coded on TV," *USA Today*, December 20, 2005. When interracial relationships do blossom on prime-time television, one recent trend is that the relationship is usually depicted with no mention of race, which is heralded by many, like the *USA Today* article. Another news article cites Yvette Walker, an African American woman married to a white man and creator of the *New People* interracial Internet magazine, who argues, "the fact that they're even bothering to write in (interracial couples) I think it is a good thing . . . if I had to pick between always focusing on race or not focusing on race, I'd say let's not focus on race." Quoted in Eric Deggans, "Too Subtle for the Small Screen," *St. Petersburg Times*, February 26, 2001.

2. Stuart Hall argues that "television is a discourse" in "Encoding and Decoding in the Television Discourse," 2005 [1973] in Darnell Hunt, *Channeling Blackness*, 49.

3. Hunt 2005, 1.

4. Gray 2004 [1995], xvii. I am extending Gray's argument about the presence of blacks in music videos, in sports, and in television/film not signaling acceptance to interracial couples.

5. While my discussion of all interracial couples on television is not exhaustive, I used a theoretical, nonrandom sampling method that I argue covers the types of depictions that exist, noting any exceptions or examples that do not fit the patterns identified. It would not have been desirable to do quantitative analysis using random sampling since interracial couples are not shown frequently or in a large selection of television shows. Instead, I conducted extensive research on all television shows through library databases, Internet databases, and by viewing hundreds of hours of television shows. Qualitative content analysis differs from quantitative content analysis of television, and some argue that since it allows the researcher to "use descriptive techniques to interpret observations in their symbolic form and to search for [inherent] meaning in content . . . [it] enables them to offer more insightful and complete analyses." Carolyn A. Stroman and Kenneth E. Jones, "The Analysis of Television Content," 275. See also Berg 2003; Fink and Gantz 1996; Gray 2005 [1995]; Hsia 1988; and Hunt 2005.

6. See Darnell Hunt, Channeling Blackness: Studies on Television and Race in America, 2005 and Gray 2005 [1995], 76–77 for an in-depth discussion of early TV images of African Americans.

7. Clara Rodriguez, Heroes, Lovers, and Others: The Story of Latinos in Hollywood (Washington, DC: Smithsonian, 2004), 93–94.

8. Daytime soap operas such as ABC's General Hospital were some of the first television shows to feature recurring interracial relationships, such as the 1980s marriage between the white doctor Tom Hardy and a black doctor colleague Simone. Interracial relationships are not common but do still occur on soap operas, though there are few characters of color on many soap operas. In April 1999, The Bold and the Beautiful featured a love triangle in which Amber, who is white, was involved with two men, Rick (white), who she is now married to, and Raymond (black), who she had a fling with, but she gets pregnant and doesn't know who the father is. The racial difference heightens the suspense, because "there would be no way for her to hide the baby's true paternity, if it turned out he fathered the child." See "The Moment of Truth: Who's the Father?" Soap Opera Weekly, Volume 10, 17 (April 27, 1999). Also in March 2000, the soap As the World Turns featured a love triangle where Denise, a young black woman, has a child with John, a white man, and when he tries to take the child from her, she is forced into a situation in which she loves Ben, an African American man, but may marry another white man, Andy, to help her chances of keeping custody. See Soap Opera Weekly, Volume 11, 10 (March 7, 2000).

9. See Gray 2005 [1995], 57–69; Du Brow 1990; Gitlin 1980; Press 1991; Taylor 1989. At this same time beginning in the 1970s, there was a new wave of depictions that emphasized lower-income black families such as Good Times, Sanford and Son, and What's Happening, yet still enforced white middle-class norms and values as well as the separate worlds of black and white.

10. See Gray 2005 [1995] for an extensive discussion of the politics of representation in network television and the changing depictions of African Americans.

11. Greg Braxton, "TV Finds Drama in Interracial Dating," *Los Angeles Times*, March 22, 2000.

12. Gray 2005 [1995], 87

13. Gray 2005 [1995], xxi; Elber 2003; NAACP 2003.

14. Darnell Hunt's "2007 Hollywood Writers Report—Whose Stories Are We Telling?" as reported in Carl DiOrio, "Report: White Males Still Dominate Writing Ranks," *Hollywood Reporter*, May 9, 2007. Accessed at www.hollywoodreporter.com.

15. Hunt 2005, 18.

16. Gray 2005 [1995], xxi and Darnell Hunt, *Channeling Blackness: Studies on Television and Race in America* (Oxford: Oxford University Press, 2005).

17. Gray 2005; Hunt 2005; and also Diane Raymond, "Popular Culture and Queer Representation: A Critical Perspective," who acknowledges the growing numbers of representations of gay/lesbian characters yet argues that these representations ignore the power and subordination as well as present certain images of homosexuality while supporting the norm of heterosexuality.

18. One example is an unaired pilot, *Pearl's Place to Play* (1994), created by four black men including Ralph Farquhar, a producer on *Married with Children*. Farquhar explained that "black response was very good, but white viewers didn't get it." The show addressed interracial dating with "some particularly bold dialogue . . . (with) a customer noting that white NBA owners don't like to see black men with 'their' women. 'Man, what you talking about?' responds Bernie. 'Every brother in sports got a white woman. . . . That's how the white man get his money back.'" Also in the mid-1990s, *The Sinbad Show* had a script rejected about interracial dating.

19. In the 2001–2002 season, there were a number of shows that were canceled soon after premiering, such as the predominantly black CBS drama *City of Angels*, which featured a relationship between a black nurse, Grace Patterson, and a Jewish doctor, Geoffrey Weiss (where the only opposition came from Grace's father). NBC's midseason drama *First Years*, which featured an interracial couple, and ABC's comedy *The Job*, which featured a married white cop with a black/biracial mistress, were also quickly canceled. Whoopi Goldberg's 2003 comedy *Whoopi* featured what a critic described as "an interracial romance involving one of the whitest black characters on television," and "an Iranian character who cracks jokes about terrorism, a white girl who acts like a hip-hop queen." The show never gained an audience and was canceled after a few episodes.

20. See *TV Guide* "Fall Preview" September 12–18, 2004, and D. Parvaz, "Paul Allen and His Beauty May Be Serious," *Seattle Post-Intelligencer*, December 7, 2004.

21. Blair Underwood discussed in an interview with Black Entertainment Television that his character on *LAX* "was not written Black. Officially they were looking for a Latin person. So I had to create my own back-story that my father was Cuban

and my grandfather was one of the original Tuskegee Airman, thus my interest in aviation . . ." James Hill interviewed Blair Underwood, posted September 30, 2004, at www.bet.com.

22. See *TV Guide* "Fall Preview" September 12–18, 2004, 38 and "Fall TV Preview," *Entertainment Weekly*, September 10, 2004.

23. See Craig Tomashoff, "CSI: Big Changes!" *TV Guide* (February 27–March 5, 2005).

24. Another example occurred during the 2006 season. The medical drama *House* introduced an interracial relationship when one of the black doctors was said to be dating a new white nurse, yet the relationship was never shown and ended within a few episodes.

25. Greg Braxton, "TV Finds Drama in Interracial Dating," *Los Angeles Times*, March 22, 2000.

26. Eric Deggans, "Too Subtle for the Small Screen," *St. Petersburg Times*, February 26, 2001.

27. In 2000, Grace dated a black man, played by Gregory Hines.

28. One media critic, Caryn James, "When It Comes to Casting, Love Conquers Color," *New York Times*, March 31, 2005, describes this *Friends* relationship as "David Schwimmer's character dated a woman played by Aisha Tyler, a situation so unremarkable that none of the friends bothered mentioning that she was black," which misses the denial of race and still-evident racialized stereotypes. On the show *Joey*, a *Friends* spin-off, Matt LeBlanc's character Joey had an on-again, off-again relationship with an Asian American woman played by Lucy Lui (who was his character's lover in the film *Charlie's Angels*).

29. On *Judging Amy*, as well as the *The West Wing*, "in well-publicized moves, minority characters were added at the last minute" before the 1999–2000 season began, according to Jonathan Storm, "Whites, Blacks Tend to Watch Different TV Shows," *Philadelphia Inquirer*, April 19, 2000.

30. Hall was quoted in "Judging from Relationships, Amy's Moving On," *Pittsburgh Post-Gazette*, February 13, 2001 (Story by Rob Owen, *Post-Gazette* TV Editor).

31. Greg Braxton, "TV Finds Drama in Interracial Dating," *Los Angeles Times*, March 22, 2000.

32. Journalist Jane Holahan writes, "Judge Amy Gray and Bruce Van Exel, her intense legal clerk, will never admit their feelings for each other . . . we were left with the two smiling at each other as if they were brother and sister. All those hints the writers threw into the scripts, all those looks the characters gave each other, all those lost opportunities will never amount to anything." "A Lament for 'Judging Amy' and Loose Ends Left Untied," *Lancaster New Era*, May 25, 2005.

33. Jing-Mei meets the black nurse Frank "Rambo" Bacon when she treats him for overexertion from running track, and she has trouble concentrating while she stares at his muscled body.

34. Prior to this baby story line, Gabrielle had an affair with a white teenage boy in the neighborhood, which helped secure her image as a very sexual being, accentu-

ated by her being the only woman without a child. Also, Carlos went to prison briefly for illegal activities. These depictions of Gabrielle and Carlos further the image of the hot Latin Lover along with promiscuousness, criminality, violence, and betrayal, though their race/ethnicity is rarely mentioned. On other shows, the Latin Lover image also appears frequently, usually as a one-episode encounter. For example, on the WB show *Charmed*, two sisters who are witches conjured up a dream lover—a Latino, brown-skinned, long-haired romantic lover—who they refer to as "Latin Lover," for a third sister.

35. There are a number of real-life examples, such as the Long Island couple who are suing because their daughter is "not even the same race, nationality, color . . . as they are." The father is white and the mother is a light-skinned Dominican. See Associated Press, "Fertility Clinic Used Wrong Sperm, Suit Claims, Baby Darker than Either Parent; Judge Allows Malpractice Case," March 23, 2007, on www.msnbc.com.

36. Eric Deggans, "Too Subtle for the Small Screen," *St. Petersburg Times*, February 26, 2001.

37. The birth mother says that now she has a better idea who the father is. As the family discusses the baby, Amy's brother refers to the baby as "black," and the wife corrects him, saying "biracial." He discusses how he is not sure they can raise him, being from "the land of baloney and milk" meaning white, which the wife thinks is ridiculous.

38. On *ER*, there is a rarely shown same-sex relationship between a white doctor and a Latina firefighter, where they decide to have a baby through artificial insemination of the Latina partner, but shortly after having the baby she dies and a custody battle erupts between her white lover and her family over the baby, highlighting gay/lesbian parenting and legal issues.

39. There are many examples, such as the commercials for a new show premiering midway through the 2005–2006 season, *Sons and Daughters*, where a white woman is telling her grown daughter that she is not prejudiced since she dated a black man, and when the daughter asks if she told anyone, the mother replies "of course not." Similarly, on the short-lived 2006 half-hour NBC comedy *Crumbs*, two white men are dealing with their mother, who is being released from a hospital after having a mental breakdown. When they pick her up, they see her in a passionate embrace with a large, black, male nurse.

40. As quoted in Ann Oldenburg, "Love Is No Longer Color-coded on TV," *USA Today*, December 20, 2005 (www.usatoday.com/life/television/news/2005-12-20-interracial-couples_x.htm).

41. Ann Oldenburg, "Love Is No Longer Color-coded on TV."

42. Leonard Green critiqued the show in "Big Fat Myths," *New York Post*, March 10, 2005,

43. Quoted in Aaron Kuriloff, "The Racial Undercurrent," espn.com (Accessed February 3, 2005, at http://sports.espn.go.com/espn/print?id=1983393&type=story).

44. On the HBO hit series *Sex and the City* in fall 2003, one of the main white characters, Miranda, becomes involved with a black man in her building, who is a

doctor for the New York Knicks. The affair was short-lived because Miranda went back to her white ex-boyfriend and father of her child, who she still loved. Beyond returning to the same-race norm, after the breakup, the black doctor angrily tells her that she used him for sex. The white boyfriend confronts the black doctor after Miranda thinks he is sabotaging her stuff because she believes he is so devastated by their breakup, but he is with two black women about to engage in a threesome, reaffirming sexual stereotypes of black men and same-race norms. Prior to the interracial affair, Miranda had become obsessed with a television program that detailed the beginnings of a romantic encounter between a black man and a white woman in England.

45. Douglas Kellner, *Media Culture: Cultural Studies, Identity, and Politics between the Modern and Postmodern* (London: Routledge, 1995), 40.

46. For a discussion of race representations on talk shows, see Corinne Squire, "Who's White? Television Talk Shows and Representations of Whiteness," 242–50.

47. Justin Saint Clair, a journalist, writes about this in "Unreality Television: Millions Watch as TV Reinforces Negative Racial Stereotypes," *Seattle Times*, April 11, 2004.

48. Roger Caitlin, "Color Commentary," *Hartford Courant* (October 14, 2004): D1, D5.

49. Another example is the *Law & Order* episode where a white young boy is found dead in Harlem, and initial clues lead to him having a black girlfriend. Many were either opposed to the relationship or didn't even know about it, but it turns out that police officers allowed him to be killed.

50. As quoted in Ann Oldenburg, "Love Is No Longer Color-coded on TV," *USA Today*, December 20, 2005 (www.usatoday.com/life/television/news/2005-12-20-interracial-couples_x.htm).

51. Oldenburg 2005.

52. In a similar way, two of the most nuanced and well-developed representations of interracial relationships on television occur in gay and lesbian relationships on HBO's *Six Feet Under*, between the previously mentioned couple, Keith and David, and on Showtime's *The L Word* where interracial relationships have been featured. These relationships already occur outside the norm of heterosexuality and also relevant is their placement on cable television networks such as HBO and Showtime.

53. On *Ally McBeal*, the Asian American character portrayed by Lucy Liu played the love interest of a white man, where the white law firm partner Richard Fish romances Liu's character Ling Woo. They have a purposefully bizarre relationship, which has been described as "subtly kinky interaction." Quoted in Greg Braxton, "Race Is No Problem in McBeal's Boston," *Los Angeles Times*, March 11, 1999.

54. Depicting black women as the object of a white man's affection on television is not necessarily new. From the 1970s through the present, there have been more than a handful of examples, starting with shows like the *The Jeffersons*. As mentioned earlier, comedies often use racial difference, pairing a white man and black woman for added humor and wackiness. For example, on the hit comedy *Spin City*, there was

an unconventional attraction between the white politician and his black secretary, and on *The Drew Carey Show*, the white lead character Drew Carey briefly dated a black woman (played by comedian Wanda Sykes).

55. There is debate over black ownership of production and what constitutes a black production. The creator of *Girlfriends* is an African American woman, Mara Brock Akil, who states that she felt that the "trend of depicting interracial love as ideal and harmonious smacked of dishonesty," pointing to how she has featured interracial couples in her shows, according to Greg Braxton's 2007 *Los Angeles Times* article "The Hot Button of a Casual Embrace." See also Kristal Brent Zook, *Color by Fox: The Fox Network and the Revolution in Black Television* (New York: Oxford University Press, 1999).

56. The producer is Kelsey Grammer, who played the character Frasier on *Cheers* and its spin-off *Frasier*.

57. Greg Braxton, "The Hot Button of a Casual Embrace," *Los Angeles Times*, February 11, 2007.

58. Braxton 2007.

59. Pornography, particularly Internet pornographic sites, play on the idea of black women, Latina, and Asian women desiring white men. These sites put forth white men as the raceless norm engaging in sexual acts with "phat booty black chicks," "Hot Latina sluts," and "submissive Asian sex slaves," further highlighting how racial and sexual stereotypes are intertwined and cannot be smoothed over with color blindness.

60. John Fiske, "Hearing Anita Hill (and Viewing Bill Cosby)," in Darnell M. Hunt, ed., *Channeling Blackness: Studies on Television and Race in America* (Oxford: Oxford University Press, 2005), 89–136.

61. One of the first episodes featuring Carter and Kem focuses on how Kem has brought a mass of sick people in to the ER to get vaccinated after Carter treated a sick neighbor who had a communicable disease. Kem is characterized as irrational and idealistic, some twist on the "noble savage" and the exotic flower. Carter is paternalistic as he reprimands her for exposing herself to sickness while carrying their baby and takes on the caretaker role. Kem is also characterized as very sexual, as evidenced in her telling Carter she can't stop thinking about food and sex. Kem is further sexualized when two male interns are looking at nude pictures of Kem that Carter received by e-mail on the ER computer and commenting on how they love to look at her. Later Carter finds printed pictures of Kem in a drawer that one of the male interns evidently has printed out to look at. In this same episode, a dark-skinned woman is brought in, who has been brutally beaten and raped. *ER* often merges discussions of race, gender, and issues with different yet intertwining stories.

62. Jhally and Lewis 2005, 79, discuss this pattern in television depictions of blacks such as Cosby in great depth.

63. Ann Oldenburg, "Love Is No Longer Color-coded on TV," *USA Today*, December 20, 2005.

64. Their union is short-lived and Yang ends up with a white man the next season through 2008.

65. According to Washington, who spoke on *Oprah* in May 2006 with some of the other cast members of the show, he first auditioned for the part of Derek Shepherd, a.k.a. "McDreamy," the love interest of the white lead Meredith Grey, but did not get the part. According to the journalist Ann Oldenburg, Washington, who plays Burke, also refused to discuss the racial difference, and Washington's publicist commented that "drawing attention to the races takes away from the fact that it's quietly and happily existing without being an issue. While we can never know the reason, it wasn't "best" to cast a black male opposite a white woman in a steamy love affair? Furthering this idea was the media reaction when Ellen Pompeo who plays Meredith Grey brought her real-life black boyfriend to a premiere, "while Ellen Pompey (Dr. Grey herself) was gorgeous in a loose flowing Jessie Kahn gown . . . it was more her company than her dress that was getting all the attention, as Ellen showed up with a surprise guest—her boyfriend of 4 years Christopher—and she couldn't stop gushing." See transcript from NBC *Access Hollywood* "Meet Ellen Pompeo's real-life Dr. McDreamy," September 6, 2006 (accessed at www.msnbc.com September 11, 2006).

66. It is important to note that Elizabeth Corday is British, because in mainstream American films that will be discussed in chapter 4 there does seem to be more tolerance for black men paired with non-American white women. See Gary Younge, "Why Love Is Never Blind," *Guardian* (London), March 29, 1999, 6.

67. Jhally and Lewis 2005 [1992], "White Responses: The Emergence of 'Enlightened' Racism," in Darnell M. Hunt, ed., *Channeling Blackness: Studies on Television and Race in America* (Oxford: Oxford University Press, 2005), 77.

68. Interview with Alex Kingston by Jeffrey Zaslow in "One Blunt Brit ER's Alex Kingston on Madonna's style, Ex-husband Ralph Fiennes' Nazi Transformation, L.A. Drivers, Interracial Love Blunt Enough?" *USA Weekend*, March 14, 1999.

69. Eriq La Salle was interviewed by Johnnie Cochran, as well as various black media outlets such as *Ebony* ("ER Star Eriq La Salle Tells Why He Balked at Interracial TV Love Affair," August 1999) where he stated he was not opposed to interracial relationships, but he objected to the fact that positive successful relationships between two black characters were not common. The black popular magazine *Ebony* called Eriq La Salle chivalrous: "I felt we were inadvertently sending a very strange message that I wasn't comfortable which is: Here's a successful Black man who can only have dysfunctional relationships with Black women. But, when he dates outside his race, he is more vulnerable, more open, sweeter, more romantic, and sensual. All the things I think are false . . . it's a shame we can't point to a positive, three-dimensional, fully developed Black-on-Black relationship . . . as a Black artist and as a Black man, I do have a responsibility to my community not to perpetuate things that are detrimental to my community and myself . . . I think Black women are so sensitive to seeing interracial relationships because they feel they're getting the short end of the stick." Aldore D. Collier, "'ER' Star Eriq La Salle Tells Why He Balked at Interracial TV Love Affair," *Ebony*, August 1999, 56. He stated that the ER produc-

ers were receptive to ending the on-screen interracial relationship at his insistence. Though in white media outlets, La Salle was more likely to be "blamed" for stopping the popular on-screen relationship and accused of being racist. Tabloids like *The Star* portrayed it as a battle, such as Janet Charlton and Stephen Viens, "Bitter Feud Tears *E.R.* Apart," *Star*, May 4, 1999, with a secondary headline of "Eriq La Salle Dumped Me as His Lover because I'm White."

70. When told by the ER supervisor that a white female patient reported that he intimidated her and touched her inappropriately during a breast exam, Pratt responds that he is being blamed as "the big black doctor," and Dr. Weaver (a white lesbian) tells him "don't turn it into a race issue . . . don't hide behind it." One of the nurses tells Pratt he is a flirt, and reiterates Dr. Weaver's assertion that this is a gender issue, referring to the white woman's complaint about the breast exam. While Pratt mentions race, the other medical staff discount the possibility and no one mentions how racial difference and racial images may have influenced the dynamics of the breast examination and the woman's perception. To further illustrate how Pratt is characterized in this same episode, a young black man and woman are brought in from a car accident that occurred during their first night together, and the woman asks for Pratt, having had a one-night stand with Pratt also months earlier.

71. Jing-Mei got pregnant from a one-night stand with a black nurse and gave the baby up for adoption. She also gets involved with Pratt, and in one scene she lets a fellow doctor borrow her sweater. While under a special light to detect bodily fluid, the sweater shows a stain on the section that covers the breast. Both white women joke about what it is, and more importantly whose it is, suggesting maybe it is Pratt's sperm.

72. John Fiske 2005 [1994], 117.

73. Christopher P. Campbell, "A Myth of Assimilation: 'Enlightened' Racism and the News," in Darnell M. Hunt, ed., *Channeling Blackness: Studies on Television and Race in America* (Oxford: Oxford University Press, 2005), 140.

74. Actors like Charlie Sheen almost exclusively play non-Latino characters, such as in *Two and a Half Men* and *Spin City*, where he has relationships with white women.

75. The long-running ABC show *Boy Meets World* featured a relationship between a young white man and a young black woman who were best friends of the two main characters, but again the executive producer Michael Jacobs explicitly stated that the race issue would not be addressed, as quoted in Kimberly Hohman, "Interracial Relationships: Hollywood Style," February 2, 2000, www.about.com.

76. Quoted in Greg Braxton, "Race Is No Problem in McBeal's Boston," *Los Angeles Times*, March 11, 1999.

77. Quoted in Greg Braxton, "Race Is No Problem in McBeal's Boston," *Los Angeles Times*, March 11, 1999.

78. Quoted in Greg Braxton's "The Hot Button of a Casual Embrace," *Los Angeles Times*, February 11, 2007. The show stars *Seinfeld* actress Julia Louis-Dreyfus and Blair Underwood, the same black actor featured in *LAX* and *Sex and the City*. Actor Blair Underwood also is quoted as saying, "These relationships are noteworthy because they

are no longer newsworthy." After starting in the 2005–2006 season, the show was slated for a mid-season return in the 2007–2008 season.

79. In the 2008–2009 season, Christine marries her black female business partner Barb to give her citizenship although neither one of them are lesbians.

80. Ann Oldenburg, "Love Is No Longer Color-coded on TV."

81. Eric Deggans, "Too Subtle for the Small Screen," *St. Petersburg Times*, February 26, 2001.

82. Deggans 2001.

83. Greg Braxton, "TV Finds Drama in Interracial Dating," *Los Angeles Times*, March 22, 2000.

84. Braxton 2000.

85. Other times, his comments are used for comic relief like "does she need 'bbl—the big black lesbian support group?'"

86. Feagin 2006, xiii.

87. Their relationship begins after he tells her that her yard is dead and symbolically she has also let her inner garden die. This is a common theme where the Other is able to renew the white person spiritually because somehow their essence is closer to nature (also meaning less civilized), beginning with white stories of Native Americans like Pocahontas. Maxine is a 65-year-old radical social worker who often challenges the system, and in many ways, is undesirable as an older, heavy-set woman who does not adhere to gender roles.

88. According to the executive producer Barbara Hall, she received some negative reactions from viewers for having Bruce and Amy kiss, highlighting African American opposition. "There's a lot of ambivalence in the African American community about Amy and Bruce's relationship, I was surprised at how little hate mail there was about the scenes where we had them kissing. But there were a lot of postings from African Americans saying they didn't want to see them (together), either."

89. In another scene, a black woman attorney Zola Nocks approaches Amy because she cannot get Bruce to participate in a class-action suit involving allegations of racism. The attorney is portrayed as hostile and expresses disdain for Amy, asking "Are you making it with him . . . if he is making it with a white woman that explains why he was playing hardball?" Amy responds that her comment is "racist" and that she "has more in common with the Black Rights movement than Bruce."

90. Patricia Hill Collins spoke about the idea of "color, safely contained" at a lecture given at Eastern Connecticut State University in spring 2005.

91. See Yen Espiritu 2000, 95–97, also Gina Marchetti 1993.

92. When whites are interviewed about interracial relationships, they often respond that they have never thought about it and do not know any interracial couples, and when interviewed in greater depth, express opposition to these unions in nonracialized statements such as "I don't have a problem with it BUT . . ." citing lack of attraction, innate differences, negative outcomes such as problems for biracial children, and opposition from others in society. See Erica Chito Childs, *Navigating Interracial Borders: Black-White Couples and Their Social Worlds* (New Brunswick, NJ: Rutgers University Press, 2005); also Eduardo Bonilla-Silva, *Racism without Racists*, 2003.

93. These images are produced in these ways, with the audience undoubtedly perceiving these representations differently "when filtered through the diverse backgrounds, cultures, and life-styles of individual audience members." Yet this does not "refute the macro level concept of encoding of dominant meanings," or in other words, certain representations and stories continue to be told. See C. Collins, "Viewer Letter as Audience Research: The Case of Murphy Brown," *Journal of Broadcasting and Electronic Media* 41, 1 (1997): 109–31.

94. Kimberly McClain DaCosta discusses the idea of "marketing multiracials" in terms of products targeted toward multiracial families such as Mattel doll Barbie's ambiguous friends, wedding cake toppers, and hair care products, as well more commercials using multiracial families such as a Nike Tiger Woods commercial, a 2004 Verizon commercial, a 2002 Tylenol ad, and a 2001 Motrin ad (2007, 154–72). Still, these commercials are few in number and do not challenge the racial hierarchy.

95. In the United Kingdom "other" has a sexual as well as an ethnic connotation. See page 467 in Stuart Hall, "What Is This 'Black' in Black Popular Culture?" reprinted from *Black Popular Culture* (1992).

96. In chapter 5, the idea of media reports choosing stories that have certain familiar characteristic will be discussed. See also Corinne Squire, "White Trash Pride and the Exemplary Black Citizen: Counter-Narratives of Gender, 'Race,' and the Trailer Park in Contemporary Daytime Television Talk Shows," *Narrative Inquiry* 12, 1 (2002): 155–72.

97. Ann Oldenburg, "Love Is No Longer Color-coded on TV," *USA Today*, December 20, 2005.

98. Gray 2005 [1995], xvii. I am extending Gray's argument about the presence of blacks in music videos, in sports, and in television/film not signaling acceptance to interracial couples.

99. Gray 2005 [1995], xix, argues that television plays a pivotal role in how individuals learn these images and representations.

100. There are numerous examples of this race/gender connection, such as in the fourth season during Benton and Corday's short-lived relationship. An old, white, male head surgeon tells Benton that Corday, as a woman, is always trying to prove something because she disagreed with the head surgeon about a procedure, and then he tells Benton, "I'm glad you're not militant minority." This scene presents gender and race equality the same, and though the white male surgeon is not presented as likable, he is able to voice a common view about minorities complaining about discrimination. Also, in terms of Benton and Corday's relationship, it links these two together as similar in terms of both being "minorities."

101. Ed Guerrero argues how in film, a similar trend exists, "Another all-too-common industry strategy for containing the range and potentialities of Black filmic talent . . . he or she is completely isolated from other Blacks or referent to the Black world." "The Black Image in Protective Custody: Hollywood's Biracial Buddy Films of the Eighties," page 287, chapter 15.

102. Hunt 2005, 21.

CHAPTER THREE

~

It's a (White) Man's World

Film representations of interracial sex and couplings have increased, and some have argued that they represent a striking improvement. In a 2003 *Time* magazine article, "Color-Blind Love," Harvard Law professor Randall Kennedy argues that "mixed marriage in the South is being accepted at all social levels—and working-class couples like the one played by Billy Bob Thornton and Halle Berry in the 2001 film *Monster's Ball* have become more common."[1] There may be more films that take as their main theme the relationship between a white man and a woman of color, yet even these films are still few in number. Yet, like television, I would argue that the production and consumption of interracial relationships on screen does not necessarily mean that these representations signal acceptance.

When looking at how Hollywood portrays interracial romance, and under what circumstances two characters of different races are paired opposite each other, the portrayal of white men and white masculinity emerge as a central component. While there were formal laws and informal rules about race-mixing scrutinizing relations between men of color and white women, film representations mirror the long-standing practice in which white men had more freedom "to cross racial boundaries and to choose freely from among women of color as sex partners." Hollywood mainly explores interracial intimacy from the perspective of the white man with an "exotic" woman of color, and particular actresses are chosen repeatedly to play opposite white male leads such as Jennifer Lopez, Halle Berry, and Thandie Newton.[2] There are certain patterns of images that exist when white men are paired opposite an African American, Latina, or Asian woman, given the relational nature of racialization and racial representations in America. While the meanings attached to interracial relationships differ depending on the race and ethnicity of the individuals involved, still there are surprising similarities of how interracial relationships are presented when it is a white man with a woman of color, despite the different ideologies associated with women from different racial groups. Not surprisingly, whites write the majority of films, considering 94 percent of film writers are white.[3]

Therefore in this chapter, I draw from popular culture depictions in mainstream American film from 1990 through 2008 of white men paired with women of color and what this tells us about attitudes about the heterosexual pairings of white men with women of color and the acceptability of these unions.[4] Most films present the story line from a white male perspective, or dominant gaze, which replicates through narrative and imagery the racial inequalities and biases that exist in society.[5] In particular, white male dominance is upheld when white men can engage in sexual relations with women of color while preventing men of color from doing the same with white women. Furthermore, a number of the films that depict an interracial relationship never mention race and instead use a color-blind discourse. The refusal to acknowledge race is common in popular-culture depictions of interracial relationships, and many such as Harvard legal scholar Randall Kennedy argue these color-blind portrayals are an improvement:[6]

> Interracial intimacy has been emerging as simply one part of a larger story in which racial difference is of little or no significance . . . because presuming the normalcy of interracial intimacy—treating it as "no big deal"—may be more subversive of traditional norms than stressing the racial heterodoxy of such relationships.[7]

While most films that feature an interracial relationship never address the issue of race, I argue that these depictions *do not* presume the normalcy of interracial intimacy, rather in true color-blind fashion, racialized images and discourses about interracial relationships and/or members of particular racial groups are put forth, all the time pretending not to be dealing with race.

In what follows I will outline the patterns in representations of interracial relationships involving white men and the types of worlds that interracial relationships happen in on screen, which fit into the three frames of deviance, privileging whiteness and perpetuating racism while denying race matters. For example, white men are most often portrayed as conquerors or saviors, either saving the woman, community, civilization, or even the entire world.

Other representations emphasize the deviance of the interracial relationship, or at the very least, the idea that these two individuals are very different. Throughout the representations, distinct messages about color blindness, the denial of racism, and the idea that people of color are racist and the source of problems are explicitly and implicitly conveyed. Lastly, I will look at two 2006 successful box-office films, *Guess Who* and *Something New*, whose plots center on an interracial relationship between a white man and black woman, to explore whether these films represent a break in the patterns of representations.

Saving Worlds by Conquest

The basic story line underlying intimate relationships on screen between a white man and a woman of color tend to revolve around the white man coming into contact with another racial community or culture, which includes falling in love or at least having sex with a "native." The woman is always an exception, usually more beautiful and good-hearted than her community, and in many instances, she saves him from himself, from his greed, his emptiness, or even her "tribe." For example, the classic Pocohantas myth, retold by Disney in a 1995 animated film, tells the historically inaccurate, highly idealized story of the English officer Captain John Smith, who comes to America and rebels against the commander as he falls in love with Pocohantas and risks his life to save her people.[8] Similarly, stories like *Miss Saigon*, the modern retelling of Madame Butterfly, also chronicles a nonwhite woman, this time a Vietnamese prostitute, who falls in love with a white soldier and is willing to live and die for him. In *The Last Samurai* set in Japan, white box-office star Tom Cruise plays an American soldier who is embraced and enthralled by the last samurais, which includes a relationship with a Japanese woman. These films often use the intimate interracial relationship as a sign or symbolic representation of a man's entry into another culture or world, even if they live in the same larger society such as in films like *Bulworth*, *The Bodyguard*, and *Year of the Dragon*. For example, in *Year of the Dragon* (1985), a white cop is determined to clean up a crime-infested Chinatown and in the process engages in a sexual liaison with an Asian American newswoman, Tracy Tzu. He convinces her to help expose the crime in Chinatown, and their relationship develops against a backdrop of violence where he is either saving her from gunshots at dinner, Asian men waiting to rape her, or engaging in rough sex with her, including slaps and verbal insults.[9]

In these films, white masculinity is reaffirmed through the retelling of conquests of other cultures, which can be symbolized through the conquest of women of that culture. By retelling this similar story of white-native contact, white masculinity is reinvented as not only kind but also physically and sexually superior.[10] In many ways, these women of color are a "racialized 'exotic treasure'" who "do not replace but merely function as a temporary 'stand-in' for white women and thus will be readily displaced," when the men leave the foreign locale they are in or when they no longer need or want her.[11] To see the power of this image in everyday life, in June 2006, a videotape surfaced of an American marine deployed in Iraq singing a song he wrote, "Hadji Girl," to a cheering military audience. The song is about falling in love with an Iraqi girl but when she takes him to her family, they shoot her and attack him so he guns down her family using her younger sister as a shield. The marine who wrote the song apologized but stated, "It was a joke that is trying to be taken seriously."[12] Yet in early July 2006, reports surfaced that a young Iraqi woman was raped and killed along with her mother, father, and younger sister, allegedly by U.S. military men not connected to the marine who wrote the "Hadji Girl" song. These incidents show how the line between reality and entertainment blurs and how dangerous these stories of conquest are.

A World Removed:
Danger, Deviance, Displacement, and Difference

Interracial relationships on-screen often emerge outside of mainstream society or the character's regular life in a temporary escape or dangerous world of infidelity, hustling, espionage, murder, and other deviant acts. Many of these films are suspense or science fiction films such as *Boiler Room* and *Mystery Men*, where white men are paired with black women, yet it is not the focal point of the story and race is not referenced.[13] In these films, the interracial relationship is used to highlight the difference of the situation, accentuate the deviance and danger, or provide additional comedy.

Some movies use racial difference as part of a process of experiencing different women. In the 2005 film *Wedding Crashers*, two white men would "crash" weddings to meet women, and before getting to the white wedding and characters in which the movie would focus on, they "crashed" Asian weddings, Hindu weddings, and Jewish weddings with ethnically matched women to briefly romance. It was "this long montage of these guys who would crash these weddings just to pick up women and it was sort of an ode to multiculturalism . . . everything but a black wedding."[14] The messages are clear, that "normal" people stick to their own kind except the wedding crashers who are "crazy." Multiculturalism is something to dabble in at best as long as you return, and even a black wedding is untouchable for these "crazy" white men. There are no interracial weddings to be crashed.

The pairing of two individuals of different races is used as a comedic tool and played for laughs, often exaggerating differences. For example, in the comedy *Napoleon Dynamite*, Napoleon's brother Kip is involved in online dating, and when he finally meets his online love LaFawnduh, he realizes she is African American, and she is presented in many stereotypical ways, including her name. In *White Men Can't Jump*, there is a white/Latina couple comprised of Rosie Perez cast as an irrational Latino woman who drank too much and spoke so fast with a Spanish accent that she could not be understood, and Woody Harrelson as an easygoing, clever white guy who made money hustling in street basketball games with mostly black men. Their relationship ended because they were too different and Billy placed more importance on basketball, making money, and his friendship with his black basketball partner Sidney.[15] It is common that the representation of the woman of color is most humorous and stereotypical, like Perez's character with her fast talking and tough attitude. Similarly, in the third *Austin Powers* movie, the black singer Beyonce Knowles's portrayal of Powers's romantic interest Foxxy Cleopatra provides laughs. Her character is a spoof on the characters in 1970s blaxploitation films, and their relationship, like much of the movie, is purposefully absurd. Another example, *Lethal Weapon 4* (1998) used the fear of interracial relationships for comedic effect while also having the black father as the one who voices concern over the possibility of his daughter being pregnant by a white man. In the scene, Murtaugh, a black LAPD officer, and his white partner, Riggs, are trapped on the street while a psychotic criminal throws explosives. Riggs tells Murtaugh that his daughter is pregnant, and Murtaugh's immediately responds, "Is he black?"[16]

Films can also dabble in interracial relationships with serious consequences rather than comic relief. In *Alfie* (2004) the white actor Jude Law plays the character of Alfie, a British limousine driver who spends his time sleeping with women. In his string of one-night stands, he sleeps with a black woman, Lonette, the ex-girlfriend of his best friend Marlon. The somewhat explicit sex scene takes place on a pool table in a dirty, smoky bar, but the next day Marlon and Lonette get back together. Alfie, who often talks to the camera, states that "no good deed goes unpunished," when Lonette comes to see him and tells him she is pregnant.[17] He says, as he waits for her to have the abortion, "if the baby was born with any white boy features. . . ." He remarks how the night they slept together he thought, "I got something for nothing, it doesn't seem to have worked out that way." Lonette and Marlon move away, but it turns out that Lonette didn't have the abortion and she had the baby who appears to be Alfie's. This makes Alfie "reflect and wonder about his life," and all his other "wrong" relationships, including a single mother girlfriend, a much older wealthy woman, and an unstable young blonde woman. The interracial one-night stand has dire consequences, and because of the racial difference that didn't matter when he slept with her but is "seen" when the biracial baby is born, Alfie's life is changed. The symbolism is clear—interracial sex has serious consequences. This theme is also used in the critically acclaimed film *Sideways*, which focuses on two white men Miles and Jack, who travel through the Santa Barbara wine country as Jack prepares for his wedding. On this trip, they meet two women, pairing Jack, the soon-to-be-married man, with Stephanie, an Asian American woman.[18] While the relationship between Miles and Maya, the white couple, develops slowly through conversation, Jack's relationship with Stephanie is immediately sexual, even showing a scene where we see him from behind naked having sex with her kitty-cornered on the bed with her legs up in the air. After she finds out that he was lying about being single, she beats him violently with her motorcycle helmet and he proceeds to hook up for one night with an obese waitress, whose husband catches them in the act. The pattern of him choosing "wrong" women further exemplifies his wrong of cheating. Race is not addressed, yet her character, beyond being racially different, also has a black daughter and a white, lower-class mother evidenced through her chain-smoking, bowling-alley, foul-mouthed behavior. The interracial pairing may signify the fleeting nature of the relationship and that it couldn't be long-term, with the difference highlighted further in the fact that she has a black daughter.[19]

There are a number of adventure and action films that feature a white man with a woman of color that revolve around danger, deviance, crime, and often graphic violence. For example, in *After the Sunset*, the white actor Pierce Brosnan is paired with Latina actress Salma Hayek as professional jewel thieves. They travel to an exotic locale upon retirement from jewel heists, where she is presented as sexually exotic, dancing in a bikini top shaking and sweating. A white police detective follows them to the island in an elaborate game of cat and mouse, where he begins his own relationship with a black police constable on the island.[20] Other action films, like *Lucky Number Slevin*, feature a relationship between a white male assassin and an Asian American female coroner, where the whole movie is filled with suspicion, intrigue, and deception. Racial and ethnic differences are never mentioned, yet the interracial pairings are arguably used to enhance the intrigue and mystery and also make the interracial relationship more acceptable in that it happens outside of everyday life.

Certain actresses such as Thandie Newton, a light-skinned biracial actress, play opposite white men quite frequently in movies such as *Interview with the Vampire*, *The Chronicles of Riddick*, *The Truth about Charlie*, and *Mission: Impossible II*. For example, *The Truth about Charlie* is a murder mystery filled with intrigue and plot twists set in France, and Newton is in the middle of the suspense with a dead (white) husband and a love interest/enemy played by white actor Mark Wahlberg. In the blockbuster hit *Mission: Impossible II*, Newton stars opposite Tom Cruise as Nyah, a known thief and ex-girlfriend of the man that Cruise needs to capture. Their initial meeting is very sexual, where he confronts her as she is about to do a heist, and they need to hide lying face-to-face. She says, "Do you mind if I am on top," and she proceeds to break in to make the heist while sitting on him. Later, she kisses him, and it fades to morning where he is shirtless in bed next to her. Though she is a highly trained thief, that is not the skill she is recruited for, instead she is asked to rekindle a relationship with the (white) ex-boyfriend who they are looking to capture. He didn't know that she would be made to do this dangerous job but he still asks her to do it, which implies she will probably have to sleep with this man. Through her relationship with Cruise, which isn't much more than the sexual encounter, she is a bad girl turned good, and the movie ends after much danger, with Cruise saving her.

One of the most prominent actresses, Halle Berry, who identifies as black yet has a white mother, is also repeatedly paired opposite white men, mainly in films where the main plot involves danger, deviance, and crime, such as *Die Another Day*, *The Rich Man's Wife*, *Swordfish*, and *Monster's Ball*. In *The Rich Man's Wife*, Berry's character appears to be an innocent woman whose distant, cold husband has been killed by a man obsessed with her, but it turns out that she masterminded his murder with his ex-partner for money. In *Perfect Stranger* (2007), Berry is paired opposite a white man, who she is pretending to like while investigating his involvement in the death and disappearance of other women. The Oscar-winning *Monster's Ball* focuses on Halle Berry's[21] character, Leticia Musgrove, who becomes involved with a white man, Hank Grotowski. The complicated story begins when Hank, a supervising correctional officer, oversees the execution of a black death-row inmate, who happens to be Leticia's estranged husband and father of her son. Tragedy foreshadows Hank and Leticia's first encounter, since Hank's son, who was also a correctional officer, commits suicide, Hank quits his job, and Leticia's son is killed when hit by a car. The relationship begins with a very graphic sex scene that Leticia initiates. The relationship is framed within a circle of deviance, including death, execution, poverty, family dysfunction, and deception (in particular the fact that Leticia doesn't know that Hank was a part of the execution of her son's father). The movie does address race to an extent, because Hank and his father are racist.[22] As Leticia and Hank's relationship develops though, the issue of race is virtually never discussed (other than a fight after his father refers to Leticia as "nigger juice"). Hank buys a gas station that he names after Leticia and he gives her a place to stay. Leticia finds out that Hank worked at the prison where her son's father was killed, yet she chooses to ignore it in order to be with Hank anyway.[23] The movie portrays the relationship in color-blind terms and reproduces stereotypes, especially with a scene at the end where Hank tells her he will take care of her and she agrees that she needs to be taken care of. Hank's actions can be read not only as his own transformation but also the redemption and ultimate goodness of white masculinity. These movies do nothing to depict the normalcy of interracial relationships, yet do solidly reaffirm the white savior role.

In most of these films, race is never mentioned, yet stereotypes are still reinforced. By pairing a white man with a black or Latina woman whose race and ethnicity is erased, or exceptionalized in the case of the light-skinned biracial Halle Berry, then interracial relationships are safely contained. Blackness or otherness is still maintained, yet it is done through markers such as class status, occupational status, or other factors, still serving as an alluring "deformity." The invisibility or slightly visible/altered race and ethnicity of the woman "generate a sexual excitement that at once defies and affirms the laws of American racial custom."[24] The context is also important because these relationships are framed in the backdrop of criminal activity, espionage, danger, and death.

Worlds of Difference: Perpetuating Color-Blind Racism

In a growing number of film representations, the interracial relationship starts when two characters who are presented as opposites meet and their differences are the main story line. These differences can be used for comedy, where the idea of a partner of another race and the confusion it causes or the absurdity is enough to make the audience laugh. Yet in these films that showcase the different worlds the white man and woman of color come from, the white man and white world are portrayed as desirable, and most often, the white man still sweeps away, saves, or otherwise enlightens the woman of color.

Stories of interracial relationships between a white man and a woman of color often involve an "authentic" woman who embodies all the racialized and sexualized stereotypes and enters into a white world.[25] The idea of difference is reinforced through the woman's dress, language, and behavior, even if racial and ethnic differences are never identified. For example, the 1999 *Snow Falling on Cedars*, a film adapted from a novel, focuses on the trial of a Japanese American fisherman charged in the 1950s with the murder of a fellow white fisherman. A white journalist possibly knows information that could clear him, but he is torn because the Japanese American man is married to a Japanese woman the journalist loved. The two loved each other yet could not be together, and like many films, the white man is in the position as a savior. Even though he is not married to her, he is her true love.

The popular comedy *Fools Rush In* plays on the religious and language differences between the white male lead and the Mexican female character (played by Salma Hayek) for comedic effect, constructing them as opposites in all areas. They meet at a local bar in Nevada, have a drunken one-night stand, and only begin a relationship months later when she shows up at his house pregnant. He is rational, hardworking, and professional, whereas she is unconventional, emotional, beautiful, and from a large family, which draws heavily on racial stereotypes. They temporarily break up because there is tension over whether they will move to New York, where he is from, for his career or stay in Nevada, where her family and community live. They eventually come back together, presumably to live in his world in New York. Another example of "a culture-clash story" is *Spanglish*, which stars Adam Sandler as John Clasky, a successful, white chef/restaurant owner married to an uptight, difficult white woman, Debbie Clasky, and they have a daughter. They hire Flor, a beautiful woman who only speaks Spanish and is described as a single-mother Mexican emigré to Los Angeles. She quickly becomes a lifesaver to the family, bringing peace to the house, sewing the daughter's clothes so they fit after the mother purposefully buys them too small to make her lose weight, and providing emotional support to the husband because his wife is too distant, more concerned with exercise than sex. Flor is portrayed as not only exquisitely beautiful but also nurturing, self-sacrificing, and morally good, which is contrasted with the selfish and unfeminine white wife. They have a romantic dinner after everything falls apart with his wife, but they never give in to their desire because it would not be right and she returns to her world, symbolically and literally. James L. Brooks, the movie's director, explains his motivation in making the film was that John is drawn to Flor but wants to be loyal to his wife, since "being moral is living with the danger of being immoral and passing the test."[26] The film presents John being with Flor as immoral, and it is significant that the test of morality that he must pass is a Spanish-speaking Mexican woman. These two are not meant to be together because of their separate positions, which can be read as a stand-in for the racial and ethnic differences. This ties in with the dangers associated with "going native," shown in earlier films such as *Mutiny on the Bounty* (1962, 1984), where the temptation of the Other is linked to renouncing one's family, community, or former life.[27] It also corresponds with images of Latina or Asian women as more attractive than white women who do not adhere to traditional notions of femininity, which not only establishes the racial dominance of white men by possessing white women and women of color, but also reinforces a gender dynamic where women are pitted against each other.

Another film, *Monster-in-Law*, plays on the differences between Latina actress Jennifer Lopez's character Charlie and her white boyfriend Kevin Fields. When Kevin's mother Viola meets Charlie, she calls her a "dog-walking slut" under her breath and then says to her assistant, "She is going to destroy him, she has no money, no career goals . . . a man's erection is usually pointed at the trampiest woman." The mother sets out to "save her son" by throwing an engagement party to ruin the relationship, and comments, "When he sees how out of place she is in his world, it is going to be over." The mother plans the party and devises a way to expose Charlie's "lower-class status," where once again class is used as a stand-in and way to deny the problems people have with racial or ethnic differences. Yet it is racialized stereotypes of women of color's buttocks that emerge when Viola buys Charlie a dress that is too small—prompting Lopez to say about the too-small dress, "I have two asses." She tells Kevin, "I don't belong here," and he says "it is just you and me, this is not my world now, you are my world." The mother questions whether she is "currently an illegal alien . . . any hereditary illnesses that could be passed on to children . . . how many men have you been sexually active with . . . would you sign a prenuptial agreement," pretending it is to include her in the will. The mother's behavior is presented as comical because she is "crazy," and she has an assistant, Ruby, who is black. Yet when Kevin's grandmother/Viola's mother-in-law Gertrude shows up, it becomes apparent that Viola's mother-in-law did to Viola what Viola is doing to Charlie. Gertrude tells Charlie, "He went out and found himself an exotic LatinA (her emphasis)," which she wishes her son had done rather than marry Viola those years ago. The racialized aspects of Viola's opposition to Charlie are further downplayed by equating it with the way Viola's own mother-in-law had treated her. Therefore, the film is able to reproduce racialized ideas while denying that race matters.

Interestingly, Jennifer Lopez is most often paired as the love interest of a white man, yet the character she plays is often not Latina. For example, in eight films, including *Gigli, Jersey Girl, An Unfinished Life, Enough, Angel*

Eyes, The Wedding Planner, Out of Sight, and *The Cell,* Lopez's character is the current or former love interest of a white man, yet her character is explicitly identified as another ethnicity such as Italian or Greek, or her character's name and family show her not to be Latina. In these films, the idea of her being from a different world than her love interest is not part of the plot. Though in *Maid in Manhattan,* racial and ethnic differences are a central focus when Jennifer Lopez plays Marisa Ventura, a maid in an expensive New York hotel who meets Senator Chris Marshall, a wealthy white politician who becomes interested in her when he mistakes her for a wealthy guest. Deception is a key element in the depiction of interracial relationships. By having him mistake her for someone she is not, the interracial relationship is allowed to happen, yet it seems that as herself he would not have even noticed her. The symbolic roles of maid and politician, and the different class levels, are emphasized as the source of their difference, but Jennifer Lopez's ethnicity is referenced a number of times. The wealthy white women who are actually the room guests she pretended to be repeatedly call her Maria rather than her name, which is Marisa, and they assume she speaks limited English. The senator refers to her as "Mediterranean" when he is trying to find her, and his aide asks her if her name is "Spanish"? The other Latina maids are portrayed in stereotypical ways and treated as invisible to the wealthy white patrons, while Lopez is repeatedly described as an exception by the other maids, by her supervisors, and by Senator Marshall, who comments on her "exceptional" beauty. She agrees to attend a large gala with him, with the intent of breaking it off because of her deception, though instead they end up spending the night together. Yet the next day the hotel finds out what she has done, and the media finds out that the Senator was dating a "maid." One reporter comments, "It will kill his career." The idea that their racial and ethnic differences would be a barrier is never mentioned; instead, the problem is centered on their separate social locations of wealthy politician and maid. This color-blind discourse ignores how hotel maids are stereotypically assumed to be Latina, and it shows the acceptability of class-based prejudice. It is only in a discussion with her mother that the relationship is explicitly defined as interracial. Near the end, when the relationship has ended and she has lost her job, her mother questions her about why she even thought she had the "right" to go out with him, and Lopez asks if she is saying that because he is "rich and white." The mom replies that she needs to stop dreaming dreams that will never happen. This scene is important because it depicts being with a wealthy white man as a dream of Latina women and depicts Latina mothers as the ones who oppose interracial dating.[28] The movie does end with them getting back together, but only after her young son goes to one of his press conferences and asks, "if someone who lies should get a second chance," and he asks the boy to take him to her. To convey that interracial relationships (or at least this interracial relationship) do not work or are at best unconventional, films often use symbolic roles such as a politician and maid or a bodyguard and client, which can be understood as metaphors for white and nonwhite (whether it is black, Latino, or Asian), conveying the message that there are still boundaries that should never be crossed.[29]

A widely popular film that exemplifies the symbolic ways interracial difference is portrayed is the 1992 box-office hit *The Bodyguard*. In the film, Frank Farmer (Kevin Costner), a white ex-Secret Service agent who is conservative and disciplined with rules by which he lives his life, is hired to protect Rachel Marron (Whitney Houston), a black music/movie superstar who is spontaneous, driven by her passions, undisciplined, and in need of protection.[30] To protect her, he immerses himself in her world. Though race is never mentioned, racial stereotypes are still perpetuated, such as the stereotype of whites as in control and blacks as needing to be controlled. In one scene, we see her surrender to him, and their relationship is portrayed as one of child and adult, with Frank tucking her into a bed filled with dolls that night. This imagery is important because it establishes who has the authority and power in the relationship. Reminiscent of the days of slavery, interracial encounters are not threatening as long as the white man is in control, which is a recurring theme in the movies discussed in this chapter. For example, while she is the one who asks him to take her out, as well as the one who initiates the sexual relationship,[31] after the night they spent together, he tells her that they cannot be together. She gets upset, asking him "if he wants her to beg" or if she "has done something wrong." This serves two purposes: it establishes her as the sexual aggressor, yet allows him to be in control of their relationship. Although Rachel should be in the position of power because she is the employer, she is ultimately an object for sexual commodification as she does not have control over Frank. Frank and Rachel's sexual encounter is not shown but rather flashes from their first kiss to them waking up in bed together the next morning.[32] Further perpetuating the image of black women as promiscuous, in a later scene, Rachel gets drunk at a party and seduces a white associate of Frank's in an effort to anger Frank after his rejection of her. Again, he is characterized as restrained while she is portrayed as desperate and needy. This sequence of events reinforces the historical construction of black women by whites as sexually insatiable and driven by their desires, which has always been linked to power to dominate.[33] As a bodyguard there are three rules that Frank lives by: "never let her out of your sight," "never let your guard down," and "never fall in love." Throughout the history of race relations, these three principles have been a part of race relations between blacks and whites, manifest in the belief that blacks cannot be trusted, whites need to keep an eye on blacks, and that whites and blacks should remain separate. The movie ends with Frank and Rachel separating because they "both know that they don't belong together." Though race is not discussed, it does not mean that the audience does not understand the film through a racial lens. *The Bodyguard* does not have to mention that Frank is white and Rachel is black for us to see it. Frank conquers her world by making it safe for her when no one else could, gives her stability and then leaves, presumably to return to his own white world and old life, rejuvenated by his success.

The award-winning and critically acclaimed film *Bulworth,* a political satire about aging white senator Jay Bulworth (Warren Beatty) who becomes disenfranchised with his political campaign and the political system in general, also uses an interracial relationship to highlight difference. Senator Bulworth begins pursuing a romantic/sexual relationship with a young black woman, Nina (Halle Berry), as part of a life transformation that includes substituting truthful remarks for his political speeches and adopting a hip-hop style through clothing and rap. While Warren Beatty coproduced, cowrote, directed, and starred in the film, he admits that when he pitched the film to Fox he never mentioned that there would be an interracial love story.[34] Unlike *The Bodyguard,* the issue of race is addressed, such as Bulworth advocating a "voluntary free-spirited, open-ended program of procreative deconstructing" to eliminate the color line through interracial sex, though in this movie the only possibility of sex is between Nina and Bulworth, and even that never happens. Therefore, while race and race relations are addressed, the issues are still coded within a comical color-blind discourse that suggests interracial sex can solve racial inequality, and as Beatty argues, "It doesn't work unless they laugh . . . the intention is always to entertain."[35] This movie can be read as an attack on the American power structure and the rigid hierarchy of the racial and class status quo of the political system, yet it also exposes certain dominant ideologies about interracial relations. A white man becoming involved with a woman of color still symbolizes "going native," where "the temptation to break the taboos against making love to the forbidden racial other and against overthrowing authority" are linked

For example, only within a groundbreaking transformation and renouncing of his former position as well as his previous (white) supporters does a prominent white man align himself with a black inner-city woman, who also happens to be much younger and extremely attractive. Yet, this relationship still affirms the power of the white male power structure and brings to mind the history of white men "eroticizing the bodies of African-American women, especially light-skinned women like Halle Berry,"[36] rather than suggesting that interracial relationships are acceptable. Black women are not threatening in this way but are readily available for sex, especially with white men. Halle Berry's character Nina also stands out as an exception from the other black women, where she is quieter, more reserved, and surprisingly intelligent to Bulworth, who is taken aback when she engages in a discussion of the political and economic problems of society. Beyond Nina, most blacks in the movie live in poverty, engage in criminal behavior, carry weapons, or sing gospel, and it is Bulworth who inspires them to do better, such as the head drug dealer who wants to make a change because of Bulworth.[37] The film allows whites to consume blackness like indulging in a fetish, as Beatty admits he became fascinated with rap music years ago. Most importantly it serves to construct white men as saviors, as Vera and Gordon have argued, who fight inequality, risk their own position and life, while attracting beautiful young black women.[38] Even while challenging certain pieces of the racial status quo, Bulworth ultimately tells a familiar story, which leads us to the question of whether there are any different stories being told.

Is There Something New?

Having looked at the different patterns that emerge in film representations of white men with women of color, these films rarely focused on the interracial relationship as the premise of the film, or even if their differences were the focal point, it was depicted in color-blind terms like *Maid in Manhattan* and *Monster's Ball*. Yet, in 2005 and 2006, two successful box-office films, *Guess Who* and *Something New*, were released, which focused on the relationship between a white man and a black woman and received considerable media attention.

Guess Who was roughly based on a reversal of the original 1967 *Guess Who's Coming to Dinner*. In the film, a black, middle-aged man Percy Jones learns his daughter Theresa is dating a white man, Simon Green. One review notes that "while the original was heavy on social commentary amid the civil-rights movement, *Guess Who* plays the interracial romance for slapstick laughs."[39] For example, in the beginning of the film Simon and Theresa are on the cab ride to Theresa's family house, and Simon asks if she told her family he was "pigment challenged," but she replies that she only told them the important things, giving the message that race does not matter. When they arrive at the house her parents think the black cab driver is her boyfriend, never even considering the possibility that Simon is her boyfriend. Simon makes a joke, "I wish Theresa would have told me you were black to save an awkward moment," which shows Simon to be open-minded and comfortable with race, while Theresa's family is portrayed as closed-minded. When her sister Keisha sees Simon, she asks, "Are we being audited?" which, along with the black father saying Simon's credit report is "a thing of beauty," reinforces the idea of whites as financially responsible and law-abiding and blacks as less financially responsible. Percy's opposition to Simon is the starting point of the comedy, and his opposition is so over the top, he seems ridiculous and Simon appears rational. At a family dinner, Percy and the grandfather get Simon to tell black jokes he has heard, and later Simon tells Theresa that "no matter what I say . . . you people are going to think that I am a racist, I say one thing and I am a racist." At the end, it turns out that Simon quit his very successful job because his white boss made a derogatory comment about Theresa, yet this is the only example of white opposition we get while there are many faces of black opposition throughout the movie. At the end, Percy bonds with Simon as a man and apologizes for his behavior, which gives the message that race does not matter and that gender trumps race—similar to the tendency to privilege gender over race discussed with television shows such as *ER*.

In this same year, a romantic comedy, *Something New* (2006), told the story of Kenya McQueen (Sanaa Lathan), a successful black career woman who had it all, except love. The movie revolves around her search for love and her ultimate decision between Brian Kelly, a white man who is everything she thinks she doesn't want, and Mark Harper, a black man who is everything she always dreamed of. The actress Sanaa Lathan says,

> We have not seen an interracial issue dealt with from a black woman and white man's perspective in this way . . . I loved the fact that it wasn't about the couple being against the world or the couple against the family. I loved the fact that it was her dealing with her own prejudices that came up, her own guilt, her own shame and embarrassment about what her peers thought.[40]

While it is refreshing to see a film from a black woman's perspective, this does not necessarily mean it presents a less problematic approach. The film begins by establishing the statistics facing black women, as Kenya sits with her three black women friends and they watch a gay black man walk by and a black man and white woman tongue kiss. Her friends discuss how educated black women hold to this idea of the "IBM-ideal black man," arguing they need to let go of this ideal. This clearly posits black women as the reason for their lack of partners, while subtly implicating gay men and black men–white women pairings, leaving white men as the only ones without blame in this story. Kenya goes on a blind date arranged by a white woman colleague, Leah, but she ends the date after she sees that her date, Brian, is white. They meet again at Leah's engagement party, and Kenya ends up reluctantly asking him to fix her lawn when she finds out he is a landscape architect. The way the film represents his drive to her house is very symbolic, as he leaves a quiet, presumably white, suburban area and drives across Crenshaw Boulevard into black urban life in a very stereotypical manner of music blaring and people hustling. As discussed in other films, the idea that they are opposites is clear—he is earthy, laid-back, natural, kind, and loves dogs while she is businesslike, uptight, and structured. The African American producer Sanaa Hamri describes her intent, "The garden is the cinematic manifestation of Kenya's life, as her garden grows, she grows." He encourages her to find herself with more color in her house while she tells him to be more financially smart because he works too much for what he charges her, which is a reversal of classic stereotypes of whites as financially savvy and people of color as more spiritual. When Kenya and Brian discuss dating and race, Kenya is the one who has a problem with interracial dating, stating that she "prefers black men . . . not prejudice just a preference." Like Simon in *Guess Who*, Brian is open-minded and wants to date her, yet she is difficult and only starts to like him as she watches him transform her yard.[41] In many ways, Brian also tries to make Kenya embrace nature, as he encourages Kenya to take out her hair weave and wear her hair natural.[42] Initially she gets angry because his hair comment represents to her the ways he cannot understand her because he is white, yet soon after she cuts off her weave and they begin dating. In this exchange, it takes a white man to get Kenya to love her own natural beauty, and he continues to help her blossom.[43] The character who plays Brian says, "For Brian it was not about race or color, it was about man and woman . . . he teaches her to be less controlled . . . more alive, more in the moment."

Still, throughout the film, Kenya and other black people are the ones opposed to interracial dating. Her brother accuses her of racial treason with comments like "skiing the slopes," and "sleeping with the enemy," which are negative ways to refer to interracial unions. Black opposition to interracial dating is highlighted when they go to a comedy show at a predominantly black club with another black couple and a black woman comedian talks about loving black men and not dating white men. While Kenya and her friend are dancing, the black man asks Brian if he is into "gardening the jungle variety" and tells him they watch out for Kenya, drawing on the idea that white men can hurt black women. When the comedian comes to the table, she calls Brian "their nightlight," and says to Kenya, "Either you're swirling or you got your probation officer with you." Kenya's black friends and family often make derogatory comments about Brian and intentionally try to make him uncomfortable or unwelcome.[44] Despite the negative comments being directed toward Brian, he remains cool and kind, whereas Kenya is the one who cannot handle it well. Black people are depicted as ignorant in their views and having a limited mind-set. Like *Guess Who*, it is black people who are rude and have a problem with interracial dating, and it is only a few bad white exceptions that are racist.

The only example of white racism shown involves a white client who does not trust her and wants the older white man in the office. She explains it to Brian as "black tax," working harder because you are black, and after work one day she tells him she is tired of "the white boys on the plantation." They argue over the realities of race, where he tells her he wasn't raised "that way" and reminds her of her success, while she explains white privilege and how whites always remind her of her blackness.[45] Brian says that they are jerks but it has nothing to do with their relationship, but Kenya wonders if she should be able to talk about "white shit" and "black shit" with him. He responds he can never be on the right side in her head because he is not black, and he points to himself, saying, "Maybe this is not what you want," and she agrees. This exchange is noteworthy for a mainstream film because it at least raises the debate over color blindness, white privilege, and different views on race.

Kenya begins dating Mark Harper, a successful black professional, and they talk about "white boys on the plantation," "black tax," and working too much because they are both up for partner. They are the same and seemingly perfect. Despite having found her "IBM-ideal black man," she is not happy.[46] The turning point for Kenya is when Mark tells her that he liked a picture he saw of her where she had long hair, and he asks her to wear her hair long with a weave. While Brian, a white man, loved her natural beauty, Mark, a black man, wants her less natural. Her friends and family, who originally gave Brian a hard time, tell Kenya, "At the end of the day it is not about skin color or race, it is the love connection, the vibe between a man and woman."[47] At her job, she takes a stand, and the white executives stand behind her, giving her the partnership. While race is discussed, color blindness still prevails, and the idea that prejudice is individual and can be overcome on the individual level, like in her job where all's well that ends well and her rantings about white privilege and Brian's lack of understanding about race seem unfounded. The film ends with Kenya going to Brian,

I know you must think I am combative, neurotic, and picky, but the real thing is I never had to be anyone but myself with you from the beginning and you make me think I can do anything, say anything, try anything, anything and that is the life I want, an adventure with you. . . . We are supposed to be together.

He responds, "Kenya, I will never be your dream man, I won't be the fall-back," and she says, "Dreams change . . . you're the one I want, Brian." She chooses a white man, not because she couldn't find an "IBM" but because she would rather have this white man.

While the movie was produced, directed, and written by black women, including the director Sanaa Hamri, one of the writers, Kriss Turner, and the producer, Stephanie Allain, the ideas and images of white masculinity are re-markably similar to mainstream films produced by whites.[48] As Hamri argued, "I didn't want to make a movie that said please go with the white man, and don't be with black men, that is not the message of this movie, . . . you should be able to be with whoever you want." Yet the white man is still idealized in this movie as not only handsome but also as a rejuvenating force who enables Kenya to find out who she really is and in many ways get more in touch with loving herself as a black woman, as exemplified with the hair experience. Unfortunately this is not new and returns to the idea that white men are supe-rior, even saviors. Though the movie claims to present this issue from a black woman's perspective and offer "something new," the end result is that the film emphasizes black people's opposition, not white racism, which created the social structure where all these relationships are problematized.

In both Something New and Guess Who, the main opposition toward the relationships is based in black families and communities.[49] This pattern of retelling the story by depicting opposition as coming from within the com-munities of color can be linked to historical practices surrounding interracial sex. During colonial times and slavery, while the real threat of interracial rape involved black and native women being raped by white men, whites spun tales of the threat of black and native men, justifying the lynching and killing by this alleged threat. In the same way, interracial relationships are discouraged by blaming the communities of color as the ones who pose the threat to contemporary interracial couples. Despite the possibilities these two films offer to present new images, they ultimately reinforce the existing ideologies about interracial relationships and black families, while maintain-ing that whites are not racist.

Conclusion

In popular culture, the images depicted in movies such as The Bodyguard, Bulworth, Mission: Impossible II, Monster's Ball, and Something New are worth noting for their representations of relationships between black women and white men, yet this increased visibility and engagement in cross-racial sexual unions does not necessarily signal racial progress or a lasting relationship. While the media may celebrate the trend of showing white men with women of color as "something new," it is more like a repackaging of something old. Representations of interracial intimacy have less to do with how acceptable these unions are and more to do with whose interests are served. By not acknowledging race, it does not mean racial stereotypes no longer exist. One might argue that all movies use these strategies of two people not meant to be, existing in deviant worlds, or having to transform to be with another. Though, when these patterns are used with interracial relationships they are more problematic because we so rarely see interracial relationships on-screen and in life, so there is less of a range of interracial images. In most instances, white men deviate from the norm, which involves entering a relationship with an exceptionally attractive light-skinned black or Latina woman while reproducing the images of these relationships as deviant and sexual.

This view of interracial relationships as deviant has existed throughout America's history, therefore it is not surprising that most films still depict interracial sexual relations as outside the realm of acceptable behavior. By constructing interracial relationships as a deviation from the norm, it is a means of privileging same-race unions and maintaining white dominance.[50] The relationships serve a purpose in the representation of whiteness. Rarely if ever does the white man look bad. These stories all depict white men as progressive and good, yet also show how only in a certain place or circumstance does the relationship occur. The dangers of interracial intimacy are clear, where the white man sacrifices his position, even his life, for the relationship. Yet the relationship is acceptable because it allows for the white man's goodness, kindness, and often superiority over others to be shown and restores the white man spiritually, emotionally, politically, economically, or in some other way. Furthermore, the white man also gains from the relationship by either solidifying his reputation as liberal and progressive, certifying his youth and coolness, or securing his image as kind and powerful. Rebecca Faery described it as "cartographies of desire" where white men "conflated with desire for a Native woman who was a representative or stand-in for the land itself."[51] By taking the woman of color, the white man symbolically also takes the community (politically in *Bulworth*), the culture, or reestablishes their superiority and moral goodness. The relationship between a white man and woman of color is acceptable as long as the white man saves her world or the woman comes to his world, either symbolically through a transformation, like Jennifer Lopez's character who goes from a maid to a business executive, or geographically, by moving into his house like Halle Berry in *Monster's Ball* or into his entire world.

Casting women of color opposite white men does not change the image of the women, but it does work as "part of a broader program of hegemonic recuperation, a program that has at its main focus the reconstruction of white masculine power." These images could also be read as affirming "white male identity against the threat of emerging feminism by warning white women to return to the 'feminine sphere'—to their duties of wife and mother—if they wish to attract and keep a man."[52] While there is no denying the different historical and contemporary realities surrounding Asian women, Latina women, and African American women, I argue that interracial depictions of white men with women of color share certain aspects. "The black-white binary is particularly powerful because it is so efficient and effective in exaggerating racial difference, in helping to establish order—a racial order,"[53] other racial positions can be understood along the continuum. What emerges is how the gaze of the film is white male and these are white male fantasies, with these depictions of interracial sex constructing white masculinity in certain ways while reinforcing certain representations of women of color. "Hollywood films rarely position audiences to question the pleasures, identifications, desires, and fears they experience as whites viewing dominant representational politics of race."[54]

Yet there are some differences between the representation of white men with black women as opposed to Latina or Asian, based on the very different histories of racialization and contemporary realities we discussed in chapter 1. While certain light-skinned African American actresses such as Halle Berry can occasionally play raceless characters, it is much more common for this option to be available for Latinas, like Jennifer Lopez and Salma Hayek.[55] The fluidity of racial and ethnic identity is clear, as we see Jennifer Lopez sometimes playing opposite a white man as a white woman or other times clearly marked as Latina. The traits and stories associated with the Latina Lopez, as opposed to white Jennifer, reveal how Latinas are represented in certain ways, but certain Latinas like Lopez have the ability to, at least temporarily, leave behind these representations. There are particular ideologies associated with Asian women as submissive, desirable exotic sexual beings, Latino women as hot, sexual, and of a lower status, and black women as sexual, untrustworthy, of a lower status, and only paired with white men if light-skinned. These representations are a "safely voyeuristic" experience that allows the audience to view what they already believe.[56] The overwhelming number of pornographic Web sites and dating services catering to these interracial fetishes of Asian submissives, black phat booties, and hot Latinas all engaging in sexual acts with white men further illustrate this argument. Interracial sex and intimacy can be consumed without a problem and without changing everyday realities or behaviors. In essence, it functions like "some of my best friends are [insert race]," which proves little more than the desire to appear accepting. For many whites in particular, Halle Berry's Leticia may be the closest they come to befriending a black woman or knowing an interracial couple, and their viewing pleasure does not seem to transfer to reality. In the end the white man remains the gentle conqueror, the savior, even if the only thing being conquered or invaded is a woman of color.

Notes

1. Tim Padgett and Frank Sikora, "Color-Blind Love," *Time*, May 12, 2003.

2. Ed Guerrero, "Spike Lee and the Fever in the Racial Jungle," in Jim Collins, ed., *Film Theory Goes to the Movies* (New York: Routledge, 1993), 125.

3. According to Darnell Hunt's "2007 Hollywood Writer's Report—Whose Stories Are We Telling?" as cited in Carl DiOrio, "Report: White Males Still Dominate Writing Ranks," *Hollywood Reporter*, May 9, 2007

4. Despite the growing trend to show same-sex relationships, there are only a few incidents of white men being paired romantically with men of color. Remarkably absent from the discussion is same-sex interracial relationships because they are rarely seen, with a notable exception in the 2005 movie *The Family Stone*, where Diane Keaton played the head of a white family with a gay son who was deaf and married to a black man. The dynamics are slightly different when there are interracial gay couples because the sexuality of the male characters may be the focus. In *The Family Stone*, one of the white sons comes home with a black partner, which is safe because it removes the relationship so far from mainstream in terms of gender, sexuality, and race that white masculinity is not threatened (read: real men like women). Given the multiple layers of deviating from the mainstream in terms of abilities, sexuality, and race, rather than challenging it simply reinforces deviance. See Christopher Ortiz, "The Forbidden Kiss: Raul Ferrera-Balanquet and Enrique Novelo-Cascante's Merida Proscrita," in Chon A. Noriega and Ana M. Lopez, eds., *The Ethnic Eye: Latino Media Arts* (Minneapolis: University of Minnesota Press, 1990), 244–59, for a discussion of an interracial love affair between a white man and a Latino man.

5. See Norman Denzin, *Images of Postmodern Society: Social Theory and Contemporary Cinema.* (Thousand Oaks, CA: Sage Publications, 1991). Hooks 1996; Margaret Russell, "Race and the Dominant Gaze: Narratives of Law and Inequality in Popular Film." Pp. 56-63 in ed. Richard Delgado, *Critical Race Theory: The Cutting Edge*, (Philadelphia, PA: Temple Univeristy Press, 1995).

6. Kennedy also identifies the movie *Cruel Intentions* as one where an interracial relationship is portrayed with race having little or no significance, yet this is erroneous. In fact, the premise surrounding the interracial relationships in the film is that a

white woman wants to discredit another young white woman, so she encourages her to have a sexual relationship with a black man, then lets her mother know, stating that the interracial affair would ruin the family name.

7. Kennedy 2002, 133.

8. *Dances with Wolves* avoids pairing Kevin Costner with a Native American woman by having him fall in love with a white woman who was raised by the tribe since she was little after her family was killed by another tribe. Yet the film still portrays whiteness as good and the white man as a savior who forsakes his position to become part of the tribe and win their undying love. Vera and Gordon 2003, 140–41.

9. See Gina Marchetti 1993, chapter 10.

10. There are a number of movies that depict a white American man with an Asian woman, often set outside the United States or set in times of war, such as *Come See the Paradise*, about a white man who falls in love with a Japanese woman just before World War II; the Oliver Stone production *Heaven & Earth* about an American GI and his Vietnamese wife; *Midway*, which has a subplot about a white son of a U.S. military officer who falls in love with a Japanese woman in an internment camp; *Sayonara*, starring Marlon Brando as a GI who falls in love with Japanese women in post–World War II Japan; and *The World of Suzie Wong*, about a Hong Kong prostitute who falls in love with a white photographer. (See www.asianwhite.org/media.)

11. Espiritu 2000, 113. For example, in August 2006, *Maxim* magazine (geared toward young men) featured Persia White (a light-skinned biracial African American actress from the television show *Girlfriends*) as "Today's Girl" with the accompanying title, "Everyone agrees this Persia should be invaded." While all women are objectified in the magazine, the particular reference to invading is used to characterize their feelings toward a woman of color, given the history of nations being invaded as well as the bodies of women of color being invaded by white men, "merely an incorporation of Blackness into the sexual/consumption networks operated by a White visual economy." Houston A. Baker, Jr., "Spike Lee and the Commerce of Culture," in Manthia Diawara, ed., *Black American Cinema* (New York: Routledge, 1993), chapter 10, 157.

12. Associated Press, "Marine Says Song about Killing Iraqis a Joke: "Hadji Girl" Video Shows GI Singing about Gunning Down Family," June 14, 2006, posted on MSNBC at http://www.msnbc.com/id/13300342/.

13. In *Boiler Room*, there is one scene where the white man tells the black woman he is involved with, "I want some chocolate love."

14. A quote from Debra Dickerson, author of *The End of Blackness*, on "Interracial Couples in America," *News & Notes with Ed Gordon* (9:00 a.m. ET) NPR, December 30, 2005.

15. There have been numerous works that address the underlying homoerotic symbolism of interracial relationships between white men and black men in films such as *White Men Can't Jump*, and the slew of interracial buddy films such as *Lethal Weapon*, *48 Hours*, and *Beverly Hills Cop*. See Norman Denzin, "White Men Can't Jump?: The Politics of Postmodern Emotionality," *Social Perspectives on Emotion* Volume 3 (1995): 33–54; Ed Guerrero, "The Black Image in Protective Custody:

Hollywood's Biracial Buddy Films of the Eighties," pp. 237–246 in Mantha Diawara, ed. *Black American Cinema* (New York: Routledge, 1993). Jacquie Jones, "The Construction of Black Sexuality," pp. 247–257 in Mantha Diawara, ed. *Black American Cinema* (New York: Routledge, 1993); and Matthew P. Brown, "Basketball, Rodney King, Simi Valley," chapter 7 in Mike Hill, ed. *Whiteness: A Critical Reader* (New York: New York University Press, 1997).

16. See Vera and Gordon (2003) discussion of *Lethal Weapon 4* on pages 5–14.

17. Two older white women who live in Alfie's building see her come to talk to him and one says to Alfie with her thumbs up, "You dating an AFRICAN American."

18. The character is played by Sandra Oh, who is often depicted in interracial relationships such as on TV's *Grey's Anatomy*.

19. This is also done in *The Lost World: Jurassic Park*, where Jeff Goldblum's character has a black daughter but there is no mention or showing of his ex-wife or if she was adopted.

20. Other examples include *The Score*, in which Robert De Niro plays a thief trying to pull off his last heist and Angela Bassett plays his girlfriend, though their relationship is shown very little. In an earlier film, *Strange Days*, which also revolves around a world of crime and murder, Bassett's character is in love with a white man who is obsessed with his white ex-girlfriend and solving a murder.

21. The choice of Halle Berry as the actress in these roles (as well as her roles in *Swordfish*, *The Rich Man's Wife*, and other films) to play opposite a white male lead is relevant because she is a light-skinned, biracial black woman. (Her mother is white, and her father is black.)

22. In the film, Hank's son Sonny, who is also a correctional officer, is kind and very different from his family. He befriends some black kids who live nearby, to Hank's dismay, who sees his son as weak. Early in the film Hank's son kills himself, which begins Hank's transformation as he begins to be nice to the black kids his son liked and decides to help Leticia with her son, recognizing her from the prison where she visited her son's father, of whom he oversaw the execution.

23. Berry won an Oscar for her portrayal and the film was critically acclaimed, with many film critics (mainly white) praising the way the film dealt with the complexities of race, family, and change. Yet, many African Americans publicly voiced their objection to the film, particularly the graphic interracial sex scene and the way Leticia's character was depicted.

24. Page 20 in "Re-membering Blackness after Reconstruction: Race, Rape, and Political Desire in the Work of Thomas Dixon, Jr."

25. Gray 2004 [1995], 157. See also Hebdige 1989.

26. Interview with James Brooks by Steve Daly, "What, Him Worry?" *Entertainment Weekly*, November 12, 2004, 63–70.

27. See Vera and Gordon 2003, 68–83.

28. This is a trend in recent movies that depict interracial relationships to depict the minority communities' opposition to the relationship with little or no mention of white opposition. (See *Guess Who* and *Save the Last Dance*.)

29. In the 2003 blockbuster comedy hit, *Bringing Down the House*, this same strategy is used by playing on the differences between an African American woman and a white lawyer and his upper-middle-class world. While Latina and Asian women are often presented as ultrafeminine, Queen Latifah's character is portrayed as loud and tough, having arrived straight out of prison. In the film, she meets the white lawyer online, but he mistakenly thinks he is interacting with her thin, white blond lawyer. She shows up at his home in an upper-middle-class white neighborhood, and the humor of the film revolves around her character not belonging and the responses of the white upper-middle-class people she encounters. For example, his short, white lawyer friend becomes obsessed with her when he sees her and pursues an intimate relationship with her. Despite the use of racialized stereotypes and ideas of difference, the movie situates the problem of race with an annoying white neighbor and wealthy white client who make blatant racist comments, which clearly marks them as the racists as opposed to the other whites. The movie ends with Martin reunited with his ex-wife, thanks to Latifah, who helped him learn to lighten up and enjoy life, and Latifah is now cleared of all charges and is visually much more refined. These movies serve the purpose of reinforcing ideas of racial difference while relegating racism to a few individuals, yet simultaneously representing whites as benevolent helpers of minorities and minorities as capable of showing whites how to be more loose.

30. Kevin Costner reportedly wanted Houston to play opposite him.

31. Even though she is the aggressor, the control is quickly returned to Frank, when Rachel says they should go out but "only if (he) wants to, you decide."

32. The reluctance to show interracial sex scenes may be based in the views of black sexuality as animalistic, immoral, and disgusting; "The prejudice, the fear, the ignorance, and the guilt concerning black sexuality have been so profound and deep-rooted in the crevices of American fantasy that, until very recent times . . . kissing was absolutely forbidden to Blacks performing on television or on the screen" (Lincoln 241). This coupled with the taboo against interracial sexuality makes showing blacks involved sexually with whites on-screen particularly problematic.

33. See bell Hooks, *Black Looks, Race and Representation* (Boston: South End, 1992) and Paula Giddings, *When and Where I Enter* (New York: Bantam Books, 1984).

34. Lynn Hirschberg, "Warren Beatty Is Trying to Say Something," *New York Times Magazine*, May 10, 1998, 34. Hirschberg interviews Beatty for this article.

35. Lynn Hirschberg, "Warren Beatty Is Trying to Say Something," 34.

36. Peter Bardaglio, "Midnight Miscegenation: Bulworth Reinforces Rather than Undercuts Certain Racial Stereotypes about White Men and Black Women," *The Sun*, June 7, 1998.

37. Beatty immersed himself in rap culture and surrounded himself with its leading producers, Russell Simmons, the black owner/creator of Def Jam Records, and Suge Knight, the owner of Death Row Records. When Simmons was asked how he felt about "Beatty making a movie about black ghetto life," Simmons responded, "[Blacks] don't care that he plays a rapper in this movie but everybody likes everybody doing certain things. They would rather see him as Bugsy," Hirschberg 1998, 36.

38. Gina Marchetti also identified this pattern of "white knights" in earlier movies featuring interracial relationships between white men and Asian women, such as *Love Is a Many Splendored Thing* and *The World of Suzie Wong*: "The relationship with the white male protagonist promises freedom of choice, material prosperity, and a Cinderella-like transformation of the ethnic female protagonist into an 'American' herself, an accepted part of the larger society who has found her American Dream through romantic love." Gina Marchetti, *Romance and the "Yellow Peril": Race, Sex and Discursive Strategies in Hollywood Fiction* (Berkeley: University of California Press, 1993), 117. See also Mary V. Dearborn, *Pocahontas's Daughters: Gender and Ethnicity in American Culture* (New York: Oxford University Press, 1986), which also documents how interracial relationships between white men and women of color are idealized.

39. See Associated Press, "'Guess Who' Tops Weekend Box Office," March 27, 2005 (www.msnbc.msn.com/id/7311968).

40. Interview with Sanaa Lathan in "Sanaa Lathan Tries Something New: Actress Faces Questions about Interracial Dating in New Film, Real Life," February 2, 2006. Accessed on www.msnbc.msn.com.

41. Another day, he tells her he is taking her hiking, which she resists because she hates hiking. They experience the outdoor beauty together, and when it starts to rain, they hide under a tree and kiss. When he takes her home, she tells him it can't go any further, but he kisses her passionately up against the wall and it changes to the next morning, lying in bed.

42. After they have sex, he asks her about taking out her weave, but she gets offended and states she thought he dated black women, to which he responds he had but they had real hair. She tells him to get out and she doesn't need his landscaping services anymore.

43. Another example is when he paints her toenails red to help her embrace color, since she usually sticks to neutral beige, and then they paint her house.

44. At a housewarming party, most of the guests are black and do not allow Brian to fit in, with Kenya's best friend's boyfriend accusing him of stealing his barbeque recipes and the black men talking about racism and getting quiet when he says, "Are you talking about the black tax?" When Kenya's parents arrive, they think he is the gardener, and Kenya says, "He is my friend." Kenya's mom criticizes her natural hair and the colors in her house as "bohemian," asking, "What has gotten into you?" Kenya's brother introduces her to his law school mentor, Mark Harper, at the party. Kenya's mother is opposed to Brian and mentions an invitation to a cotillion party that Kenya did not want to go to with Brian. Brian asks what a cotillion is and she shows her pictures. He asks to go but she says she will skip this year, and he asks is it because of me. He says they would not be comfortable, and he says, "We or you won't feel comfortable."

45. He reminds her she is at the whitest firm and went to Stanford/Wharton and is more successful than he and 98 percent of people; she cites white privilege, saying whites only have to think about it when they are in a room full of black people and

she is always in a room full of white people who have to "regroup" when they find
out she is in charge of their multimillion-dollar accounts.

46. In an interview about the movie, Sanaa Lathan acknowledges that "when you
see a black man with a white woman there is a feeling that you have and I think the
feeling is an instinctual feeling of you want her you don't want me. I don't look anything like her so you don't like. . . . But then you think about it, you should love who
you love." Interview with Sanaa Lathan in "Sanaa Lathan Tries Something New:
Actress Faces Questions about Interracial Dating in New Film, Real Life," February
2, 2006. Accessed on www.msnbc.msn.com.

47. Her father ends by encouraging her to be with Brian because she loves him,
"He's just white, he's not a Martian . . . we carry on like we are a pure race . . . white,
black, brown, yellow mutts, all of us, nothing pure about none of us."

48. Like *Something New*, the film *Joy Luck Club*, written by Amy Tan, was critiqued by an Asian American male as portraying negative images of Asian men as
"monstrously evil or simply wimpy . . . we are used to this message coming out of
Hollywood, but it disturbed . . . to hear the same message coming from Amy Tan and
Wayne Wang." In the *Joy Luck Club*, a white man is portrayed as wealthy, successful,
and ultimately ends up happily reunited with his Asian American wife.

49. This ties in to the contemporary debates over race relations and language,
where the media presents debates over who is allowed to say what words when a
white commentator like Don Imus makes a racist comment and he blames the fact
that blacks routinely use the same racist language.

50. Gina Marchetti, *Romance and the "Yellow Peril": Race, Sex and Discursive Strategies in Hollywood Fiction* (Berkeley: University of California Press, 1993), 320.

51. Rebecca Faery, *Cartographies of Desire: Captivity, Race and Sex in the Shaping
of an American Nation* (Norman: University of Oklahoma Press, 1999), as cited in
Nagel 2003.

52. See Espiritu 2000, 113.

53. Hunt 2005, 3.

54. Page 296 in Henry Giroux, "Racial Politics and the Pedagogy of Whiteness."

55. Some actresses like Cameron Diaz, whose father is Latino, is not referred to as
a Latina and always plays a white woman.

56. Joe White, a journalist, makes this argument about white Sony executives
with the movie *Boyz n the Hood* in 1991 in "John Singleton and the Impossible
Greenback of the Aassimilated Black Artist," *Esquire* (August): 65.

CHAPTER FOUR

~

When Good Girls Go Bad

Men, particularly white men, have historically been conquering worlds and women both off- and on-screen. Accompanying these conquests, the myth of white womanhood as the epitome of beauty, femininity, and purity emerged as part of the fabric of American society and popular culture. As Feagin and Vera argue, "The same white male mind that transformed African men and women into slaves transformed white women into possessions that must be protected and repressed."[1] Whiteness was bound in white womanhood, and therefore keeping white women and whiteness "pure" by keeping white woman safely away from men of color became a prerogative. Early captivity tales of white women being stolen by Native Americans, lured away by devious Asian men,[2] seduced by Latin Lovers, or pillared by black men served the purpose of legitimizing the treatment of these racial groups, while also reinforcing patriarchal dominance and control over white women as well as women of color. Those white women who willingly encountered blackness or any man of color were tarnished and fell from grace.[3] In the past few years, media attention on white women who disappear illustrates how this particular preoccupation with the plight of white women and their safety still exists.[4] As one journalist describes,

> It's something seen as precious and delicate being snatched away, defiled, destroyed by evil forces that lurk in the shadows, just outside the bedroom window. It's whiteness under siege. It's innocence and optimism crushed by cruel reality. It's a flower smashed by a rock.[5]

While men and women of color are also victims, the media chooses to seize upon stories of the plight of white women who are middle class or higher, petite, and attractive who disappear.

Given this privileging of white womanhood and the focus historically on preventing relationships between men of color and white women, not surprisingly relationships between white women and men of color have been largely ignored on the big screen, with few depictions in mainstream films until recently. The 1967 classic *Guess Who's Coming to Dinner*, where even the title has become a pop-culture slang used any time someone unwelcome or shocking is brought home, is widely viewed as a sign of the change in contemporary representations of interracial unions between a black man and white woman. *Guess Who's Coming to Dinner* came out in 1967, following on the heels of the civil rights movement and the 1967 Supreme Court ruling that any laws banning interracial marriage were unconstitutional. It was remarkable in contrast to the invisibility of interracial unions on-screen between white women and men of color, or the other trend of showing problematic images of men of color capturing, terrorizing, or raping white women or at least desiring to, such as in various other films discussed earlier like Westerns depicting Native American tribes capturing white women, D. W. Griffith's 1915 *Birth of A Nation*, and the 1919 *Broken Blossoms*. In *Guess Who's Coming to Dinner*, Joanna, the white daughter of Matt Drayton, played by Spencer Tracy, and his wife, played by Katharine Hepburn, surprises her parents when she comes home with a black fiancé, Dr. John Prentice, played by Sidney Poitier.[6] While many heralded the movie for showcasing an interracial marriage between a black man and a white woman, many of the racial strategies used in this film are still used today. For example, the Draytons represent whiteness and all that is good, while racism and opposition is relegated to a few unlikable whites and various black individuals. The white parents are depicted as liberal and defenders of injustice, as evidenced in Ms. Drayton firing a white woman who works with her for making a racist comment. Dr. Prentice's black father objects to the marriage and never comes to accept it the way the white father does, and the Drayton's black maid is depicted as vehemently opposed.[7] By having a black character express negative views and racist comments, it allows opposition to be voiced without implicating whites. Like the television depictions discussed earlier, Prentice was an "exceptional" man, a widowed 37-year-old public health doctor who refuses to sleep with Joanna until they are married. The audience learns this not only through his actions but also after Joanna's father does a background check, validating the idea that even a white liberal man is justified in being distrustful of a black man trying to marry his daughter. Prentice is also a "tamed black man" in that he clearly defers to the white father's decision, stating that he will heed whatever decision the white father makes. The film does not deal with the actual interracial couple very much and the film does not culminate with a beautiful wedding as many films do, but it instead focuses on the reactions of others, particularly the white father. The father's objections to the marriage are not depicted as racial, but realistic concerns about how fast this happened and concerns that their plans have not been well thought out. To further sanitize this treatment of interracial relationships, the movie depends upon "sight gags and double takes, weak jokes, visual ironies and snappish, cynical humor."[8] The film ends having done more for affirming whiteness than promoting a greater acceptance or understanding of interracial relationships.

Despite the popularity of *Guess Who's Coming to Dinner*, this did not usher in a wave of interracial representations. Still "good" women, particularly "good" white women, are not involved in interracial relationships with men of color on-screen (or off-screen), unless it is under very specific circumstances. In chapter 3, I argued that black women are often saved or improved by their on-screen relationship with white men who dominate different worlds, yet white women paired with men of color on screen symbolize something different, often a downward spiral or destructive life. The three patterns that emerge overlap with the frames discussed in both the television representations and the film representations, which include the impossibility of interracial relationships between white women and men of color (and the more acceptable alternative of "not quite white"); the tendency to show interracial relationships and the individuals involved and the social environment in which it occurs as deviant; or the infrequent depiction of an interracial relationship with an exceptional man of color. Also, the ways these relationships between white women and men of color play out in films written, directed, or produced by filmmakers of color will be discussed.

Interracial Impossibilities

On-screen, interracial relationships between white women and African American, Latino, or Asian men occur so infrequently that it can be argued that there is an implicit censorship of these unions that demonstrates how certain subjects are rendered outside the realm of what is speakable.[9] Even films that do pair a white woman with a man of color tend to keep the relationship platonic or avoid showing any intimacy in their relationship. For example, interracial weddings are rarely seen or celebrated on-screen, even though weddings are a particularly popular tool used in Hollywood films to end a movie or serve as a backdrop of the narrative. Since weddings legitimize and solidify relationships, the avoidance of legitimizing interracial unions through marriage can be read as a symbolic ban, like the legal ban on interracial marriage overturned in 1967 by the Supreme Court.

Prominent black actors such as Cuba Gooding, Jr., Will Smith, and Denzel Washington have commented on Hollywood's tendency to avoid the issue of interracial intimacy and the hesitancy of white executives to place a black male lead opposite a white female lead for a romantic story line.[10] When Denzel Washington was asked how people would react to a black man and white woman in bed on-screen, he replied "I don't know. . . . I wouldn't do it just for the reaction. If it's a good story, I'd do it. . . . I haven't turned down any scenes like that because I haven't been offered any. So again that's a question for some guys [waves his arm toward the Hollywood Hills] behind those big gates."[11] While black male actors are often blamed or rumored to avoid love scenes with a white woman, Denzel Washington, as well as Will Smith and Cuba Gooding, have all acknowledged that it is the filmmakers who make these choices.[12]

Even if a man of color—black, Latino or Asian—is paired opposite a white woman, the relationship will rarely be consummated. For example, the Asian actor Jackie Chan often plays opposite white women in movies such as *The Medallion* and *The Tuxedo* with barely a hint of romance, reinforcing the stereotype of Asian men as kung fu masters with no sexual presence. Also, the younger Asian actor Jet Li played opposite the white actress Bridget Fonda in *Kiss of the Dragon* with no relationship, and even when he played Romeo in *Romeo Must Die*, a loosely based contemporary version of *Romeo and Juliet* produced for the MTV generation opposite the African American singer Aaliyah, the two never moved past flirting.

In Hollywood today, a black man kissing a white woman is still largely a taboo as far as studio executives are concerned,[13] as evidenced in the large number of movies that pair a black man opposite a white woman that do not include a romantic relationship. Films based on books that contained an interracial relationship, such as *The Pelican Brief* and *Kiss the Girls*, altered the story lines from the books they were based on to eliminate any sexual tension or relationship between the white and black lead actors.[14] In *Kiss the Girls*, as well as another movie *High Crimes*, the black actor Morgan Freeman plays opposite Ashley Judd, a much younger white actress, and though they have great chemistry, they do not even come close to becoming intimate. *The Pelican Brief*, originally a novel that included a romantic relationship between the two main characters, featured the white actress Julia Roberts opposite Denzel Washington, yet they had a platonic friendship on-screen.

Similarly in *The Bone Collector*, Washington played opposite Angelina Jolie, where they did exchange sexual innuendos, yet there was no danger of the two actually having sex since Washington's character was a quadriplegic who couldn't leave the house. The Oscar-nominated and popular box-office black actor Will Smith has also been paired against white women in movies such as *Men in Black*[15] and *I, Robot*, yet the closest it came to a romantic or sexual encounter in either film was suggestive comments. This phenomenon occurs in a string of films such as *Murder at 1600* (1997) with Wesley Snipes and Diane Lane and *The Long Kiss Goodnight* (1996) with Samuel Jackson and Geena Davis, who "inch toward embrace, then are separated by the script or editing."[16] Similarly, in *Finding Forrester* (2000), there seems to be a romance developing between the African American male star and his white classmate, but the movie stays focused on his relationship with the elderly white man because it is safer and nonsexual, not to mention affirming the white savior role discussed in the last chapter, where white men help blacks achieve success. As Vera and Gordon argue, "Middle-class American family norms include a guarantee against miscegenation"[17] and interracial sex is most problematic if it involves a white woman, given the gendered way that white women paired with men of color are often rendered outside the realm of possibility while white men paired with any woman is a possibility.[18]

One way that this "problem" is addressed is by casting a man of color, particularly a black man, opposite a woman who is almost white or "not quite white." For example, in the popular 2005 romantic comedy *Hitch*, Will Smith plays a "love doctor" who helps other men get women to fall in love with them, focusing on his work with an awkward white guy in love with a beautiful blonde. While able to help other men by teaching them his moves, Will Smith clumsily pursues a character played by Cuban American actress Eva Mendes. One journalist describes Mendes in the following way:

> (she has) the burden of (convincing movie producers she is more than) "ethnic/ exotic" . . . on the other hand, (her) career has been pushed along by her dark good looks, which also happened to solve an awkward little industry problem: what to do with highly bankable African American stars like (Denzel) Washington and (Will) Smith who are strapped for romantic leads.[19]

Film critic Tom Carson calls it the "Latin Option," arguing "It's Hollywood's favorite way of dabbling in cross-racial sexuality without scaring moviegoers." Latina actresses like Eva Mendes, because of their ambiguous racial and ethnic identities, can be used to diversify a movie for maximum appeal without alienating anyone. As "the love interest of an African American star, she's a stand-in for a Caucasian woman; opposite white actors, she's a stand-in for a black one."[20] Similarly, Denzel Washington has often been paired opposite Latina women, such as in his Oscar-winning performance in *Training Day* and *Out of Time*, or a Middle Eastern woman in *Mississippi Masala*, a romantic comedy specifically about the problems that arise from their relationship.[21] Another strange twist was used in Denzel Washington's *Devil in a Blue Dress*, where he plays a detective looking for a white woman who is engaged to a powerful white man, yet it turns out that the woman Washington is pursuing is actually biracial and "passing" as white. This highlights how the woman paired opposite a black man can look white, as long as she really isn't. As *Hitch* director Andy Tennant argues, "Unfortunately, if you paired Will with a white woman, that would overpower the romantic comedy. It would suddenly become an interracial love story, and that wasn't the movie we were making."[22] Will Smith also commented on the racial politics of casting in an interview with a British paper, the *Birmingham Post* while promoting *Hitch* overseas:

> There's sort of an accepted myth that if you have two black actors, a male and a female, in the lead of a romantic comedy, that people around the world don't want to see it. . . . We spend $50-something million making this movie and the studio would think that was tough on their investment. So the idea of a black actor and a white actress comes up—that'll work around the world, but it's a problem in the U.S."[23]

Therefore, racial policing of on-screen relationships can be tricky business, especially when a black male actor is featured, and the fear of the white producers is that pairing him with a white woman will "overtake" the movie or more likely alienate some, yet pairing him with a black woman would change the film into a "black film." Rather than acknowledge racism, white directors like Tennant problematize interracial unions and excuse the avoidance of these unions as good storytelling.

Yet the illusion of interracial sex, or the possibility of it, remains an acceptable indulgence. The film *Full Frontal* (2002) starring Julia Roberts and Blair Underwood plays with the idea that Hollywood avoids showing intimate scenes between black men and white women. In *Full Frontal*, Roberts and Underwood play actors who are starring in a film together, and in this film-within-a-film they are supposed to fall in love. *Full Frontal* brings together many different people around the plotline of the making of a film and a big birthday party for the director. The plot is purposefully confusing, as Roberts plays Catherine, an actress playing the part of a journalist named Francesca, who is interviewing Underwood's character, Nicholas, who is playing an actor named Calvin. As Calvin, he discusses racism in Hollywood and the reluctance to show an intimate relationship between a black man and white woman. The film-within-the-film shows a quick peck between the two actors, and ends with the two putting their faces cheek to cheek, smiling suggestively and mocking the trend in Hollywood to not show intimate interaction on-screen. Despite addressing opposition to interracial relationships in films, *Full Frontal* still never shows any sexual relationship between Roberts and Underwood, not even in the film-within-the-film. Yet Underwood's character Nicholas is involved with many women, including the white wife of one of the writers, but the sex scene is blurred, shown through the inside of hotel air vent—in essence doing exactly what the film accuses the rest of Hollywood of doing.

Another way interracial unions are indulged on-screen without actually being seen is through cartoon or nonhuman characters. For example, media scholars have argued that films like *Star Wars* "repeat the 'blood and purity' mythology of *The Birth of a Nation*."[24] Cartoons such as *Who Framed Roger Rabbit* and *Shark Tale* pair various characters together, which are often meant to represent different racial and ethnic characterizations. While movie producers avoid pairing Will Smith opposite a white woman in films such as *Hitch*, in the cartoon film *Shark's Tale*, the fish Will Smith provides the voice for is clearly marked as African American through his dress, talk, and community and is romantically linked with two different fish played by white actresses Angelina Jolie and Renée Zellweger. Scholars have also discussed how *King Kong* "has been read as the tragic story of a heroic beast and/or the fate of a black man punished for desiring and engaging with a white woman."[25] By symbolizing interracial unions through cartoon or animal characters, not allowing interracial unions on-screen between white women, and substituting Latina women for white women, the idea that interracial relationships do not happen and should not happen, at least for white women, is reinforced, which ties in with the next pattern of representations of interracial deviance.

Symbolizing Deviance and Destruction

Like the early captivity tales of white women being stolen by Native Americans, lured away by devious Asian men,[26] seduced by Latin Lovers or pillared by black men that served the purpose of legitimizing the treatment of these racial groups, contemporary representations still imagine white women being destroyed by their contact with men of color. Relationships between men of color and white women are rarely depicted as long-term or successful and are often submerged in deviance. Furthermore, interracial sex is used to symbolize a major transformation or turn in the lives of young white women on-screen. This is reminiscent of the way white womanhood was viewed as a potential source of crisis after the Civil War, where along with "the threat of the black rapist . . . the fear of uncontrollable white womanhood was already a point of contention . . . turn-of-the-century white women who asserted identities beyond the domestic space were figured both as race traitors and as diseased bodies, perhaps equally capable of spreading infection in their midst."[27] A number of contemporary movies such as *Bad Company*, *Cruel Intentions*, *Freeway*, *Pulp Fiction*, and *Ricochet* include an interracial sexual encounter or relationship, yet it is submersed in a deviant world of crime, prostitution, and inner-city motels.

Pairing a white woman, particularly a young white teenage girl, with a young man of color is used to signify her downward spiral. The film *Freeway* (1996) begins with the white main character, Vanessa, with her black boyfriend living in a seedy motel with her prostitute mother and perverted mother's boyfriend, which she soon leaves after her black boyfriend is shot. In two other critically acclaimed films, *Thirteen* (2003) and *Traffic* (2000), young, white, teenage girls who are honor students get involved in drugs and deviant subcultures that include interracial sex. Film critic Tom Carson describes how "hooking up with black guys is clearly supposed to mark a new stage in the pubescent heroine's degradation, to the audience's combined horror and titillation."[28] Similarly, in the MTV-produced teen blockbuster *Cruel Intentions* (1999), a group of wealthy teens manipulate each other's lives, with a subplot where one young white teen wants to ruin the reputation of a fellow white classmate, so she encourages a relationship between this girl and her black cello instructor. According to the black actor Sean Patrick Thomas, who played the cello instructor, the writer/director "Roger Kumble intended for it to be played by a black actor, because in this situation something had to be there between his character and the white girl that would scandalize her socially prominent mother."[29] Other films also show the interracial relationship to correspond with one's downward spiral even if the interracial relationship is not contributing to it. For example, the film *Crazy/Beautiful* (2001) featured a white teenage girl from a successful family who is destroying her life through deviant behavior while romancing a smart Latino teen who never gets in trouble (which will be mentioned later in the section on exceptional men of color).

Films that focus on adult underworlds of drugs, prostitution, and gangsters also have a pattern of pairing a white woman with men of color. In the cult classic *Scarface* (1983), a Cuban emigré Tony Montana comes to Miami and becomes a major player in the drug trade, including taking the blond, white girlfriend of the drug boss Frank Lopez. *Empire* (2002) features a Latino drug dealer trying to get out of the business, and in the process he gets mixed up with a corrupt white businessman, where he ends up having a sexual encounter with his white female companion, despite his Latina wife. The white women are often portrayed as sexually promiscuous by nature or a prostitute by profession. Films such as *Ricochet* (1991) use a sexual encounter between a black man and a white prostitute to mark the degradation of Denzel Washington's detective character, who is being set up by a psychotic, revenge-hungry white man he had arrested years before.[30] In the Oscar-nominated *Hustle and Flow* (2005), an African American pimp/rapper Djay has a white prostitute, Nola, who he pimps out to black men, along with his pregnant black girlfriend prostitute. In *Kiss of the Dragon*, the Asian actor Jet Li plays opposite Bridget Fonda's character, who is a white, American prostitute in France, though the characters are actually never intimate. It is also significant that the pairing takes place outside of the United States, or with a non-American white woman, such as in Spike Lee's *Mo' Better Blues* (1990), where one of the black saxophonists who plays in Denzel Washington's character's band has a French girlfriend. Similarly, in *U.S. Marshalls*, a 1998 sequel to the blockbuster hit *The Fugitive*, the black actor Wesley Snipes has a white, French, waitress girlfriend, though they are never shown together because he spends the movie running from federal agents. In *He Got Game* (1998), the black filmmaker Spike Lee featured a Russian-born white actress, Milla Jovovich, as a prostitute opposite Denzel Washington, because as Jovovich states, "Spike's whole point in wanting me . . . (was) to push people's buttons."[31] By portraying the white woman who is paired with a man of color as sexually promiscuous or a prostitute, these representations reinforce patriarchal dominance and control over white women (as well as women of color), while signaling the dangers of being involved with men of color. Furthermore, the interracial relationship is not threatening because the white woman is undesirable or deemed less deserving of "protection" because of her looks or behavior.[32]

Even if interracial relationships do not include prostitution and drugs, interracial encounters often happen in deviant worlds such as *8 Mile* (2002), the semiautobiographical film of the white rap sensation Eminem, set in the underbelly of Detroit, where Eminem's character discovers his close black friend having sex with his white girlfriend in a recording studio. In *One Night Stand* (1997), where even the title implies that the relationship is not a normal date or relationship, Max, a married black man, and Karen, a married white woman, meet and have a one-night extramarital affair, yet reunite months later through coincidence and continue their affair. Their entire relationship evolves within an alternative lifestyle that mainstream society considers "deviant," such as homosexuality, AIDS, and the use of illegal drugs. Another example, *The Object of My Affection* (1998), depicts a relationship between a black man and white woman as part of a string of unsuccessful and unconventional relationships, without ever mentioning race. In *The Object of My Affection*, a white woman, Nina, is initially engaged to Vince, a demanding and controlling white man. After getting pregnant, she leaves Vince to raise their child with her gay roommate, George, who she eventually falls in love with. Unfortunately for Nina, George still desires male companionship, so she finally accepts that they cannot be together. Ultimately, the film ends with Nina in a relationship with a black man yet still in close contact with George and his lover. The movie revolves around the idea that Nina always chooses men who are not "suitable" for her, based on personality, sexuality, or race. The final scene of the movie exemplifies this idea when the white father of her child, Vince, tells her "You know I was the only one who made sense." Since they shared no similar interests and were completely incompatible, it leaves the viewer to contemplate why they "made sense": was it simply because he was a white, heterosexual man, while her other choices were deviant according to norms of sexuality and race relations?

Similar to television's use of interracial couples for shock or comedy, films such as the *Object of My Affection* also present white woman-black man pairing as a readily visible means of placing the relationship or circumstance outside the norm for comedic effect. For example, in *Me, Myself, & Irene* (2000), Jim Carrey plays Charlie, a white police officer whose white wife, Layla, leaves him for their wedding limousine driver, Shonte Jackson, who is a black short person. Racial differences are played for laughs, especially in the scenes where everyone but Charlie realizes that their three young sons are obviously not fathered by him, as they are black and presumably fathered by Shonte.[33] Early in the film Layla runs off with Shonte, leaving Charlie to raise their three black sons.[34] Following what Vera and Gordon identify as the "white savior role," while Shonte and Layla abandon their children, the film is about Charlie who raises them, though this is a very small subplot of the film. In a youth classic film *Sixteen Candles* (1984), the interracial pairing is also purposefully absurd, with an Asian male high school exchange student who finds a tall, unattractive, full-figured white female student irresistible, which is especially comical because she is clearly not desired by other American (read white) students. These two films offer distinctly different racial messages that correspond with the historical construction of black and Asian men, where in *Sixteen Candles*, the Asian young man can only win the affection of an undesirable white woman, whose tallness further emphasizes the symbolic smallness of the Asian man's attractiveness, yet in Me, Myself, & Irene, the black man, despite his short stature and unpleasant personality, is able to steal an attractive, intelligent, married white woman from her white husband, reaffirming the hypersexualized threat of any black man.[35]

The idea of a white woman's insatiable attraction to black men is also used for comedic effect in films geared toward black audiences, but the images are slightly different. For example, in the film Soul Plane (2004), which had a predominantly black cast, there was one white family, consisting of a man, his two kids, and his second wife, a very young, sexy blonde. The white father is concerned about his daughter partying on the plane with black men (which she does attempt to do), but while he is looking for her, his blonde wife looks through a magazine that shows black men to be well endowed and she runs to have sex with one of the many black men on the flight. This idea of a white woman seeing a black man and immediately wanting him sexually also surfaces in the film How High (2001), where the two black men have a brief encounter with two white women who have sex with them immediately after watching a black guy on television. Further illustrating how ingrained these ideas are, a popular genre of Internet pornographic Web sites feature "white sluts" who can't resist having sex with black men.[36]

In films geared toward black audiences, black men who desire or engage in relationships with white women are often portrayed negatively.[37] This scenario plays out in numerous films, including White Chicks (2004), where a large, muscular, yet somewhat deranged black man is so obsessed with white women that he chases after a black man impersonating a white "chick." In another comedy, Don't Be a Menace (1996), a black man who espouses pro-black sentiments and is dressed in traditional African garb knocks over a black woman to get to a white woman, who he proceeds to try to talk to. Pairing a black man with a white woman symbolizes the black man is a "sell-out" who is not committed to black communities or issues affecting black people, Black men dating white women are also characterized in certain stereotypical ways, such as corny, stuffy, and conservative in movies such as Mo' Money (1992), where one of the black characters who is conservative is shown with a white woman. In a number of films, such as Undercover Brother (2002), Bamboozled (2000), and Livin' Large! (1991), the main black character's transition into a more corrupt, less socially conscious person is accompanied by a relationship(s) with a white woman.[38] Therefore, blacks who do cross the racial divide to date are often depicted as "selling out" the black race, not being "black" enough, and overall, their commitment to the black community is questioned as a result of their relationship with a white individual. In Livin' Large!, a young black man from an inner-city neighborhood becomes a newscaster by being

at a scene of a breaking news story and loses touch with the black community in his pursuit of success. To illustrate he has "sold out," he has an
affair with his white female coanchor, starts speaking "proper English," is
accused of "acting white," and when he looks in the mirror he sees himself
as whitened.[39] Similarly, *Undercover Brother*, a 2002 successful, mainstream
box-office comedy, tackled a number of racialized stereotypes, including the
images surrounding black men, black women, and white women.[40] Satiriz-
ing the blaxploitation films of the 1970s, the film features black comedian
Eddie Griffin as the "Undercover Brother," a black hero who is out to fight
the white "man" responsible for oppressing blacks.[41] In this battle, "The
Man" sends in "black man's Kryptonite," which is Penelope Snow, a white
woman he cannot resist, and he slowly changes the way he talks, the music
he listens to, and the foods he eats, quickly becoming "more white." When
the other black men he works with at the "Brotherhood" hear that he has
been with a white woman, they can barely conceal their envy and respond
like adolescent boys asking how it was, then quickly reverting back to their
professional composure and criticizing him for "selling out." Undercover
Brother's relationship with Penelope brings forth outrage from "Sistah
Girl," his black female partner who is the main source of opposition, and she
ultimately rescues him from the white woman's house and influence.

While a comedy and spoof, these representations still reinforce ideas
about black men and white women, as well as black women's responses
(which will be addressed in greater detail later in the chapter). These films
use these commonly held beliefs about white women and black men and
how associating with a white woman is part of a transformation in which
the black man becomes less black and sells out. Ironically, this corresponds
directly with the "tamed" black man, who is represented as the acceptable
person by white standards: eligible, qualified, even good enough to be with a
white woman. In his classic work *Sex and Racism in America*, Calvin Hernton
draws upon these same ideas when he argues,

> to almost all black men, no matter how successfully they hide and deny it. . . .
> there arises within almost all blacks a sociosexually induced predisposition for
> white women. The fact that few blacks will readily admit this is due more to
> their knowledge that black women and whites in general bitterly disapprove
> of it, than to their honesty.[42]

Regardless of whether these images and ideas are true, they are reproduced
and influence the perceptions and understandings of black-white relationships. Therefore, films geared toward black audiences do not necessarily pro-

vide any less stereotypical representations. Still, in films directed and written by black filmmakers, different perspectives on interracial relationships can surface, such as Spike Lee's film *Bamboozled*, which offers a serious critique of contemporary popular culture and uses an interracial relationship to show how a black male character compromises his black identity and black people in general through the development of a television show on the lines of *Amos 'n Andy*.

Exceptional Exceptions

While there are few depictions of successful unions between men of color and white women, those that are shown usually include an "exceptional man of color," continuing in the tradition of Sidney Poitier's character in *Guess Who's Coming to Dinner* and the television characters discussed on *ER* and *Grey's Anatomy*. In film, Latino men are included in these exceptions, especially when their racial or ethnic heritage is minimalized. There are less depictions of white women with Latino or Asian men, yet there seems to be some acceptance of the Latin Lover, as evidenced in the characters played by the popular film star Antonio Banderas, who is originally from Spain. In Hollywood, Latin Lovers are often European and also able to "pass" as white, such as Emilio Estevez, Charlie Sheen, Jimmy Smits, Lou Diamond Phillips, and Benjamin Bratt. For example, in *Love Actually* (2003), which is set in London, one of the subplots involves a white American woman who is "not-so-subtly" pursuing "the office hunk," who is Latino. Also the film *Crazy/Beautiful* mentioned earlier pairs a smart, handsome Latino youth opposite a rebellious, downward-spiraling, young white woman.

There are virtually no examples of a black man paired in a successful relationship with a white woman on-screen, no matter how exceptional he may be. One of the only exceptions is the 2001 MTV-produced blockbuster film *Save the Last Dance* (2001), geared for the teen/college-aged generation, which grossed over 90 million dollars. The film fits many of the patterns presented such as deviance and opposition, but it also fits the pattern of partnering a white woman with an "exceptional" man of color. In the film, Sara, a white teen, has to move in with her father in a predominantly black neighborhood in Chicago after her mother dies. At the high school in this new neighborhood she becomes friends with Chenille, a popular black teen, and develops a relationship with Chenille's brother, Derek.[43] Derek stands out in the high school because he is smart, ambitious, and awaiting acceptance to Georgetown in preparation for medical school, while the other black students at the high school, including Derek's sister Chenille, are underachievers, teen parents, not college-bound, promiscuous, and/or involved in illegal activity. The idea that Sara does not belong in this black world is depicted through her innocence, her clothing, her vocal contributions in class while other students are silent except Derek, and her classical ballet training, thereby fostering distinctly different images of white women and black women. This ties in with the historical tradition of depicting whites, particularly white women, as sexually innocent and pure, especially in contrast to black women.[44]

The movie highlights all the problems that erupt as the relationship between Sara and Derek intensifies, and it clearly problematizes black communities and black people, making black students the ones who oppose the relationship and the black community Sara moves to as one plagued with drugs and criminals. Derek and Sara have bonded over school and dance, yet they encounter problems from Derek's best friend, who accuses him of letting his relationship with Sara make him "soft." Chenille, Derek's sister, agrees with other black students that good black men like Derek shouldn't be with white women. Eventually Chenille acknowledges that her opposition comes from her own inadequacies and that of the father of her child, and she tells Derek that striving to leave the neighborhood (and having a white girlfriend) is not selling out, but rather just trying to succeed. This conversation is important because it characterizes Sara and Derek's relationship in individual terms and reproduces the idea that anyone can succeed if they are a good, smart, hardworking person regardless of race, which shows Derek as a positive person while implicating the rest of his black community as responsible for their lack of success. The complexity of interracial relationships and societal responses is illustrated because this movie depicts both support and opposition for interracial relationships, yet ultimately it reproduces many of the negative images of black women and black men that are referenced in qualitative studies of how black men and women feel about interracial dating and why interracial relationships are problematic.[45] The movie ends with the message that echoes the color-blind discourses prevalent in society that reduces the problem of race to individuals, and like the color-blind discourse that dominates American society, the movie concludes that despite the opposition of blacks, these two individuals can come together and find happiness because Derek is not like other black men. Like the black television characters on *ER* and *Grey's Anatomy*, a few good black men who are "tamed" like Derek, because of their exceptional intelligence and character and difference/distance from other black people, are qualified to engage with a white woman. Derek "proves" that anyone can make it, affirming the idea that those who do not succeed are personal failures and that the ultimate success for black men includes a white woman, which has long been a belief in white society.

Black Takes, Something Different?

Given that one of the main patterns of representation of interracial relation-ships relates to the privileging of whiteness, it is important to consider if mainstream filmmakers of color may produce distinctly different images. Yet as discussed in chapter 3, the film *Something New*, written, produced, and directed by black women, as well as film comedies that have predominantly black casts and include representations of interracial couples, tend to contain similar images of interracial couples, though with slightly different mean-ings. Spike Lee, whose films challenge the racial hierarchy and racist images rampant in society, produced the film *Jungle Fever* (1991), which presents interracial intimacy as a sexual animalistic attraction, likened to a disease that can be caught and cured, as the title implies. When portraying the is-sue of interracial relationships, Lee's depictions of the ways black and white communities respond to these relationships simultaneously reproduce the idea of interracial unions as undesirable and problematic.[46] Yet the difference lies in the justification for the opposition: Lee documents an oppositional black perspective based on "black political ideas ranging from Afrocentricity and black separatism to a subtle refrain of black neo-conservatism."[47] Lee even dedicates the film to Yusef Hawkins, a black teenager who was killed in the Bensonhurst section of Brooklyn in 1989 by a group of white teens who believed he was coming into this predominantly Italian section to see a white Italian girl (media coverage of this murder will be discussed in chapter 5). Unlike most white filmmakers, he does provide a sharp critique of the racism that exists in white communities and the strong opposition against interracial relationships that still exists among whites, while representing interracial unions as dangerous and destructive.

In *Jungle Fever*, Flip, a successful, married black architect, and Angie, his new white temporary secretary, develop a relationship over late-night take-out dinners at work, which leads to a sexual encounter on top of his desk. Ironically, Flip had not wanted Angie as a temp because he always demanded black assistants, and in other comments showed that he was committed to black issues, yet similar to the *Undercover Brother* premise, he ends up abandoning this in his sexual attraction to Angie. Lee does devi-ate from dominant Hollywood strategies by including an erotic and highly visual interracial sex scene between a black man and a white woman, yet it only serves to emphasize the sexual aspect of interracial unions. This sexual encounter results in Flip's wife throwing him out of the house, while Angie is severely beaten by her father for her indiscretion with a black man. The relationship begins as an extramarital affair and seems to have nowhere to go from the start since Flip loves his wife, not Angie. The temporary nature of their relationship is conveyed through the scenes that show the apartment that the two are staying in is never unpacked or decorated. In *Jungle Fever*, the interracial affair begins amidst stereotypes as evidenced in their initial conversations about her ability to cook spaghetti and lasagna, Harlem, skin color, and sexual stereotypes about penis size and sexual practices. When Flip ends the relationship with Angie, he tells Angie that she got with him in spite of her family only because she was "curious" and that he was "curious about white."[48] At the time the movie came out in 1991, Lee stated that the film was "an attempt to look at some myths . . . the (black) man buys into the belief that to be successful you have to have a white woman . . . and the (white) woman buys into the myth that the black man is a sexual superman. The stud, you know, the animal . . . since their union, their initial union, was not based on love, but was based on sexual mythology." Flip and Angie's relationship does not last, and the two ultimately separate, with Flip returning to his wife and Angie returning to her family house. Though Spike Lee shows how complex the responses to interracial unions may be, his portrayal of Angie and Flip's relationship (like other films) still serves to reproduce the image of interracial unions as sexual and not based on love and respect.

In many ways, interracial relationships are portrayed as an unacceptable alternative for both blacks and whites.[49] *Jungle Fever*, like *Undercover Brother*, presents interracial relationships as a betrayal of the black community, and what makes the betrayal more painful is that the black individual is betraying the race with the "enemy" who is a member of the group that has oppressed them for centuries. This idea also surfaces in the popular film *Waiting to Exhale* (1995), based on the best-selling novel by African American writer Terry McMillan. When Bernadine, a married mother of two, finds out that her husband is leaving her for another woman, she asks her husband if it is the "white bitch" from his office, and her husband asks if it would be better if she was black. Bernadine responds, "No, it would be better if you were." His blackness is questioned because of his relationship with a white woman. Later in the film, once again a white woman is a barrier to Bernadine's happiness when she meets a man with whom she immediately bonds and is attracted to, though it is revealed that he is also married to a white woman. Both *Jungle Fever* and *Waiting to Exhale* contain a scene where a group of black women discuss black men and relationships, focusing on the "problem" of white women. For example, in a scene from *Jungle Fever*, Flip's wife, Drew, and her friends discuss the "low class white trash white women" who throw themselves at black men. The issue of black men's obsession with white women and light skin is explored, with the black women referring to the white standards of beauty and femininity that have been used to devalue black women. The women conclude that if it wasn't for the "29,000 white bitches . . . who give up the pussy" and are "stealing" all the black men, they would have men to date and marry. Intermarriage is understood as a rejection of blackness and an internalization of the dominant belief held by whites that blacks are inferior. In *Waiting to Exhale*, the same issues are raised, and the conclusion is that white women (along with incarceration, drug abuse, homosexuality, and homicide) are the reason they can't find a "good black man." Through these different images, opposition to interracial unions among black women, collectively speaking, is conveyed. Like the films *Something New* and *Guess Who* that featured white men with black women and the trend in television shows such as *Judging Amy* and *ER*, placing opposition to interracial relationships with communities of color serves to deflect attention from white opposition and justify why interracial relationships do not occur. Therefore, even though filmmakers like Spike Lee may argue that he is representing views found in black communities toward interracial relationships, these representations of black opposition support the color-blind discourse of whites that simultaneously problematizes interracial relationships while denying white opposition and racism. Furthermore, black women are characterized as angry and confrontational, particularly in relation to interracial relationships, which contribute to the problematic stereotypes of black women as aggressive and ignorant.[50] While you may see slightly different images, the bottom line that interracial relationships should not happen does not change.[51]

Conclusion

The chapter has focused primarily on white women with men of color because the representations center on constructing whiteness and what whiteness should and should not be. It is also about what blackness, or the Other, can and cannot be. Too often, interracial relationships symbolize chaos, unevenness, the unknown, fitting right into a postmodern or post-postmodern disarray of lives. Beyond what representations we see, it is more about what we don't see. Interracial weddings are rarely seen or celebrated on-screen, even though they are particularly popular tools used in Hollywood films to end a movie or serve as a backdrop of the narrative.[52] Since weddings legitimize and solidify relationships, the avoidance of legitimizing interracial unions through marriage can be read as a symbolic ban, like the legal ban on interracial marriage overturned in 1967 by the Supreme Court. There are virtually no films that include a happily partnered white woman and man of color within the context of a stable, middle-class world. If a white woman is paired interracially, most often it occurs in a deviant setting, it causes problems, and/or is met with opposition, usually from communities of color who are used to symbolically represent the potential problems.

Protecting white women even in the movies remains a prerogative of the predominantly white male producers who control the film images we see. Not showing, deviantizing, or creating very unique exceptions of interracial relationships between white women and men of color serve to reinforce the dominance of whiteness and white masculinity. This tradition began as "the effort to 'protect' white women from the presumed desire of dark men, both Indian and African (as) a coded insistence on the rights of the colonists to territory already taken or not yet taken but desired."[53] Yet in film representations this remains true, with the battle now over the territory of identity, image, and symbolic power. While the earliest films showed the dangers of interracial sex, with a white woman jumping off a cliff rather than be defiled by a black man, today's white women who engage in sexual relations with a black man on-screen are also damaged, yet now it is symbolized through drugs, prostitution, and disengagement with school or family.

The representations of interracial unions between men of color and white women do little to challenge racial boundaries, and often it is safer to pair a man of color with a Latina woman, who is almost, yet not quite, white. Black men can be sexual predators, but they cannot be charismatic sexual partners, especially to white women, as we see in how few romantic movies a prominent star like Denzel Washington has been in. In *Hitch*, the problem of who to cast opposite Will Smith and the solution of pairing him opposite Eva Mendes shows what filmmakers think will alienate viewers and allows the familiar story to be told of a black man who is sexually savvy and slick teaching a white man how to get a girl without the threat of Will Smith wanting a white woman too (thereby also not posing a threat to the white man who he instead is helping). What emerges is that not only is interracial sexuality involving whites, particularly white women, problematized, it also points to how the sexuality of people of color or loving sexual relationships between two people of color are also dangerous and unappealing to white audiences. Even in films made by African American filmmakers, or films directed toward a black audience, these stereotypes of interracial relationships are reproduced, and while they may alter the representation, these images still do not challenge the idea that races should not mix.

Furthermore, there is little room for the representations of interracial images to be critiqued in contemporary discourse. For example, when black actor Blair Underwood was asked about his brief kiss with Julia Roberts in

Full Frontal for her "first big-screen interracial coupling," he replied, "Look at *Monster's Ball*. That's a story about racism in the South and still [race is] not so much of an issue [in the romance]. It's something that exists. . . . I don't even have tolerance for the conversation, really. . . . it's really about human beings and who connects and who clicks."[54] The cult of color blindness makes discussion of race problematic and any interracial pairing is celebrated, particularly by the media, even if it simply reinforces negative views. Interracial sex and relationships can be tolerated and consumed for entertainment, but only in very particular ways. In the next chapter, we will look at how these issues play out in media coverage of interracial events and what stories the news media chooses to tell.

Notes

1. Feagin and Vera, *White Racism*, 123.
2. Gina Marchetti, *Romance and "The Yellow Peril."*
3. See M. Frye, *Willful Virgins: Essays in Feminism, 1976–1992* (Freedom, CA: Crossing Press, 1992); and Elizabeth B. Higginbotham, *Righteous Discontent: The Woman's Movement in the Black Baptist Church, 1880–1920* (Cambridge, MA: Harvard University Press, 1993).
4. In a *Providence Journal* article, August 7, 2005, "Critics: Media Coverage Skewed to Missing White Women," Mark Effron, MSNBC News Daytime Programming, said, "The stories of missing women typically bubble up from local network affiliates who are covering the stories based on the public outcry they generate in their home communities . . . usually there's an involved family that tends to be sophisticated in how to use the media . . . we have never, ever, ever turned down a story based on race or any of those factors." Yet "one media-savvy relative said her efforts to draw attention to the disappearance of her niece, 24-year-old Tamika Huston, failed to win the attention of local media outlets whose stories might be picked up by national news." Despite the denial of race, it clearly seems that news media knowingly or unknowingly are drawn and identify with the stories of white women. See also Erin Texeira, "Fleeing Bride to Be's Tale Opens Old Rracial Wounds," Associated Press. Accessed at www.msnbc.com.
5. Eugene Robinson, "(White) Women We Love," *Washington Post* (June 10, 2005).
6. The choice of actors is very significant since Spencer Tracy and Katharine Hepburn were "one of the best loved American couples of their generation . . . the apogees of whiteness and project the Establishment seal of approval." (Vera and Gordon 2003, 87). Sidney Poitier "was well recognized and acceptable to the white audience" and as one critic wrote, "in 1966, he was the only black actor who could convincingly woo a white girl without alienating a large portion of the American film public" (Vera and Gordon 2003, 87, citing Gary Carey, *Katharine Hepburn: A Biography* (New York: Pocket Books, 1975), 208.

7. James Baldwin noted how the explicitly racist *Birth of a Nation* depicted a black maid who virulently told the black congressman she didn't like "niggers" who got above themselves, and *Guess Who's Coming to Dinner* uses the same scene of a black maid attacking and degrading a black man. See Vera and Gordon 2003, 87–88; also James Baldwin, *The Price of the Ticket: Collected Nonfiction, 1948–1985* (New York: St. Martin's Press, 1985), 602.

8. Vera and Gordon 2003, 86.

9. Butler 1997.

10. "Wild Will Smith on the 'Race Thing,'" *Providence Journal Bulletin*, July 3, 1999.

11. Quoted on pages 129–30, "The *George* Interview: Denzel Washington," *George* magazine (December /January 2000): 88–93, 129–30. In a *Chicago Sun-Times* article, he denied he had ever said he wouldn't do an interracial on-screen scene, but he responded, "The audience has the right to feel the way they want to feel," quoted in Stephen Schaefer, "Milla Jovovich Defends Denzel Sex Scene," ABC News Internet, May 1, 1998, at http://mrshowbiz.go.com.

12. Most films are still written, directed, and produced by white men, and the same powerful, white elite largely own the movie production companies. Blaming the black actor for not appearing opposite a white woman, even though the actor rarely has the power to make those decisions, is a similar strategy to presenting families and communities of color as the main opposition to interracial relationships.

13. See Nicholas D. Kristof, "Blacks, Whites and Love," *New York Times*, OP-ED, April 24, 2005; Michael Janusonis, "Solid Performance Is Bright Spot in 'Cruel Intentions,'" *Providence Journal Bulletin*, sec. E3 (March 5, 1999); Saada Branker, "Black in White Film," http://www.iconn.ca/zone451/issue07/verticals/saada.html.

14. *The Pelican Brief* movie was based on a John Grisham book that involved a romantic relationship between the two main characters. According to Denzel Washington, Julia Roberts wanted him to play the role, and in an interview he discussed how when he got the script there was no romantic relationship in it. As he describes, "It wasn't right for the story. (Robert's) boyfriend had died like three days before." Quoted on page 129, "The *George* Interview: Denzel Washington," *George* magazine (December /January 2000): 88–93, 129–30. Black actor Sean Patrick Thomas also argues that in *The Pelican Brief*, "If that had been a white guy playing the role, there would have been something between them. But because it was Denzel, they made it very platonic." Quoted in Michael Janusonis, "Solid Performance Is Bright Spot in 'Cruel Intentions,'" *Providence Journal* (March 5, 1999). *Kiss the Girls* was also based on a book that involved a romance between the two main characters.

15. In the sequel *Men in Black II*, Smith is given a romantic lead, a Latina woman played by Rosario Dawson.

16. Donna Britt, "Even on 'ER' Race and Love a Touchy Mix," *Washington Post* (April 9, 1999): BO1. Also in *Rising Sun*, Wesley Snipes's character flirts with a character played by Tia Carrere, who plays "the daughter of a Japanese woman and a black American," but still does not have a romance because she is secretly involved

with a white man played by Sean Connery as discussed in Charles Taylor, "Black and White and Taboo All Over," at www.Salon.com.

17. Vera and Gordon 2003, 6.

18. Films that offer serious treatment of interracial unions do not necessarily challenge dominant ideas, as the interracial relationship between a white woman and a black man often causes deleterious consequences for all involved. Historical pieces such as *Rosewood* (1997) document how allegations of rape by a white woman against a black man resulted in white men attempting to burn and destroy an entire black community, which was based loosely on historical facts. While the whites who participated are depicted negatively, there is one white man who risks his own life to help a group of black community members to escape. Another film, *Far from Heaven* (2002), depicts a white couple in the 1950s who realize that the white husband is gay and the wife becomes interested in a black man in the community, though their relationship could not happen because of the opposition. These films simultaneously place opposition to interracial relationships in the past, while reinforcing the idea of these relationships as deviant and dangerous impossibilities.

19. Interview quote from page 368 in Joseph Hooper, "The Education of Eva," *ELLE*, March 2005. See also Jeanette Walls, "Was Race an Issue in *Hitch* Casting?" www.msnbc.msn.com/id/7019342/ February 24, 2005

20. Tom Carson, "Skin Flicks," GQ, June 5, 2005. Other columnists such as Nicholas Kristof wrote an Op-Ed piece, "Blacks, Whites and Love," *New York Times*, April 24, 2005, where he argues, "But it's hard to argue that America is becoming more colorblind when we're still missing one benchmark: When will Hollywood dare release a major movie in which Denzel Washington and Reese Witherspoon fall passionately in love?", also noting that it is more acceptable to pair an African American with a Latina.

21. Other movies where the Latina/black pairing occurs include *Four Brothers*, a film about four men who consider each other brothers (two are white, two are black). There is a relationship between one of the black brothers and a light-skinned Latina woman, whose Latina ethnicity is emphasized. When Jennifer Lopez plays opposite a black man in films such as *Money Train*, her character is clearly marked as Latina, through her language, her name, and her neighborhood, yet when she is opposite a white man, her race and ethnicity are more ambiguous or clearly marked as white, non-Hispanic.

22. Interview quote from page 368 in Joseph Hooper, "The Education of Eva," *ELLE*, March 2005.

23. "Wild Will Smith on the 'Race Thing,'" *Providence Journal Bulletin*, July 3, 1999.

24. See page 459, Isaac Julien and Kobena Mercer, "De Margin and De Centre," originally appeared as the introduction to "The Last 'Special Issue' on Race?" *Screen* 29, 4 (1988): 2–10.

25. See Gail Dines, "King Kong and the White Woman: *Hustler* Magazine and the Demonization of Black Masculinity," in Gail Dines and Jean M. Humez, ed., *Gender, Race and Class in Media: A Text-Reader* (Thousand Oaks, CA: Sage Publications, 2003),

451–61; J. Snead, *White Screens, Black Images: Hollywood from the Dark Side* (New York: Routledge, 1994); see also page 460, Julien and Mercer, "De Margin and De Centre."

26. Gina Marchetti, *Romance and "The Yellow Peril."*

27. See Gunning, page 26–27, chapter 1, "Re-membering Blackness after Reconstruction: Race, Rape, and Political Desire in the Work of Thomas Dixon, Jr."

28. Tom Carson, "Skin Flicks," *GQ*, June 5, 2005, 120.

29. Quoted in Michael Janusonis, "Solid Performance Is Bright Spot in 'Cruel Intentions,'" *Providence Journal*, March 5, 1999.

30. This ties in with the exceptional-man-of-color representation, where good black men safely prefer black women, and only the most exceptional examples, who are usually disconnected from black communities and are symbolic representations of blackness, can on rare occasions pair with a white woman.

31. See Stephen Schaefer, "Milla Jovovich Defends Denzel Sex Scene," ABC News Internet, May 1, 1998, at http://mrshowbiz.go.com.

32. Charles Ramirez Berg identified this as one of the strategies used in films, in what he calls "the alluring but flawed gringa," with the example of the early film *My Man and I,* in which the white actress Shelley Winters plays a troubled woman who is the object of fascination of a Latino character, Chu Chu.

33. *Me, Myself & Irene* contains many problematic racial stereotypes, including an opening scene where the limo driver, Shonte, accuses Charlie of racism (enforcing the idea that black people make everything a racial issue). Shonte is a limo driver, yet then for comedy it is revealed that he also a member of Mensa (the high-IQ society) and a professor (making it unexpected and comical that he would be so intelligent), and the three black sons are shown as little boys watching profanity-laced comedy by Richard Pryor and teaching their dad to appreciate this profanity—implying that it is a natural trait of African Americans to say "motherfucker."

34. Layla and Shonte both have T-shirts with each other's picture on it, and Shonte tells Charlie that she will be "eating plenty of whale blubber," referring to his sexual prowess.

35. Pornographic films and Web sites that feature interracial sex often focus on the image of white wives (implying the white wives of white men) who can't resist "big, black cocks," including some reality sites where white men film white women who want black men, who they describe in degrading terms.

36. Most of these sites are created by white men and the presumed audience is white men. I discuss the themes of these pornographic sites in depth in *Navigating Interracial Borders: Black-White Couples and Their Social Worlds* (Rutgers, 2005), see pages 173–78.

37. Films that are geared toward black audiences do not mean that they were written or produced by black filmmakers or that the messages are any different than those produced by white filmmakers, since the images and representations are part of the fabric of American thought and culture.

38. *Bamboozled* is a Spike Lee production and is a critical commentary on the media images of African Americans, as it centers on a black television executive

who becomes increasingly successful after he chooses to support more stereotypical depictions of blacks on TV. Beyond connecting the black man's choice in white women to his decisions to portray negative images of blacks on the television show, the white producer, who thinks he is hip and connected to black culture, has a black wife, further offering a critical commentary of interracial relationships and black individuals.

39. The short-lived television show *Whoopi*, created by Whoopi Goldberg, featured a black character who was involved with a white woman as part of him being "the whitest black character" as described by Eric Deggans, "Can New Comedies Deliver for NBC?" *St. Petersburg Times*, July 26, 2003.

40. See also Jeff MacGregor, "TV, the Movies' Abused (and Abusive) Stepchild," *New York Times*, Sunday, October 8, 2000, 11, 34.

41. See review in Ann Hornaday, "Going with the 'Fro: Witty 'Undercover Brother' Takes a Trip to Funky Town," *Washington Post*, May 31, 2002, CO5. *Undercover Brother* was originally the protagonist of an animated Web series created by novelist John Ridley, who cowrote the screenplay.

42. Calvin C. Hernton, *Sex and Racism in America* (New York: Anchor Books, 1988), 66.

43. Sean Patrick Thomas states that he wants "the kind of roles that aren't specifically defined by color," though he acknowledges "ninety-nine percent of scripts . . . are specifically defined by color," in *Ebony* article "Hottest TV Hunks," Volume 59:9 (July 7, 2004): 172.

44. Many scholars have discussed this issue, such as Vincent Rocchio, *Reel Racism: Confronting Hollywood's Construction of Afro-American Culture* (Boulder, CO: Westview Press, 2002).

45. It appeals to interracial couples in particular, as Kimberly Shearer Palmer, a white woman dating a black man, recounts in *USA Today*: "*Save the Last Dance*, steps out of the Hollywood stereotype to more accurately portray the challenges facing interracial couples. By doing so, it makes audience members consider the complexities of interracial relationships and may help them avoid making hurtful comments themselves." Somehow it seems white women in interracial relationships need protection from the hurt black women inflict on them when their "frustration can turn adversarial" as she writes. Kimberly Shearer Palmer, "Movie Reflects Interracial Issues," *USA Today*, January 22, 2001. This perspective is sympathetic to white women and constructs black women as the problem.

46. Spike Lee has openly discussed his views on interracial unions and commented that the couple in *Jungle Fever* came together only "because of sexual mythology." See Cardullo 1992. Annabella Sciorra, the white actress who portrayed Angie, revealed in an interview that she fought with Lee over the character because she wanted to portray her interest in Flipper as more complex than just sexual curiosity. See Taylor 2000.

47. Ed Guerrero, "Spike Lee and the Fever in the Racial Jungle," in Jim Collins, ed., *Film Theory Goes to the Movies* (New York: Routledge, 1993), 174.

48. While overall the movie begins and ends with the idea that these two were sexually attracted and "curious," through a gradual process of overcoming prejudice, comparing experiences, gaining confidential insights, and becoming familiar, the two are drawn together. Flip continues to spend time with Angie even after his wife finds out, taking her to his family's house and various spots such as a black soul food restaurant in his neighborhood. Angie breaks up with her long-time boyfriend because of her relations with Flip and even raises the question of children with him. See also William A. Harris, "Cultural Engineering and the Films of Spike Lee," in *Mediated Messages and African-American Culture: Contemporary Issues*, Venise T. Berry and Carmen L. Manning-Miller, eds. (Thousand Oaks, CA: Sage Publications, 1996), 3–23.

49. In the black community, there is a painful and complicated history attached to black-white unions, and the roots of the opposition are markedly different from white communities. "While blacks clearly enjoy some agency in constructing and marketing the representations of blackness that circulate today, the 'increased control' view fails to acknowledge the underlying consumer needs that make black 'excess' a viable commodity in the first place . . . (and) likely constrain the domain of representational options . . . (and) black 'control.'" See Hunt 2005, 7.

50. See Erica Chito Childs 2005, "Looking Behind the Stereotypes of the Angry Black Woman," and Erica Chito Childs 2006, "Can We Stand to Ignore the Perspectives of Black Women on Their Own Experiences?"

51. This is due to white control and ownership of most media, even in films written and produced by people of color, and also it is a reflection of how interracial relationships are understood and received in communities of color. For an in-depth look at black communities' views on interracial relationships, see Childs 2005, *Navigating Interracial Borders: Black-White Couples and Their Social Worlds*.

52. See Teresa de Laurentis, *Technologies of Gender: Essays on Theory, Film and Fiction* (Bloomington: Indiana University Press), 1987. For a discussion of weddings and queer representations, see Patricia White, *Uninvited: Classical Hollywood Cinema and Lesbian Representability* (Bloomington: Indiana University Press), 1999; and Elizabeth Freeman, "'The We of Me': The *Member of the Wedding*'s Novel Alliances," Jose Munoz and Amanda Barrett, eds., *Queer Acts: Women and Performance* 16 (1996): 111–36.

53. Rebecca Faery, *Cartographies of Desire: Captivity, Race and Sex in the Shaping of an American Nation* (Norman: University of Oklahoma Press, 1999).

54. Daniel R. Coleridge, Interview with Blair Underwood, *TV Guide Insider*, accessed at www.tvguide.com/newsgossip/insider/020306a.asp

CHAPTER FIVE

~

Playing the Color-Blind Card: Seeing Black and White in News Media

As we have seen from the film and television representations, certain ideas about interracial relationships exist, having been constructed historically and continually produced and reproduced as the circumstances surrounding different racial and ethnic groups changed. Media is not much different, telling very specific stories about race and interracial relationships. In recent years there has been a trend for news outlets to do lengthy pieces on the "changing face of race."[1] These articles tout color blindness and how the increasing numbers and acceptance of interracial marriages have altered the racial landscape, making race and racism barely visible, despite interracial marriage rates remaining low. For example, the 2007 Associated Press article, "Interracial Marriage Flourishing," which was picked up by newspapers across the country, reports:

> Coupled with a steady flow of immigrants from all parts of the world, the surge of interracial marriages and multiracial children is producing a 21st century America more diverse than ever with the potential to become less stratified by race.[2]

This color-blind optimism is quite common in news reports that tend to make headlines, yet inside most of these news pieces, there is at least a footnote that contradicts the headline, describing some opposition and evidence against their color-blind argument. In the middle of the article referenced above, a few paragraphs acknowledge that interracial couples do face opposition and even identify black families as a big part of this opposition, yet these revelations do not change the celebratory tone of the piece.

Media reports on race and racism in very particular ways. There is often a focus on past incidents or an effort to explain away present-day racism as the extreme acts of one individual or group.[3] While that may be the desired story that the media tells, there are other stories happening, yet they receive less media attention. For example, there have been a number of recent cases of interracial violence enacted primarily by whites against interracial couples or men of color involved with white and desirable women that have received brief media exposure, including incidents in Arkansas, California, Connecticut, New York, Ohio, South Carolina, Texas, and Wisconsin.[4] Yet the ways the media emphasizes or even mentions interracial relationships in these cases varies, and they virtually never discuss the events together to highlight a possible pattern of violent incidents, or threats of violence, the way the media does about patterns of color-blind love and the growing number of interracial couples. This oversight is part of a pattern where the media is more likely to ignore stories in which the alleged victim is a person of color, such as separate cases where white men either kidnapped, raped, or tortured black women.[5] Also, there is tendency to present whites accused of being involved in interracial crimes in a more sympathetic light, such as the numerous white women, many of them teachers, accused of having sex with underage boys of color from Mary Kay Letorneau to Tammy Imre.[6] Despite these documented incidents, the media most often ignores the racial implications, questions others' discussions of incidents as racial, and prefers to categorize these incidents as an isolated case or an extreme example of racism, while continuing to focus on color blindness, the opposition of minority communities, and the public relations shot of a smiling interracial couple.

Media outlets also emphasize the idea of "playing the race card," an accusation that race is being used as an unfair advantage or argue that race is used as an explanation when it clearly does not matter. While there are always racial meanings attached to any story involving people of color, the racial implications can be emphasized or denied, yet it usually affirms a "white reality."[7] The media presents issues involving individuals of different races in particular ways, and the audience understands these racialized images and ideas differently depending on their social location. Furthermore, as Lynn Chancer argues, it often leads to a partialization where there is an either/or way of looking at the event, influenced by the two-sided structure of the legal system and other involved parties such as prominent community leaders, protesters, politicians, religious leaders, and family members, who also participate in how the media frames the event.[8] Looking at these events on a continuum, we can see the "articulation of different elements into a distinctive set or chain of meanings," or in other words, the dominant ideologies on interracial relationships.⁹ When it comes to events that involve an interracial pairing with allegations of sex, rape, or even sexual desire, there are competing, contradictory, yet intertwined representations of black men and women, essentially all men and women of color, as dangerous and feared yet also titillating and desired. Not surprisingly, "the most prized news stories [are] those that threaten the boundaries of social safety while encouraging feelings of moral superiority in the audience."¹⁰ It is against these varying news stories and realities that we begin this chapter.

There have been a number of high-profile interracial occurrences that have caught media attention over the last twenty years and been consumed by the public, highlighting the intricate way the world is constructed as color-blind yet clearly racialized and sexualized. In media coverage of interracial sex, seeing when and how race is used, ignored, and manipulated can tell us about our underlying views on race. We will look at what interracial "stories" the news media covers, how the news media reports on incidents involving interracial intimacy and sex, and whether these reports use the same frameworks found in film and television images. Therefore, I begin with a brief discussion of the numerous high-profile crime cases over the last decades in the media where race and sex intersected such as the Central Park jogger case, the Yusef Hawkins murder, the Tawana Brawley case, and the O. J. Simpson case, as well as coverage of other "interracial" events. Then the 2003 Kobe Bryant pretrial rape case and the 2006 Duke University lacrosse rape allegations will be analyzed in great depth, reviewing the different media accounts and the ways that race was (and was not) addressed.¹¹ In media coverage, I argue that stories tend to deviantize interracial relationships and people of color, privilege whiteness and whites, and emphasize how race no longer matters. In these cases, the interracial nature of the accusation and the way that race is emphasized or avoided by the media will be addressed, arguing this is representative of the way that racial groups deal with interracial relationships in society and racial groups in general. In matters of race and sex, the meanings attached to these events often vary by group and can be highly contested and debated.

History Repeats Itself

Before Internet news blogs, twenty-four-hour news channels, or even daily newspapers, stories of interracial romance or allegations of interracial sex or rape circulated, often resulting in those involved, particularly men of color, being fined, banished, physically punished, or even killed. As we discussed in chapter 1, these stories or accusations were handled quite differently depending on the race of those involved. For example, while black men were executed and imprisoned for raping, allegedly raping, or even having consensual sex with white women throughout the mid-1900s, white men were rarely charged for sexual assaults against black women, even when the evidence was overwhelming.[12] "Black bodies in pain for public consumption have been an American national spectacle for centuries . . . from public rapes, beatings, and lynchings to the gladiatorial arenas of basketball and boxing . . . (where) white men have been the primary stagers and consumers of the historical spectacles."[13] Still today when we hear about interracial rape or sexual misconduct, the alleged or real sexual misconduct, deviance, assault, or rape is that of black men and white women. While interracial sex or relationships are no longer *legally* punishable by violence or death,[14] the way interracial unions and allegations of interracial sex or rape are handled by the media reflect how the public understands and responds to interracial relationships and communities of color. Contemporary media messages are subtle, even silent, yet they still have the power to construct reality.

Recently, historical incidents involving racial injustices and interracial sex have received renewed interest. The media has less difficulty highlighting historical events that included opposition to or even crimes associated with interracial sex because it does not contradict the color-blind message that today's race relations have improved so dramatically that any lingering racial issues are minute at best. Through media coverage of a number of high-profile events, the strategy of addressing past injustices, rather than present ones, is clear,[15] such as the media attention surrounding the January 2005 documentary *Unforgivable Blackness* on Jack Johnson, the black heavyweight champion who was notorious for cavorting and marrying white women. Most mainstream newspapers and news programs highlighted the Ken Burns documentary, which provides original footage and news accounts of Jack Johnson in the early 1900s, when he was hated in America for being able to defeat any white boxer and was depicted as a dangerous predator of white women. The federal government selectively applied the Mann Act, which "criminalized interstate transportation of women for immoral purposes," to convict Johnson[16] for being with white women. On the CBS *The Early Show*, the host asked Burns why he called it "unforgivable blackness," and he replied it was because he was outraged at what he learned:

not just the usual Ku Klux Klan corner or Jim Crow South, but from the *New York Times* and the *Los Angeles Times* and the *Detroit News*, just out-and-out racism . . . it will curl your hair to hear this stuff coming out of the most reputable newspapers of the day. But to their credit, on Friday the *Los Angeles Times* did an editorial that said, "Shame On Us,"[17]

The *Los Angeles Times* editorial "A Word to the Black Man" that he is referring to was published on July 6, 1910, after Johnson defeated a white boxer
to keep the title, "Do not point your nose too high . . . you are on no higher
plane, deserve no new consideration, and will get none. No man will think
a bit higher of you because your complexion is the same as that of the victor
at Reno."[18] The *Los Angeles Times* lamented their own participation in "the
nation's collective amnesia," while also giving credit to these predecessors
for describing the match as between individuals, not races, which leaves
racism as a thing in the past to be ashamed of, not a thing of the present.[19]
Besides the *Los Angeles Times* apologizing, other papers like the *New York
Times* acknowledged their past racism in articles reviewing the documentary
and covering the story. Racism toward black men, opposition to black men
having sex with white women, and constructing black men as dangerous
predators are all placed in the past and used to argue how far we have come
from this racist past where black men were prosecuted because of their race
(and the race of their partner). Later in the chapter, as contemporary media
coverage is reviewed, the idea that men of color no longer receive the "Jack
Johnson treatment" will be challenged.

The Politics of Interracial Sex in the Media

While the media denies that racism and opposition to interracial unions still
exist, the symbol of interracial sexuality is still used, especially in the realm
of politics. During the 2006 elections, a media debate arose in the Tennessee
Senate race over commercials that aired against black Democratic candidate
Harold Ford, who was running against white Republican Bob Corker. The
television ad featured a scantily clad, white, blond woman saying she met
"Harold" at a Playboy party, and ended with her saying "Harold, call me,"
which alleged that Ford attended Playboy parties and accepted money from
pornographers. Furthermore, the Corker campaign argued that he "truly
embodies the values of Tenesseeans more than Ford."[20] The ad was quickly
picked up by the news media, raising the possibility that the ad struck some as
"sleazy and racially nuanced" and was "playing on racial fears."[21] Chris Matthews, the host of MSNBC news program *Hardball*, interviewed Democratic
Senator Dick Durbin from Illinois about whether he believed this ad was
meant for angry white voters, while an Associated Press/Local Wire article
included an interview with the white actress in the ad who stated that the
ad was not racist.[22] Media reported that Democrats and other organizations
such as the ACLU considered it racist, while Republicans including Corker
and the Republican National Committee described it as ill conceived but not

racially motivated and did not contain racial connotations. News reports also tended to discuss these ads along with other ads as part of the overall trend to run negative ad campaigns.[23] Very few media outlets explicitly made the connection between using a white woman making sexually suggestive comments to a black politician and the history of the use of allegations of interracial sex or desire to destroy a black man, often literally by lynching.

Racial fears, particularly the threat of black men to white women, has been used many times recently, including the 1988 advertising campaign of George Bush, Sr., against Michael Dukakis for president. The Republican strategist Ken Duberstein used the image of William "Willie" Horton, a black man who was convicted of murder but escaped during a 48-hour prison furlough and raped a woman in Democratic candidate Michael Dukakis's state of Massachusetts, to clearly symbolize the threat of not only Dukakis and liberal politics but also unleashed black male sexuality.[24] His expertise in constructing black male sexuality must have been known because he was also used to strategize the contested nomination of Clarence Thomas to the Supreme Court. The proceedings received intense media coverage when Thomas, a conservative embraced by the political right who is married to a white woman, was accused of sexually harassing Anita Hill, a black woman, during the Supreme Court confirmation hearings. Republican supporters like Duberstein argued the "decisive charge that the hearings had become a 'high-tech lynching of an uppity Black man.'"[25] The imagery of lynching served Thomas well even though a black man was never lynched for sexually abusing a black woman. Ironically, the same white men who used the media to convey racially charged images of black men as sexual predators to win a presidential election now argued against these images to support Thomas.[26] In both instances, the media was used to convey certain ideas about race and sex.[27] When a sexually suggestive ad ran showing a blonde woman seeking to romance Harold Ford, a black Senate candidate, the sponsors denied any racial intent or consequence, yet the idea of lynching is thrown around when it serves the purpose of those in power. The media, along with the powerful people whose words and actions affect how media construct issues, can present interracial sex along with whiteness and blackness or otherness in whatever way to best fit the stories that they want to tell. In what follows we will look at how men of color and in some instances women of color are still symbolically lynched in the media, particularly when they are tangled up in interracial liaisons, whether it be consensual, accidental, or forced. I will begin with a synopsis of the interracial incidents that made headlines from the 1980s through the 1990s, followed by a discussion of media coverage of ordinary interracial couples and an in-depth discussion of two contemporary interracial spectacles, the Kobe Bryant and Duke University lacrosse team rape allegations.

A Snapshot of Interracial Events: 1980s and 1990s

Looking at mainstream (white) media's coverage of incidents involving interracial sex, a complicated and contradictory relationship with race exists. In the late 1980s there were a number of incidents involving interracial sex that received widespread media attention. In 1989, a white, upper-middle-class woman was brutally beaten and raped while jogging in Central Park,[28] and it became known as the "Central Park jogger case." In response, the media reported widespread incidents of "wilding" in New York City, describing the alleged dangers presented by black and Latino young men who were likened to "wolf packs." At the time of the attack, the media seized upon the story, with some reporters arguing it was because of the vicious brutality of the crime, the famous location of the crime, or the reports that it was a gang. In *High-Profile Crimes: When Legal Cases Become Social Causes*, Lynn Chancer interviews a reporter who covered the story for a national newspaper:

> she was a white, upper-middle-class young woman, almost beaten to death by a group of young blacks and Hispanics. Everybody's worst nightmare . . . it wouldn't get the same coverage if she was black or Hispanic . . . if you read about a young black woman who was raped by a bunch of blacks and Hispanics in Central Park, I doubt very much whether you would be interested in that story . . . as you would be if it was your college roommate . . . so who's reading newspapers in this country? Eighty-seven percent white.[29]

While Chancer does not identify the race of the reporter, it seems quite clear that the reporter is white and aligning the preferred white audience's concern (and his own) with attacks on whites, the fear of blacks and Hispanics, and the desire to protect whiteness. The outrage over a white woman being raped and beaten by men of color was expressed in the one-page ad Donald Trump took out in the *New York Times* demanding the death penalty for those responsible.[30] Representing a different view, the black newspaper *Amsterdam News* ran a piece condemning the Trump ad, in which an African American attorney Colin Moore, who represented one of the accused young men, compared Trump's reaction to white southerners of the earlier 1900s and other cases like the Scottsboro Boys, where young black men were executed for the alleged rape of white women.[31]

The significance of allegations of interracial rape in terms of media and societal response is clear in the Central Park jogger case, especially in light of the lack of attention other rapes that occurred the same week received, including a black woman who was raped and thrown off an apartment building by a group of black and Latino men. Also most importantly, the five black and Hispanic young men who were originally vilified by the media, convicted by the justice system, and imprisoned in 1989 and 1990 for the Central Park rape were released in 2000 based on DNA evidence, and the confessions of a different man, Mathias Reyes, that he had acted alone.[32] While at the time the media could present the case as one divided by racial lines, in hindsight the black press's claims of racism and overzealousness to punish the teenage boys for the crime of raping a white woman are validated. There was very little media coverage of the reversal of the five convictions, and it rarely addressed how and why these five youths were demonized by the media, police, and prosecution and wrongly imprisoned.[33] The Central Park jogger's revealing of her identity a year after the convictions were overturned received more media attention, and it was reported that she still questioned the absolute innocence of the five men. For example, in a CBS *News* report on Trisha Meili "coming out" as the Central Park jogger, the five men were described in the following way:

> Five teenagers, Yusef Salaam, Raymond Santana, Antron McCray, Kharey Wise and Kevin Richardson . . . made incriminating videotaped statements to police about the attack. Genetic evidence found on Meili later failed to connect the attack with the youths, but they were eventually convicted and served up to 11½ years in prison. Last year, however, Mathias Reyes, a man serving time for murder and serial rape, claimed that he was the attacker, and DNA evidence linked him to the crime. The five men's convictions were thrown out at the district attorney's request. The police department said it was possible both Reyes and the teens attacked the jogger, but the prosecutor's office said there was "substantial reason" to believe Reyes' claim that he acted alone.[34]

One of the only accounts that addressed and sought to explain how these five teens could be erroneously charged ran in the alternative New York paper *Village Voice*, which highlighted how the FBI evidence presented at the time of the rape confirmed that the semen in the jogger's cervix did not come from any of the five defendants and that the semen from the cervix and the semen found on the sock were from the same person, yet not the five defendants. The *Village Voice* argues, "In hindsight, the FBI disclosures should have exploded a bomb in the heart of the prosecution case. But the testimony set off no fireworks. The disturbing confessions were what had captured the minds of the jury and the press."[35] As defense attorney Rogher Warehman stated, "When a white woman is attacked or accused of being attacked by someone who is black or Latino, then logic, sense, justice, evidence go out the window. It becomes a question of 'lets get one of them,' any one of them—and that's what happened here. Just get them."[36]

Further illustrating this fear of men of color, the media covered another racially charged incident in 1989, the racially motivated murder of Yusef Hawkins, a young black man who was killed by a group of young white men in the Bensonhurst section of Brooklyn. There was intense media coverage, and significant attention was paid to the role of a white, Italian, young neighborhood woman, Gina Feliciano, who did not know Yusef Hawkins. Still she was accused of instigating the incident because she was known to associate with black men and had allegedly told the group of white youth that black men would be coming to her party that night. News accounts reported, "Fueled by jealousy and hate, a gang of up to 30 white teens . . . shot and killed a black youth they mistakenly thought was dating a young white woman in their Brooklyn neighborhood . . . (police) said there also was a confrontation Saturday night, in which the woman was warned to stop bringing blacks to the predominantly white neighborhood."[37] Another *New York Times* article reported, "The fault, in the eyes of much of the neighborhood, lies with Gina Feliciano . . . who, among other things, violated the mores of the Italian-American community by dating black and dark-skinned Hispanic men."[38] By connecting Yusef Hawkins to interracial sex, his murder by the white young men is given an explanation, even a justification. In particular, media reports represented the views of the white defendants' lawyers and community members who argued that these white young men were "defending their turf" rather than highlight that the killing was racially motivated.[39] Rather than describe these young white men as "wilding" like the black and Hispanic men accused in the Central Park jogger case, the media made at least some attempt to present them as part of a community and explain how they could have committed such a crime.

During this time, there was also another allegation of an interracial crime that eventually made headlines. This time a black teenage girl, Tawana Brawley, alleged that she was smeared in feces, covered in racial slurs, raped, and brutalized by a group of white men who were possibly police officers or some other officials. Yet the case was suspect from the beginning by the police, prosecution, and the media. Mainstream media did not begin extensive coverage of the case until these allegations were seen as a hoax, which signals "the story of a black girl's extreme racial and sexual victimization was not by itself sufficiently newsworthy for the mainstream press," and this "became an important bone of contention in later coverage by some of the black press."[40] In terms of credibility, "the public appears to be more willing to believe someone White who says they were victimized by someone Black than someone Black who says they were victimized by someone White . . . from the beginning, many suspected that the Brawley . . . (incident was) fabrications."[41] Even if Tawana's allegations were false, the media coverage never seemed interested in explaining why a 15-year-old would fabricate this story and engage in disturbing behavior such as smearing feces on herself, and there was virtually no humanistic or sympathetic coverage of the young teen.[42]

One early editorial in response to the Central Park jogger case critiques the difference between the media responses to the Tawana Brawley case and the Central Park jogger case:

> From the very outset of the case it was clear what the intent was: to use an undeniably heinous crime, whose victim still is hospitalized and comatose as a result of her injuries, to fan the flames of racial divisiveness and hatred . . . that same media that refused to print or say that Tawana Brawley was raped had no difficulty summarily in stating so in the case of the Central Park victim. The same media that demanded Brawley "prove" her sexual assault . . . that had no difficulty identifying the underaged Wappingers Falls teen-ager by name, invading the sanctity of her home to show her face and even televising semi-nude pictures of her while she was in the hospital have been careful to avoid identifying the Central Park woman.[43]

As the editorial points out, the media (as well as the criminal justice and legal systems) treated this white woman and young, black, teenage girl quite differently. While there were certainly differences in the injuries they suffered, the racial difference between the women as well as the attackers undoubtedly played a role. The media seized upon the story of black and Latino gangs raping an upper-middle-class white woman because it fit the long-standing ideas of black men as savage rapists who prey on white women that have been produced and reproduced since African slaves first were brought here. The dismissive media treatment of Tawana Brawley and refusal to even consider her accusations are part of the historical tradition of not seeing black women as capable of being raped, or even if they were raped, not holding white men accountable. While "the Central Park jogger" was rightfully protected, the young teen Tawana Brawley was victimized by the media and demonized, which was unjustified whether or not she fabricated her story. Given that the five black and Latino young men who were arrested and convicted in the Central Park jogger case were eventually released, it strengthens the argument that the media (and others) were eager to punish any black and Latino teens for this crime. There was virtually no attempt in mainstream media to present stories of the wrongly convicted teenage boys or of their families and communities like was done for the young men found guilty of killing Yusef Hawkins.

Putting it all in context, it was also during this time that the Bush presidential campaign and organizations that supported his candidacy used "Willie" Horton to capitalize on the white fear of the black male rapist. As mentioned briefly, ads paid for by George Bush and the Republican National Security Political Action Committee[44] accused Democratic presidential candidate Michael Dukakis of being soft on crime by distorting the Willie Horton case, about a black man who raped a white woman after never returning from a weekend prison furlough where he was serving time for murder. As Feagin and Vera describe, the ads featured a "blurred photograph of a Black man being arrested" as the words "kidnapping," "stabbing," and "raping" could be seen and heard, which played on the threat of not only Willie Horton but also blackness and interracial rape. After the campaign was over, Susan Estrich, Dukakis's campaign manager, commented, ". . . it was very much an issue about race and racial fear . . . you can't find a stronger metaphor, intended or not, for racial hatred in this country than a black man raping a white woman. And that's what the Willie Horton story was."[45] William Horton was chosen not only because of his race but also because of the race of the woman he raped.

Just as powerful whites use racialized stereotypes of black men as dangerous like in the 1988 presidential campaign, everyday white individuals draw on this widespread belief of the criminal black man to cover their crimes or behavior, such as Charles Stuart, the white man who murdered his pregnant wife; Susan Smith, the white woman who drowned her two young sons; and Jennifer Wilbanks, the runaway bride, who disappeared and then reappeared saying that she had been kidnapped by a Hispanic man and a white woman at gunpoint.[46] These stories "work because they tap into widely held fears about crime and about who one's likely attacker might be."[47] Whites are able to accuse an unidentified black man of having committed a crime to cover their own wrongdoing, which must carry significant weight and credibility if it is used so often and could more accurately be called "playing the race card," yet this is not the story the media weaves for us. Katheryn K. Russell details the pattern of these "racial hoaxes" by whites, with a subtheme of fabricated rape claims by white women that they were raped by a black man (or men), which taps in to the historical construction of black men as potential rapists of white women. It is illustrated in two infamous racial hoaxes, the 1931 Scottsboro incident where nine black youths were sentenced to death based on the accusations of two white women, one of whom recanted, and the 1923 Rosewood Massacre of a black community based on the false claim of a white woman that she had been raped by a black man.[48] Despite this documented pattern of whites falsely accusing imaginary black men of committing their crimes, people of color are the ones most often doubted and discredited when they make accusations against whites before their accusations are even completely investigated by the media (and law enforcement officials). This is particularly true when black women accuse white men of rape, as discussed with the Tawana Brawley case.[49]

The sexual threat of the black man continually resurfaces in media stories, emphasized, exaggerated, and vilified. A media frenzy erupted in 1997 when an African American man, Nushawn Williams, was publicly identified and aggressively prosecuted for knowingly transmitting the HIV virus to teenage girls in Chautauqua County. "That Williams is African American and was having sex with teenage white girls, transmitting HIV to some of them, in a small-town subculture that was infected with drugs, was simply irresistible to the media given the narratives, symbolisms, and representations that were (and are) in place."[50] While race was never mentioned as the problem, the case was racialized in the media obsession with Williams and the zeal to punish him. Williams was demonized not simply because he transmitted HIV but also for having sex with white, young girls in a suburban area far from the urban ghetto of Brooklyn where Williams came from, and in the eyes of white America belonged. The media highlighted Chautauqua County as "idyllic and nostalgic, a place of past innocence, a (white) world violated by a (black) big-city thug."[51] Without explicitly using racial language, Williams was described as an unattractive, "scary, nasty mouth,"[52] dangerous sex predator who maliciously infected young girls with HIV. Yet it was his ability to seduce "typical, good-looking, middle-class kid(s)"[53] and his reported oversexed nature and sexual prowess that made him a "monster." Nushawn "crossed boundaries . . . transgressed limits . . . the very fact he did not use force made him dangerous . . . it was this very attractiveness that made him such a threat and turned him into monster."[54] The racialized stereotypes of bad black men and victimized naive white women are clear. The interracial nature of the case undoubtedly influenced the media attention, especially considering how other similar stories received almost no attention, such as another African American man, Darnell McGee, who allegedly had sex with more than a hundred African American women and infected at least thirty with HIV and who was later killed by one of these infected lovers.[55] The elevated media focus on the danger or damage done to white women, and the lack of concern and coverage of black women who are victimized is a pattern that clearly exists in media coverage of interracial incidents.

Undoubtedly, the most widely covered interracial spectacle intertwining race and sex was the brutal murder of Nicole Simpson and Ron Goldman and the ensuing O. J. Simpson "trial of the century." Despite the obvious racial dynamics of a popular black male athlete accused of brutally murdering his white ex-wife and her white male friend, there was a peculiar dance played between both sides of emphasizing and denying race. A number of reporters such as Leo Wilensky of the *Los Angeles Times*, Ed Boyd of the *Los Angeles Times*, and Michael Janofsky of the *New York Times* emphasized the brutal double homicide and celebrity status and lifestyle as what brought this case to the forefront of media attention, while others such as Dennis Schatzman of the black newspaper *Los Angles Sentinel* argued that "to say that a high profile case such as this involving all those elements has no racial factor involved is just bull shit."[56] As Lynn Chancer documents, "two contemporary social problems, gender inequities and racial injustices, were symbolized on either side of this now famous case: feminist concerns about domestic violence were aligned with the prosecution, while the specter of racism came to characterize the defense's position," and I would add the prosecution and concern for women/domestic violence was constructed as white and the defense and concern about race was viewed as black.[57] This will be a recurring theme in the more recent media spectacles we will explore.

When looking at the O. J. saga, race was written all over it. As George Lipsitz reported, "Even *Time* magazine agreed with arts curator Thelma Golden that 'if Nicole had been black, this case would have been on a cover of *Jet* magazine not much more.'"[58] Yet in the media coverage of this case, race was most often discussed in the debate over "playing the race card," and Johnnie Cochran took center stage as the one who was accused of playing it.[59] If Simpson's defense team was playing the race card, the prosecution was playing the color-blind card, pretending that race played no role in how the case was unfolding, though media accounts rarely accused the prosecution of ignoring race.[60] Media coverage of the O. J. Simpson case reveals many things about how interracial sex is imagined and represented, since "the same things that made O. J. a symbol of fulfilled desires also made him a focal point for rumination about unrestrained appetites, about cocaine use, indiscriminate sex, and violence."[61] As Richard E. Lapchick argues in an ESPN article,

> O. J. Simpson was the first African American athlete to be widely used in commercial and endorsement deals, to star in movies and seemingly be accepted into the homes of white people around the country. Now O. J. Simpson is described as the African American athlete who most divides the races in America.[62]

O. J. also tells a story that we have heard before, dating back to Shakespeare's *Othello*, where you have a powerful, successful, black man who becomes consumed by his jealousy and kills his white lover. O. J. Simpson became a media obsession because he embodied all the stories about interracial sex that we know. First, O. J. was the "tamed Black man" who was accepted and lived in a white

world devoid of blackness with a white wife, in a world where color was safely
contained. Then after the murders, O. J. was darkened—even literally by *Time*
magazine—and he became the dangerous predator representing the threat that
black men posed to white women (and white men). As the July 1996 *Weekly
Standard* mainstream print journal reported after Simpson was acquitted, "the
cover depicts a dark, sinister-looking caricature of O. J." accompanied by the
headline "Why He Still Haunts Us" and begins with a declaration that O. J. is
a murderer.[63] More than ten years after the trial, O. J. Simpson and issues surrounding the murders and the victims' families still make news headlines.

The O. J. Simpson case, and presumably other high-profile cases involving
African American or other minority defendants, come to represent much more
than one person, or one alleged crime, but rather can be used to speak about or
even silence race. The media focused on the racial divide between whites and
blacks in terms of views of guilty/not guilty, distorting and creating the image
that "The Black Viewpoint" was untrustworthy, "slightly crazed and fanatical."[64]
As Derrick Z. Jackson, a *Boston Globe* reporter wrote, "O. J. Simpson may not be
unfairly prosecuted because of his race, but that doesn't mean that race does not
matter, but rather it matters more in other places where the average black man
is being profiled, unfairly prosecuted, over-sentenced and abused, while a handful of privileged African American men like Simpson, and Clarence Thomas are
receiving support from the black community."[65] In many ways, media accounts
used the O. J. Simpson acquittal to "prove" race does not matter, as many whites
argued and reinforced the idea that blacks and people of color "make" everything
about race, are "race-obsessed," or in other words, are the real "racists."[66] As we
look at the contemporary examples, we see how these issues play out in very
similar ways, where the mainstream media often seems to be unwilling or unable
to clearly address how interracial pairings, especially when a crime is involved,
change people's understandings. Simultaneously, in mainstream media reports,
race is presented as something that is used, manipulated, and played, usually for
the benefit of the minority, except in the small number of black or minority publications. Whites, even those accused of rape and murder, are given the benefit of
the doubt and presented in the media as multidimensional people with families
and communities while people of color, even alleged victims, are more likely to
be doubted and demonized, with no attempt to humanize them.

Contemporary Comparisons: Kobe Bryant and the Duke University Lacrosse Team

Media stories that receive high-profile coverage draw from dominant stories
that are familiar, and often the cases are juxtaposed, "revers(ing) the racial

identities of victims and perpetrators from one case to the next."[67] The 2003 Kobe Bryant rape allegations and the 2006 Duke University lacrosse rape allegations received extensive media coverage and can be juxtaposed to look at the different ways high-profile incidents involving interracial sex, particularly allegations of rape, are handled by the media.

When the story broke that the Los Angeles Lakers basketball star Kobe Bryant was accused of raping a young woman at a resort in Colorado, the media frenzy immediately began. This case had many of the necessary sensational elements: a famous person, upscale locale, sordid stories of sex, high-powered attorneys, and arguably, most importantly it involved an allegation that a famous black male athlete raped a young white woman. As virtually all media outlets responded, media correspondents such as Christine Brennan from *USA Today* reported:

> Kobe has been the Boy Scout, in many ways, for the National Basketball Association . . . you know, Mom and Pop in Omaha. I can't imagine that they are loving the NBA today . . . the NBA is certainly predominantly black. . . . I don't know that I see that here because Kobe has already transcended race and has become such, had become such a star.[68]

Other news reports also described Kobe Bryant as "young, talented, wholesome, exactly the image the NBA seeks to promote . . . a positive image and used in many cases as a way of—of critiquing some of the more hip-hop-inspired players."[69] In essence, Bryant had been a "tamed Black man," an exception to the blackness of the NBA.

Mainstream media addressed issues of race, racial difference, or any racial implications in the Bryant case at particular points during the pretrial, often arguing against the relevance of race, if it was mentioned at all. The intentional or unintentional avoidance of race does not mean it did not play a role, yet it made it easier for whites, in particular, to dismiss the role that race played, especially given the support Kobe had.[70] While early news reports presented the case without discussion of race, the media characterized this as "a long, high-stakes legal battle for Kobe Bryant's freedom."[71] Beginning in early July 2003, when the rape allegations were reported, the case received extensive coverage throughout pretrial hearings, covering issues such as what evidence would be allowed in, the sexual and mental history of the accuser, what role Bryant's basketball fame, celebrity, and wealth played, the relevance of rape shield laws and the gendered implications of how and why women are raped/claim to be raped, yet there was virtually no discussion of the racial dimensions of the case.[72] It was common to hear news reports like Dan Rather on the CBS *Evening News* begin his reports with statements that emphasized the gendered aspects, "Bryant's lawyers have taken very public aim at the private life of his teen-age accuser, trying to damage her reputation, and some say that accounts for an overall drop in reports of sexual assault in the area."[73] The media highlighted an open letter to the judge from the accuser's mother that detailed how much the young woman had gone through. As Kirk Johnson reported in a *New York Times* article, the accuser had been "besieged" despite rape shield laws and "her anonymity obliterated partly by the celebrity culture that surrounds Mr. Bryant."[74] Echoing these sentiments, Lorraine Dusky wrote a piece in one of the local papers, *Vail Daily*,

> as if the woman's right to privacy in such a situation was of no importance. And (Bryant's lawyer Mackey) injected racism into the trial with her offhand comment (about the history of black men being falsely accused of rape by white women) . . . the women-hating, race baiting tactics of this defense.[75]

Protecting women's rights is positioned in opposition to issues of race when both can be operating at the same time.[76]

Very few media stories delved into discussions of America's racialized history, and rarely was the racial difference of the individuals involved discussed as relevant. For example, Kirk Johnson wrote in a *New York Times* article, "Attitudes about race are so deeply entwined in American culture . . . that the effects can never be entirely discounted. But so are attitudes about gender, and the case presents those issues in bewildering abundance as well." Most importantly his article is headlined "In Kobe Bryant Case, Issues of Power, Not of Race."[77] At the same time media reports largely ignored the racial meanings attached to certain images even though racialized stereotypes were routinely used in the mainstream press. News reports with headlines like "Sources: Evidence of Bruising, Vaginal Trauma in Kobe Bryant Case" detailed the woman's injuries, suggestively arguing that the bruising came from a very large penis.[78] Yet most articles ignored race completely, instead characterizing the case as a "a starkly illuminated laboratory, feminists and legal scholars say, for questions of celebrity justice and gender fairness."[79]

The question of race was first discussed in media coverage over the debate of where the trial would be held. Newspapers and news programs covered the issue of the overwhelmingly white population in Vail and the 1995 racial profiling settlement against the Eagle, Colorado, police department.[80] From local newspapers such as the *Vail Trail* to larger metropolitan newspapers like the *Los Angeles Times*, journalists argued that Vail could definitely provide an unbiased jury and provided interviews with a handful of minority residents, including one who no longer lived there, to attest to the color-blind society and how they "did not even see race."[81] Media stories also focused on how the predominantly white Vail community suffered from this unfair spotlight on race, arguing "residents have reacted with emotions ranging from indignation to saddened disbelief at being labeled on a national stage as a racist community. And the race card is being dealt even more cavalierly in the past week."[82] In this race debate, the reporter clearly outlines that race is an excuse used or "played," and the sympathy is placed with the white community, who is portrayed as being unjustly labeled racist.[83] Whiteness is normalized, such as the words used by different white journalists "not how *we* are around here."[84] There is no mention that Vail residents don't think about race because the area is racially homogeneous, where blacks make up less than 1 percent of the population according to the 2000 Census. Yet what media almost always misses is that it is not just that Bryant is black, but his blackness combined with the accuser's whiteness. As history has shown us, being a black man brings consequences, but being a black man who is accused of assaulting a white woman can bring even worse consequences. For example, many whites, including those who espouse color-blind attitudes and report no problems with blacks as friends and coworkers, still draw the line at interracial relationships for their family, friends, and community,[85] never mind the idea of interracial rape.

The role of race was also debated in the media in response to the statement made by Bryant's lawyer, Kathryn Mackey, during pretrial hearings that they be able to use the accuser's sexual history since "there is lots of history out there about men, black men, being falsely accused of this crime by white women."[86] Most mainstream media outlets referred to this as "playing the race card" and described Mackey's statements as *injecting* race into the trial, rather than presenting it as an accurate assessment of the role race plays in society.[87] On the popular ABC morning show *Good Morning America*, the African American host Robin Roberts poses the question, "Is Kobe Bryant's lawyer playing the race card? Or is a courtroom comment being blown out of proportion?" The reporter Tony Perkins answers, "Her saying these words gives it a different credibility than if she were a Black male. A lot of people, for instance, were offended at the way that Johnnie Cochran approached the O. J. Simpson trial, and they talked about the race card being played." Another reporter, Tania Hernandez, adds, "This may not be the last mention of race in the Bryant trial . . . and some argue Mackey's statement was not an accident, that portraying Bryant as a victim of racism may balance the defense team's aggressive moves toward his accuser."[88] In this typical media exchange, black men being falsely accused of raping white women is never discussed as actually having relevance but rather the lawyer's motives for saying this is explored. Mentioning race, or portraying a black man as being affected by racism, is depicted as a tool that can be *used* but is not *in use* in everyday life. When questioning the lawyer's mention of race, the reporter clearly states the "race" comment was more credible coming from a white woman even though it was a statement of historical fact, not opinion. Also, the media discussed Mackey's comments as simply stating that the accuser's motive was racial rather than acknowledging institutionalized racism, where as a black man Bryant may be treated differently by the court, police, and jury. On MSNBC, Norm Early, a former Denver district attorney, argues, "We've had the defense accuse this victim of being morally unsound, of being mentally unsound. And now accusing her of being a racist . . . if this is a case of a white woman and a black man, everyone in the world can see that it's a case where a white woman is accusing a black man. . . . It certainly was a race card . . . to say that this woman is falsely accusing a black man of rape only crystallizes the race card in this case and probably inappropriately so."[89] In comparison, during the Supreme Court nomination hearings, Clarence Thomas, and the white Republican senators supporting him, successfully claimed that accusations that Thomas sexually harassed a black woman were a "lynching," linked to the historical tradition of black men being lynched.[90] Yet when Bryant's lawyer makes the same connection, arguably in a situation that much closer resembles the lynching of black men in the past for transgressions with white women, the media presents this statement as appalling.

Illustrating the pervasiveness of racism, during the time that Mackey made these statements the district attorney, Hulbert, also admitted that "someone in his office had ordered T-shirts . . . lampooning Bryant" with pictures of the game Hangman and sayings like, "I'm not a rapist; I'm just a cheater," which were given to prosecutor Hurlbert.[91] News media outlets debated the significance of these T-shirts, such as the following exchange between NBC correspondent Dan Abrams and Karen Russell, a criminal defense attorney:

> Karen Russell: . . . the racist T-shirts. I mean these T-shirts are of a black man hanging, and there's the issue of whether or not law enforcement. . . .
> Dan Abrams: But, see you know this company makes these T-shirts, you know, all the time about everyone.
> Karen Russell: It's only one T-shirt . . . of a lynched black man.

The debate continues with how the T-shirts relate to Mackey's statements about black men being falsely accused by white women, and NBC/MSNBC media personality Dan Abrams refers to Mackey's statement as "a pretty inflammatory statement," and "bringing out the race card," concluding that

Mackey's statement and the T-shirts are "only relevant . . . if they can actually show that there's some nexus between that and what happened in this case."[92] There is no discussion of how the T-shirts are relevant in that they reflect the lens through which individuals, including the police, the prosecutors, and even potential jurors may view and understand this case.

A related issue emerged when media reports discussed the deputy district attorney Dana Easter's argument that it was inappropriate for the defense request to have three questions about interracial relationships on the prospective juror questionnaire, stating, "The defense would like to find out about societal views regarding race, interracial relationships and dating, this was not a relationship. This was not a date."[93] On the NBC *Today Show*, Matt Lauer presents the issue of juror questions as another "race card" that is being played, stating "Kobe Bryant's attorneys inject that explosive issue into this trial," mentioning the prosecutor's objection to asking potential jurors "What do you think of interracial marriage and relationships?"[94] These media comments show an inability or unwillingness to recognize that jurors and the larger society may see the case based on how they perceive interracial relationships, with those who oppose interracial relationships potentially more likely to be prejudiced against Bryant for having consensual or forced interracial sex. On CBS, two legal analysts, Andrew Cohen and David Lugert, discussed this interracial issue:

> Cohen: Obviously the defense would be more interested in trying to vet out potential jurors who might have a problem with interracial couples, because in essence, what happened in that room was an interracial event.
> Lugert: (the) defense was trying to start the classic O. J. Simpson defense, blame everything on the police.[95]

Other media reports, such as NBC's Dan Abrams's, also made the connection to the O. J. Simpson case, arguing "this really could become another sort of O. J.-style defense where law enforcement is put on trial,"[96] referring to the defense's claims about the sheriff department's racial profiling accusations years earlier. Also, the *New York Times* ran a piece where the author draws a connection to O. J. Simpson in discussing the Bryant defense strategy of using the accuser's past, "As far as Mr. Bryant and his counsel are concerned, from the moment the district attorney . . . labeled him a rapist, his life was over . . . you just don't meet a lot of babies named O. J. anymore."[97] These are interesting parallels given that race is not acknowledged to matter and rape is different than double homicide, yet one of the only similarities is that the two cases involve a famous black male athlete and a white female victim.

While mainstream media sidestepped race in various ways, the black press, such as the *Amsterdam News* and *BET News*, presented race as ever present and relevant. Wilbert A. Tatum, the publisher emeritus and chairman of the board of *Amsterdam News*, wrote an editorial, "Invitation to a Legal Lynching," where he defended Bryant's lawyers using the accuser's history to prove their case, stating:

> A lot is riding on this case: Kobe Bryant, the young woman who has accused him of raping her, the entire Black community, and Black America. That is how far the media can interpret an accusation against a Black celebrity, in order to tarnish all Blacks, with a stroke of "animal, sex-crazed, lawlessness, and indifference to the rights of others" . . . the press in America is avidly anti-Black.[98]

News reports and commentaries in newspapers like the *Amsterdam News*, the *Tavis Smiley* show, *Ebony* magazine, and *BET News* connected the Bryant case to the other prominent black men being tried at the same time, including Michael Jackson, and to the history of black men being accused (usually falsely) by whites such as the Scottsboro Boys.[99] In black newspaper editorials and even more on black Internet boards on media coverage, there is no doubt that a black man accused of raping a white woman still brings about a legal lynching.[100] Despite all the debate, eventually all charges against Kobe Bryant were dropped, yet it wasn't long until another interracial media spectacle emerged.

In 2006, media attention turned to a new set of interracial allegations that members of the Duke University lacrosse team assaulted and raped a woman at an off-campus party, which has parallels to the Kobe Bryant and Tawana Brawley case. While media reports varied how they presented perceptions of Bryant's guilt or innocence, especially as the case continued, there were doubts about the Duke University rape allegations in the media almost from the beginning.

Early coverage of the case described the individuals involved as a black stripper/exotic dancer and members of the Duke University lacrosse team members. From the very beginning, the woman's allegations and her character were called into question, even in the decision to identify her first and foremost as a stripper. Based on the limited information being released and the initial hesitancy of Duke University to respond, media highlighted the student protests, with headlines such as "Protests Continue over Alleged Duke Gang Rape," which discussed the allegations, police investigation, and student protests at the University Provost house, quoting the Duke president as stating, "'physical coercion and sexual assaults are unacceptable in any setting and have no place at Duke' but reiterated the school's position that the facts of the case are in dispute."[101] For example, most news reports headlined their coverage with statements such as "Lacrosse Scandal: The Duke Accuser—New Credibility Questions," and "Doubts about Duke," documenting possible inconsistencies in the accuser's story and the district attorney's handling of the case.[102]

The media decides how to tell a story and can imply many things, especially with a headline. In media coverage, racialized views of black women and white men were reinforced even if race was never mentioned. For example, in *Newsweek*'s extensive front-cover coverage, "A Troubled Spring at Duke," the case is laid out with the visual of the lacrosse team practicing. The article discusses how there are "at least two different scenarios" and "heavy overtones of race and class," where either the black woman who is referred to as "the stripper . . . who told (another newspaper) that she is a student at a local black college and a mother of two" was raped, sodomized, strangled, and beaten by three of the Duke lacrosse team, or this is "a tale of a prosecutor exploiting racial tensions with a trumped-up charge."[103] In particular, the way the Duke accuser is characterized is problematic. MSNBC's news personality Tucker Carlson argued, ". . . the testimony of an ordinary person is different from the testimony of someone who hires herself out to dance naked in front of and, yes, sometimes sleep with . . . (her) testimony about matters of sex is to be taken by ordinary commonsense people a little differently than the testimony of someone who isn't a crypto-hooker."[104] While the accuser in the Kobe Bryant case was depicted as a 19-year-old former cheerleader at her high school, who had many friends and family and was an accomplished singer who even tried out for *American Idol*,[105] the Duke accuser was commonly referred to as a stripper, exotic dancer, or in news personality Tucker Carlson's words, "crypto-hooker." The mother and father of Bryant's accuser received significant coverage and wrote letters to officials and media, which received media coverage. Facts about her past such as being mentally unstable and suicidal were brought to light, but it was more explanatory than defamatory, while the Duke accuser had very little coverage and her identity was constructed as first and foremost a stripper,[106] fitting into a pattern where black women are devalued or presented in negative stereotypical ways throughout the media and popular culture.[107] The "relative invisibility" of black women as rape victims "began with the systematic sexual abuse to which they were subjected during slavery and upon which the institution of slavery depended," and still when black women allege they are raped, it is more likely to either be ignored by the media (like the other rapes of black women the same week of the Central Park jogger case) or retold by the media in a way that discredits the women and gives the white man accused the benefit of the doubt. The media has trouble accepting black women as victims of "good" white men.[108]

Despite being accused of rape, media coverage emphasized the "good upbringings" of many members of the Duke lacrosse team and details the elite private schools and communities they were raised in.[109] The media also interviewed family, former teachers, coaches, and hometown pastors of the Duke University lacrosse team, like the accused Collin Finnerty's Catholic prep school coach and Reade Seligmann's headmaster of the Catholic prep school he attended and the mayor of his hometown of Essex Fells, New Jersey, who is good friends with his dad. They all expressed their belief in the young men's innocence and offered characterizations of the men as "great kid(s), and good students and players.[110] One lacrosse player's father, a Duke alumni, stated, "I think it's clear to anyone with brains that they did not do what they are accused of doing to this woman."[111] During the Kobe Bryant case, the family and friends of the white woman accuser were interviewed, part of this pattern where the white parties involved are portrayed in a more in-depth way whether they are the alleged victims (the Kobe Bryant case, Central Park jogger case) or the alleged perpetrators (Yusef Hawkins, Tawana Brawley, and Duke). Even months after the media coverage had lagged, there was an Associated Press story that ran "Coach K Breaks Silence on Duke Lacrosse Case," where the well-known white Duke University basketball coach Kryzewski states that he withheld speaking until now but he supports the players and empathizes with the Duke lacrosse team coach, Mike Pressler, who resigned, yet he never mentions the accuser.[112] Coach K, Tucker Carlson, and the media identify better with these young men than this black woman, who at this time it is believed may have been raped.[113] In fact, as one source reports, "Most students seemed primarily worried about the stain on Duke's reputation." As Feagin and Vera documented, media has a tendency to seek to explain the background of middle-class or higher whites who become involved in a criminal case or investigation, yet the media is less likely to look for an explanation to account for a black individual's alleged or proven crime.[114] It becomes about protecting whiteness. When a black man like Bryant is accused, it becomes "another one bites the dust," as the black newspaper *Amsterdam News* editorial was titled, and the idea is that he might not actually have been the exception we thought he was. With the Duke men accused of rape, not only were the men's backgrounds as "good boys" emphasized but also a *Washington Post* article, "Lacrosse Players' Case a Trial for Parents," lamented the ordeal this rape accusation was causing the Duke parents, noting Washington's connection to nine of the players who are from the area.[115] Particular attention was paid to the ordinary lives of the Duke men before the accusation, the parents' unwavering faith in their sons' innocence, the parents' constant stress, and how they watched while "in a fell swoop—a lightning bolt—everything is taken from them."[116] In contrast, the black and Hispanic young men wrongly convicted of the Central Park jogger case never received this sympathetic coverage even after having served years in prison for a crime they did not commit. The difference between how the white Duke lacrosse players and the black and Latino young men accused in the Central Park jogger case highlights white privilege and illustrates how media operates not only from a white perspective but also in defense of whiteness, as evidenced in the following passage from the *Washington Post* article:

> Their lawyers told the parents to keep quiet, no matter how difficult. There were former headmasters, coaches and priests who spoke on their son's behalf. The contrast was sharply drawn: privileged white athletes against a black single mother putting herself through college while moonlighting for an escort service . . . her elderly parents with only a screened porch on a shotgun house . . . came out to say how much they loved their daughter. The NAACP was calling for justice. In the court of public opinion, the lacrosse players were losing. . . . (another father) talked to his cousin, Bob Bennett, President Bill Clinton's lawyer in the Paula Jones case. . . . Bennett worked behind the scenes. . . . The one news outlet they felt was challenging the prosecutor's narrative was *The Abrams Report* on MSNBC, hosted by Dan Abrams, a Duke alumnus. They started funneling him tips.[117]

This article repositions, essentially reverses, the story where the Duke young men are the ones who are disadvantaged, with the accuser's lower status and low-income parents rewritten as an asset, similar to the arguments that affirmative action is reverse racism. Yet the article also explicitly states the contradictory fact that the Duke men and families have a prominent and influential news personality who they have direct access to and have close contact to prominent political lawyers. When their news "friend," MSNBC's Dan Abrams, first reported on "the sex assault scandal at Duke," he ended the program by stating, "This is a dark day for my University, which I love very much, and you know, sorry to have to cover a story like this, but I can't let my personal affiliations prevent us from covering what is an important story."[118] Soon after these initial reports, he took a special interest in the case, and his coverage became more critical of the prosecutor's case, even having the opportunity to look at all of the defense's documents. On the NBC program *Dateline*, he reported that the accuser's story did not add up and he believed the rape did not occur based on the documents he saw. Yet based on the parents' statements and Abrams's own statement of allegiance, we see how the media's social location, who they identify with, and who they talk to undoubtedly affect how they frame the story.

On one hand the media covers the events that happen, yet the media also has the power to shape the discourse and provide a lens through which to understand the events that happen. The question that the media does not adequately explore is how the stereotypes of black women may have contributed to the representation of the alleged rape and the ensuing media coverage. The media does report that there was a rush to judgment about the young white men's guilt and an unfair accusation that Duke University and the surrounding community were racist and at fault, seemingly implying whites are privileged but rather are the ones being "stereotyped." Yet there is little media discussion of how problematic the stereotypes of blacks are and how they affect behaviors and attitudes. The desire to protect Durham's image was even clearly written about by the Associated Press in an April 2006 piece, "Officials Try to Protect Durham's Image," quoting Rosemarie Kitchin, the director of media relations for the Durham Convention & Visitor's Bureau, and Reyn Bowman, president and chief executive of the Convention & Visitors Bureau, who said, "Their aim is not to put a positive spin on the story, but to provide an accurate context for national depictions of their city."[119] The blatantly racially motivated behavior of the white young men in hiring two separate black strippers and by the neighbor's account hurling racial comments, "Hey bitch, thank your grandpa for my nice cotton shirt," is an important piece, yet most media reports overlooked the historical connections. One of the few articles to address the raced and gendered aspects was "Duke Case Reopens Wounds for Black Women," which featured interviews with young black women and reports, "The facts about the Duke case remain in doubt, but the image of a black woman stripping for a room full of white athletes shouting racial epithets is painful to many black women."[120] While black women interviewed recount experiences where white men disrespected them and treated them as sex objects, even this piece ends with a discussion of how *Black Entertainment Television* features videos made by black men where "no one forces black women to disrobe."[121] Despite the attention to the pain experienced by black women, the news piece falls in line with other media coverage and ends by placing the blame back on black women. Similarly, in another article, Sally Fogarty, the mother of Duke lacrosse player Gibbs Fogarty, "a powerhouse fundraiser for Duke" and wife of Robert H. Fogarty, president of Sport Chevrolet Company, answers that accusation of the racist comment at least one of the men made, by stating, "One of the dancers hurled her own racially and sexually demeaning remarks."[122] Some Duke players acknowledged to *ESPN* that "racial slurs and bad language" were used when "a dispute over money and the length of the performance led to the argument between players and two exotic dancers."[123]

Whenever there is an allegation of interracial rape, someone is accused of playing the race card, and this time it is the white district attorney who is up for reelection in a diverse area and one of his opponents is black. In this case we see some emphasis on racial difference in the media, but the race element is often implied to be an excuse rather than a reality. Furthermore, the most widely heard argument about race was that District Attorney Nifong was using this case to win his reelection with his largely black constituency and that blacks held the racial advantage. We see this in the media accounts of the Duke case as the story becomes how could this happen at Duke, and disbelief that it did happen, so the news accounts seek to answer these questions as well as present evidence that the boys are good boys, that Duke is not racist, and by extension, whites are not racist. While the media coverage died down by the summer of 2006 before any date for trial had been set, the news reports that were popping up emphasized how the case had fallen apart. The case was finally dismissed in early 2007 with major news coverage presenting the damage done to the white lacrosse players.[124] Ultimately District Attorney Mike Nifong resigned and was disbarred and charged with intentional prosecutorial misconduct for pursuing charges against the three Duke students.[125] As one lawyer for the players stated, "This rush to judgment, which has created a lynch mob mentality, which has hurt the University, Duke University, unfairly, which has hurt the community of Durham unfairly, is just unfortunate, at best, and un-American, if I might say so."[126] While Nifong very well may have engaged in unethical behavior, what about the prosecutors in the Central Park jogger case who wrongly prosecuted and won a conviction against young men who did not commit the crime? It seems as if falsely accusing whites, particularly well-connected and wealthy whites like the Duke lacrosse players, will not be tolerated and is seen as a violation of the ethical foundation of our justice system and society, playing to ideas of belonging and citizenship and the notion of whites as the true Americans, and thereby to treat white men in this way is un-American, as one of the Duke lawyers argued.

Lessons Learned

In both instances, the charges against the Duke University lacrosse players and Kobe Bryant were dropped without a trial, yet the truth of the allegations and the innocence or guilt of the accused does not justify the different types of coverage. The media weaves stories before the "story" is actually known, and how they decide to present the little bits of information they receive shows us the stories they assume to be true. We see how the media approaches race as something that is played for a reason and manipulated for advantage, rarely acknowledging the extent to which race affects any interracial case. The reports are contradictory, where we hear that a white lawyer "playing the race card" carries more credibility, but we still hear from journalists that race does not matter and they "never think about race." The role of race is denied, yet people in Vail, Colorado, live in a area where there are virtually no black people and we have darkened faces on magazine covers and Hangman T-shirts made of black athletes who have supposedly "transcended race."

The media coverage shows a pattern of focusing on matters involving interracial sex, while denying, minimalizing, or trying to explain why race does not matter, or at least not matter much. These contemporary stories are cultural narratives that draw from historical images of "the myth of the promiscuity of slave women allowed white men to rape them . . . and the rape of a frail white victim by a savage black male must be avenged by the chivalry of her white male protectors."[127] Black men, even those with wealth and power, who are accused of sexual impropriety with white women receive what could be called a legal lynching by the news media. For black women who accuse white men of raping them, they are symbolically raped in the media, even before their accusations are explored. These examples, beyond showing how interracial sex still matters, also continue to show that "contemporary racial ideology in the U.S. is that it is considered bad taste, a violation of protocol, for blacks to identify racism where racism exists."[128] When blacks are accused or believed to have committed an "interracial crime," they will be (per)prosecuted harder, but their immediate community, and to an extent the entire black race, also comes under scrutiny. When black women are the victims of rape, particularly by whites, their story seems to be quickly doubted by both the criminal/legal system, and the media passes on this doubt. Also problematic are the countless stories that the media lets pass under their radar from the twenty-eight other women raped the same week as the Central Park jogger to the July 2006 South Carolina separate brutal serial rapes and attacks of black women by two white men in a spree of racially motivated attacks that never garnered much attention. Therefore for whites, accusations of a crime that involves interracial sex can actually serve as an excuse (such as in the Yusef Hawkins murder) or makes it less likely the "crime" will be believed. Furthermore, by using the Kobe Bryant case (or O. J. trial) to argue whether or not race matters, it makes it easier for whites to affirm that race no longer matters, especially since the media pays little or no attention to the unknown black men who have been falsely accused or received stiffer penalties for crimes against white women; "the real racism that millions of people face every day is thus either too localized or generalized" and not the story that fits the white imagination.[129] There emerges a pattern that when whites are accused—white young men in the Yusef Hawkins murder, the white Italian community of Bensonhurst, the white community of Vail, Colorado, during the Kobe Bryant case, and the white lacrosse players, Duke University and Durham—the media participates in the protection of whiteness either through the characterization of those accused or the validation of the white communities. Through the media coverage, the protection and privileging of whiteness is clear.

Men and women of color are simultaneously desired and despised, envied and reviled. "This schism in white subjectivity is replayed daily in the different ways black men become visible on the front and back pages of tabloid newspapers, seen as undesirable in one frame—the mugger, the terrorist, the rapist—and highly desirable in the other—the athlete, the sports hero, the entertainer."[130] With Kobe Bryant, and even O. J. Simpson, they are both operating simultaneously and at different times to different groups. Allegations of rape take on different meanings and reveal the differential value of women's bodies in capitalist societies based on race, as well as class and other factors.[131] "Sexuality gives a special power and meaning to ethnic and racial tensions; the introduction of race into a charge of sexual assault can be explosive, reminding us once again that sex and race are a volatile mixture."[132] If we believe for a moment the media's premise that we are color-blind, we only need to look at these supposedly "isolated" incidents that we often wouldn't hear about if we weren't scouring the back pages of local papers and the high-profile incidents we hear about endlessly (for why they are chosen and how they are presented), where the racist beliefs weave in and out of the story. The media will only minimally address race in historical terms like the pardon of Jack Johnson, or in individual terms like the extreme "racist" who burns a cross on an interracial couple's lawn, or address race to argue how much race no longer matters in a color-blind world. Yet most media refuses to address how racism operates in contemporary society on an institutional level that permeates every aspect, never more clearly than when interracial sex is involved.

Notes

1. *Newsweek* had an entire cover and stories devoted to this "phenomenon," *Boston Globe* had a 2000 article, "Changing Face of the Racial Divide, Mixed Marriages Alter Longtime Boundaries," and *Seattle Times* had "Interracial Couples Becoming More Common," by Dawn Sagario, page L2, December 29, 2002. "Special Report: A

New America," *AARP Magazine*, May/June 2004, reports on its cover that "71% now approve of interracial marriage—even for their own children. Are we close to Martin Luther King Jr.'s dream of a 'beloved community'?" See also Associated Press, "After 40 Years, Interracial Marriage Flourishing," April 13, 2007, http://www.msnbc.msn.com/id/18090277/page/2/.

2. Associated Press, "After 40 Years, Interracial Marriage Flourishing," April 13, 2007, http://www.msnbc.msn.com/id/18090277/page/2/.

3. News coverage contributes to the production of contemporary racism where previous studies have found that news reports tend to present prejudicial information regarding allegations of wrongdoing, and in particular racial differences where blacks are overrepresented as defendants and whites as victims. See Sears 1988 and Christopher Campbell 2005 [1995], "A Myth of Assimilation: 'Enlightened' Racism and the News," in Hunt, *Channeling Blackness*; Travis Dixon and Daniel Linz, "Television News, Prejudicial Pretrial Publicity, and the Depiction of Race," *Journal of Broadcasting and Electronic Media* 46, 1 (2002): 112–36. See also Robert Entman and A. Rojecki, *The Black Image in the White Mind: Media and Race in America* (Chicago: University of Chicago Press, 2000); Travis Dixon and Daniel Linz, "Overrepresentation and Underrepresentation of African Americans and Latinos as Lawbreakers on Television News," *Journal of Communication* 50, 2 (2000): 131–54; Travis Dixon and Daniel Linz, "Race and the Misrepresentation of Victimization on Local Television News," *Communication Research* 27, 5 (2000): 547–73; and D. Romer, K. H. Jamieson, and N. J. De Coteau, "The Treatment of Persons of Color in Local Television News: Ethnic Blame Discourse or Realistic Group Conflict?" *Communication Research* 25 (1998): 268–305.

4. D. Parvaz, "Paul Allen and His Beauty May Be Serious," *Seattle Post-Intelligencer*, December 7, 2004. The story was covered in most newspapers across the country, such as the *Chattanooga Times* (TN), *Daily News* in New York, *Herald Sun* (Durham, NC), *Houston Chronicle*, *Los Angeles Times*, *Providence Journal* (RI), *New York Post*, and *St. Louis Post Dispatch*; Roberto Gonzalez, "Five Men Charged in Attack on Interracial Couple," *Hartford Courant*, January 8, 2004; and Associated Press, "3 Arkansas Men Indicted in Cross-Burning Case," May 7, 2006, www.msnbc.msn.com/id/12677315/from/RS.1/.

5. The media reported how the local NAACP president Bobby Fleming even remarked that these were "isolated incidents of racism and didn't see cause for further alarm." Mike Gellatly, "Hate Crime? Pair Charged with Rape, Kidnapping, Attempted Murder," *Clarendon Today*, July 13, 2006. See also Associated Press, "More Details Arise in W. Va. Torture Case," by Tom Breen and Shaya Tayefe Mohajer, September 19, 2007; "Details Emerge in W. Va. Torture Case," John Raby at www.abcnews.com; Cash Michaels, "West Virginia Victim Was Captive for a Month," *Wilmington Journal*, September 26, 2007; Katrina A. Goggins, "Deputies: Assault of 15-year-old Clarendon County Girl May Be Hate Crime," July 10, 2006. Accessed www.clarendontoday.com.

6. Tammy Imre is a white woman who had a sexual relationship with an 8-year-old black child. In the news article, "Woman Blames Boy, 8," *Connecticut Post*, by

Daniel Tepfer, November 9, 2004, Imre's employer is interviewed and states she was a "dedicated mother," who was a good, dependable worker and "the firm intends to hold Imre's job for her and 'hope for the best.'" See also Daniel Tepfer, "Woman Accused of Sex with Boy," *Connecticut Post*, November 6, 2004; Daniel Tepfer, "Bizarre Case of Boy-Woman Sex Moves Forward," *Connecticut Post*, November 11, 2004; Daniel Tepfer, "Lawyer: Imre's Story on Boy Sex Not Told," *Connecticut Post*, November 17, 2004; "Woman Charged with Abusing 8-Year-Old Boy," *Los Angeles Times*, November 9, 2004; See also Marian Gail Brown, "Why Did She Do It?," *Connecticut Post*, November 14, 2004. "Teacher Sex Scandal Spurs Cries of Racism," Associated Press, March 28, 2007. Accessed at www.cbsnews.com.

7. Hunt 2005, 18, 19. As Hunt argues, "People who control television news—as we saw with television fiction—are overwhelmingly white. Decisions about which stories are newsworthy and how the chosen stories are to be framed are routinely made with little or no input from nonwhites . . . combined with the reliance upon mostly white official sources, the relative paucity of nonwhites in the newsworker corps results in a white-washed depiction of reality—a reality populated by nonwhite Others who are often rendered in ways that reflect the black-white binary and its related chains of equivalence."

8. While gender is undoubtedly also very important, the focus here is not on how issues of gender surface in allegations of rape and how women are revictimized through the process, yet I realize how important and well documented those issues and realities are. See Earl Smith and Angela Hattery 2006 for a discussion that looks at gender and race in interracial rape allegations, particularly against athletes

9. Hall 1981, "The Whites of Their Eyes: Racist Ideologies and the Media," page 89.

10. Thomas Shevory, *Notorious H.I.V: The Media Spectacle of Nushawn Williams* (Minneapolis: University of Minnesota Press, 2004), 3.

11. This analysis is based on an extensive and comprehensive review of news materials relating to the media events discussed. For each case, occurrence, or event, a LexisNexis search was conducted on interracial couples, as well as each individual case yielding results from all media sources. Additional searches of coverage by major metropolitan newspapers such as the *New York Times*, *Los Angeles Times*, *Atlanta Constitution*, *Chicago Tribune*, *Boston Globe*, and television news coverage by NBC, ABC, CBS, Fox, BET as well as coverage by the local newspapers where the event occurred (such as Vail, Colorado, during the Bryant case and Durham, North Carolina, during the Duke case) and minority-owned news sources such as the *Amsterdam News* were also conducted. General Internet searches of the covered events were also done, yielding additional media coverage and Internet discussions of the topics. The news articles and transcripts were read and coded based on their description of the event, the sources quoted, and most importantly, whether or not they mentioned race.

12. See Martha Hodes, *Sex, Love, Race: Crossing Boundaries in North American History* (New York: New York University Press, 1999).

13. Page 83 in Elizabeth Alexander, "Can you be BLACK and Look at This?": Reading the Rodney King Video(s)," Black Public Sphere Collective, ed., *Black Public Sphere* (Chicago: University of Chicago Press).

14. I emphasize the word *legally* because interracial couples are still the target of violent attacks and threats that sometimes receive media coverage, such as the biracial black man who was beaten by off-duty white police officers at a party where he was with two white women and another black man, which will be discussed later in the chapter.

15. For example, the U.S. Senate offered an apology to the victims of lynchings and their families for their failure to act and reopened the 1955 murder case of Emmett Till and exhumed his body. Also in 1998, there was passing media coverage of South Carolina's voter resolution to end the state constitutional ban on interracial marriage, which had been useless since the 1967 Loving Supreme Court decision. See Lyn Riddle, "South Carolina May End Ban on Mixed Marriages," *Atlanta Constitution*, April 19, 1998.

16. Richard Sandomir, "Forgiving 'Unforgivable Blackness,'" *New York Times*, Section D, Column 4, January 18, 2005.

17. Transcript of CBS *The Early Show*, 7:00 a.m. ET, January 17, 2005.

18. As quoted in Martin Miller, "A Boxer's Last Battle Royal," *Los Angeles Times*, Part E, January 15, 2005.

19. See "Shame on Us," *Los Angeles Times*, editorial pages Part B, 10. The original editorial was published on July 6, 1910, *Los Angeles Times* editorial.

20. See Edward Lee Pitts, "Corker Says He Reflects Tennessee More Than Ford," *Chattanooga Times Free Press*, November 3, 2006.

21. There was another Republican ad during the 2006 Senate elections that shows a close-up of a white girl's face with her mouth covered by a noticeably darker hand with the caption, "Family Values Are under Attack. If the Democrats Take Control . . . Our Values Will Be Destroyed." See Beth Ridner, "Latest Republican Ad Strikes Some as Playing on Racial Fears," Associated Press, October 25, 2006, and Erin McPike, "Ad Spotlight: Steaming over Stem Cells in MO," *National Journal* (October 30, 2006).

22. See transcript of MSNBC Hardball with Chris Matthews, October 25, 2006, at www.msnbc.com and "Actress Says Anti-Ford 'Bimbo' Ad Not Racist," Associated Press and Local Wire, November 8, 2006.

23. For different examples, see CBS *Evening News* transcript, "Looking at Campaign Ads," October 29, 2006; the Fox *Hannity & Co.* news program, "Campaign Commercials Get Nasty," 9 p.m., October 25, 2006; and Beth Ridner, "Latest Republican Ad Strikes Some as Playing on Racial Fears," Associated Press, October 25, 2006.

24. See "Compounding a Political Outrage," *New York Times*, Section A, Column 1 (October 27, 2006), 18.

25. John Fiske 2005, "Hearing Anita Hill," 94.

26. Thomas was a "tamed Black man," like the television depictions on *ER* and *Grey's Anatomy*. See Fiske, *Media Matters: Everyday Culture and Political Change* (Minneapolis: University of Minnesota Press), 94.

27. During the same time in the 1980s *Hustler* magazine featured four cartoonists who all regularly featured caricatures of black men with big, dark bodies, small heads,

and exaggerated facial features, often with sexually suggestive pictures and captions. For a discussion of *Hustler* magazine cartoons of black men see Gail Dines, "King Kong and the White Woman: *Hustler* Magazine and the Demonization of Black Masculinity," in Gail Dines and Jean M. Humez, eds., *Gender, Race and Class in Media: A Text-Reader* (Thousand Oaks, CA: Sage Publications, 2003), 451–61.

28. For an in-depth discussion of coverage of the Central Park jogger case, see Lynn Chancer, *High-Profile Crimes: When Legal Cases Become Social Causes* (Chicago: University of Chicago Press, 2005), chapter 2; and Valerie Smith, "Split Affinities: The Case of Interracial Rape." See also original news articles such as Jimmy Breslin, "Violence in the Night Grabs Lone Jogger," *Newsday*, April 21, 1989; Dennis Hamill, "Like Bambi in Hunting Season," *Newsday*, April 21, 1989; Craig Wolff, "Youths Rape and Beat Central Park Jogger," *New York Times*, April 21, 1989; "Wolf Pack's Prey," *Daily News*, April 1989, 1–3, 29.

29. Page 33 in Lynn Chancer, *High-Profile Crimes; When Legal Cases Become Social Causes* (Chicago: University of Chicago Press, 2005). She references a September 26, 1994, interview with an unnamed national reporter on the "Central Park jogger" case.

30. The full-page ad ran in the *New York Times* on May 1, 1989, page A3, signed by Donald Trump.

31. See J. Zamgba Browne, "Trump's 'Kill Them' Ad Condemned," *Amsterdam News*, May 6, 1989.

32. See Harold Jamison, "Another Woman Raped and Strangled to Death: Police Have No Suspects, Motive for Killing," *Amsterdam News*, May 1989; Don Terry, "A Week of Rapes: The Jogger and 28 Not in the News," *New York Times*, May 29, 1989, 25. Valerie Smith, "Split Affinities: The Case of Interracial Rape," also discusses the invisibility of the mostly black and Latina twenty-eight other women raped the same week as the Central Park jogger.

33. The lack of outrage over having imprisoned the wrong young men who lost years of their lives will be compared to the outrage that surfaced over the Duke lacrosse young men who were wrongly charged with rape.

34. See CBS News, "Central Park Jogger Reveals Identity," March 28, 2003. Accessed at www.cbsnews.com.

35. Sydney H. Schanberg, "A Journey through the Tangled Case of the Central Park Jogger: When Justice Is a Game," *Village Voice*, November 20–26, 2002.

36. See transcript from online *NewsHour with Jim Lehrer*, December 24, 2002, "Central Park Justice," featuring Betty Ann Bowser.

37. Chancer 2005, 65, quoting Stuart Marques, "30 Teens Chase, Shoot Youth, 16," *Daily News*, August 25, 1989, 1–3.

38. John Kifner, "Bensonhurst: A Tough Code in Defense of a Closed World," *New York Times*, September 1, 1989, as quoted in Chancer 2005, 147–48, 294.

39. See chapter 3, "The Murder of Yusef Hawkins," in Chancer 2005 for an in-depth discussion of the high-profile media coverage and communities' responses to Yusef Hawkins's murder.

40. See Jonathan Markovitz, *Legacies of Lynching: Racial Violence and Memory* (Minneapolis: University of Minnesota Press, 2004), 42. The grand jury declined to issue indictments and the case was widely described as a hoax, particularly by the mainstream media, despite Tawana Brawley standing by her story.

41. See page 83 in Katheryn K. Russell, *The Color of Crime: Racial Hoaxes, White Fear, Black Protectionism, Police Harassment, and other Macroaggressions* (New York: New York University Press, 1997).

42. The *New York Times* reporters who covered the case wrote a book, *Outrage: The Story Behind the Tawana Brawley Hoax* (1990), which put forth the idea that Tawana had lied about the rape with the help of her mother to cover up for running away and to gain sympathy from her mother's live-in boyfriend, who had a violent past and was potentially abusive to Tawana and her mother. Also see Markovitz 2004.

43. Editorial, "It's an Outrage," *City Sun*, April 26–May 2, 1989.

44. Feagin and Vera, *White Racism*, 115–24.

45. As quoted by Feagin and Vera, 117.

46. Jennifer Wilbanks's use of a Hispanic man paired with a white woman may signal the growing perception of Hispanics as threatening and linked to increases in the Hispanic population and growing anti-immigrant sentiment.

47. Erin Texeira, "Fleeing Bride-to-be's Tale Opens Old Racial Wounds," Associated Press article accessed at www.msnbc.msn.com.

48. Page 79 in Katheryn K. Russell, *The Color of Crime: Racial Hoaxes, White Fear, Black Protectionism, Police Harassment, and other Macroaggressions* (New York: New York University Press, 1997.

49. On April 25, 2007, the *New York Times* article, "For Indian Victims of Sexual Assault, a Tangled Legal Path" by Ralph Blumenthal discussed the high rates of rape of Native American women by non-Native American men and the difficulty and unwillingness of courts and authorities to handle these incidents.

50. Fiske 1994, 13.

51. Fiske 1994, 24.

52. George, Tara, "Panic over HIV Spree," 7. *Daily News*, October 27, 1997: 7.

53. Rick Hampson, "AIDS Scare Rips through Upstate NY: Teenagers Outbreak Blamed on One Man, Puts Communities in Shock," *USA Today*, October 29, 1997, D1.

54. Shevory 2004, 77.

55. Shevory 2004, 20.

56. See page 80 in Lynn Chancer, "O. J. Simpson and the Trial of the Century?: Uncovering Paradoxes in Media Coverage," 78–103 in Gregg Barak, ed., *Representing O. J.: Murder, Criminal Justice and Mass Culture* (New York: Harrow and Heston Publishers, 1996).

57. Page 13 in Lynn Chancer, *High-Profile Crimes: When Legal Cases Become Social Causes* (Chicago: University of Chicago Press, 2005).

58. See George Lipsitz, *The Possessive Investment in Whiteness: How White People Profit from Identity Politics* (Philadelphia, PA: Temple University Press, 1998), 111–12, citing Jack White, "A Double Strand of Paranoia," *Time*, October 9, 1995, 39.

59. Lipsitz (1998) argues how the way race is handled by whites is illustrated in the way Mark Fuhrman's racism was dismissed as a personal problem, not something relevant to the case.

60. Jury pools were questioned before selection in the Simpson case about general race relations and the prevalence of racial discrimination, as well as specific questions about interracial marriage. See Lynda Gorov, "Prospective Jurors in Simpson Case Get Lengthy Quiz," *Boston Globe*, October 1, 1994.

61. Lipsitz 1998, 8.

62. Richard E. Lapchick, "Sadly, Stardom Often Only Skin Deep," *ESPN*, February 28, 2002, accessed at www.espn.go.com/gen/s/2002/0225/1340490.html.

63. Page 53 in Katheryn K. Russell, *The Color of Crime*, for an excellent analysis of the media response to the O. J. Simpson case in chapter 4.

64. Page 51 in Katheryn K. Russell, *The Color of Crime*.

65. Derrick Z. Jackson, "So Who Really Gets the Juice?" *Boston Globe*, July 29, 1994.

66. Scholars argue that the media seeks stories that are intriguing, yet only slightly different from the types of stories that are usually told. See Gaye Tuchman, "Making News by Doing Work: Routinizing the Unexpected," *American Journal of Sociology* 79 (1973): 110–31; Gaye Tuchman, "Objectivity as Strategic Ritual: An Examination of Newsmen's Notion of Objectivity," *American Journal of Sociology* 77 (1972): 660–79; Chancer 2005: 34, 28; Todd Gitlin, *The Whole World Is Watching: Mass Media in the Making and Unmaking of the New Left* (Berkeley: University of California Press, 1980); Stuart Hall, Charles Critcher, Tony Jefferson, John Clarke, and Brian Roberts, *Policing the Crisis: Mugging, the State, and Law and Order* (London: Macmillan, 1978).

67. Chancer 2005, 38.

68. Christine Brennan was interviewed on a panel on ABC's *Nightline*, July 18, 2003, in response to questions about whether Kobe Bryant making a public statement that he did cheat on his wife tarnished his image and whether there was racial dynamic to the case.

69. *NBC Nightly News* (6:30 p.m. ET) July 19, 2003, with Don Lemon reporting, and the "positive image . . . players" was quoted during the news broadcast by Professor Todd Boyd. See also NBC *Dateline* (8:00 p.m. ET), July 18, 2003. NBC News called him a "hometown hero . . . reputation as a homebody," NBC *Nightly News* (6:30 p.m. ET) July 7, 2003.

70. Numerous scholars have demonstrated how American sports, like the larger society, is based on ideas of racial difference, and in particular blackness. See C. Richard King and Charles Fruehling Springwood, "Body and Soul: Physicality, Disciplinarity, and the Overdetermination of Blackness," 185–206, in Darnell Hunt's *Channeling Blackness*; and John Hoberman's *Darwin's Athletes: How Sport Has Damaged Black America and Preserved the Myth of Race* (Boston: Houghton Mifflin, 1997).

71. Reported by Jim Avila on NBC *Nightly News* with the headline, "Kobe Bryant Admits to Adultery but Claims Innocence of Rape Allegations," anchored by John Seigenthaler, July 19, 2003.

72. In a review of transcripts from ABC *Good Morning America*, ABC *World News Tonight with Peter Jennings*, CBS *48 Hours*, CBS *60 Minutes II*, CBS *Early Show*, CBS *Morning News*, *Dateline NBC*, NBC *Nightly News*; NBC *Today Show* and news reports from *Los Angeles Times* (Mike Bresnahan, Tim Brown, Anna Gorman, Steve Henson, David Kelly and Henry Weinsten), and *New York Times* (Harvey Araton, Kirk Johnson, Alex Markels, David O. Williams, Mike Wise).

73. This broadcast on CBS *Evening News*, 6:30 p.m. ET on January 23, 2004.

74. This article appeared in the *New York Times* on March 26, 2004.

75. Lorraine Dusky, "Defense Tramples Rights of Alleged Rape Victim," *Vail Daily*, March 12, 2004. Accessed www.vaildaily.com.

76. Interestingly, this was done on television shows such as *ER*, where gender bias was confronted, racial bias denied, and in films such as *Guess Who*, in which the movie concludes by linking the male characters of the black father/white boyfriend by gender and overcoming the perceived racial boundaries.

77. Kirk Johnson, "In Kobe Bryant Case, Issues of Power, Not of Race," *New York Times*, August 27, 2004, 12.

78. David O. Williams, "Sources: Evidence of Bruising . . . ," *Vail Trail*, September 19, 2003.

79. Kirk Johnson, "Criticism Takes Toll on Judge in Bryant Sexual Assault Case," *New York Times*, August 14, 2004. See also NBC *Dateline* (7:00 p.m. ET), July 20, 2003, where they report, "America is going to be very interested in this because it deals with everything we love: Sex, celebrity, athletes, all of it is in this mix."

80. Different examples include NBC *Dateline*, which reported, "Some people in Eagle County who don't follow basketball will see Kobe Bryant as a big black guy who took advantage of a young white woman in their community." NBC *Dateline* (7:00 p.m. ET), August 3, 2003. See also *Fox News*, August 1, 2003, and on Fox's *O'Reilly Factor*, August 1, 2003, Rita Cosby reports that after talking to the sheriff, she "knew" an assault took place and the host John Kasich asks, "Will the race card be played?"

81. Boyd recounts how he interviewed an African American store owner weeks ago and "only this past week, when we were looking around for African Americans to interview for our race-oriented cover story, did I realize that (he) is black. Race never crossed my mind even once. It simply doesn't occur to me. That's how we are around here." See Tom Boyd, "IF You Move It, I'll Lose It," *Vail Trail*, August 8, 2003. Similar articles appeared nationwide in the *Los Angeles Times*, with interviews with these same small groups of minority Vail residents. See Steve Henson, "Still Waters May Run Deep," *Los Angles Times*, August 10, 2004.

82. David O. Williams. "The Great Race Debate," *Vail Trail*, August 8, 2003.

83. A similar sentiment emerged when the mayor of the Louisiana town of Jena argued that his town was being unfairly portrayed as racist after white kids hung nooses on a tree. See Associated Press, "Jena Mayor Calls Song Inflammatory," www.apgoogle.com.

84. The district attorney Mark Hulbert said in response to the jury pool in Eagle County, "Racially, the people of Eagle County are some of the fairest I've ever seen.

They've always decided on the facts. . . . (noting the significant Latino population in the county) every time I've done a case with a Latino jury or a Latino victim, the jury has decided on the facts." Quoted in Mike Wise and Alex Markels, "Bryant Case Puts a County in the Spotlight," *New York Times*, July 20, 2003.

85. See Erica Chito Childs, *Navigating Interracial Borders: Black-White Couples and Their Social Worlds* (New Brunswick, NJ: Rutgers University Press, 2005); Eduardo Bonilla-Silva, *Racism without Racists* (Lanham, MD: Rowman & Littlefield, 2003); Joe Feagin and Eileen O'Brien, *White Men on Race* (New York: Beacon Press, 2003).

86. See also BET *Nightly News* transcript, January 23, 2004.

87. The news account covering the story made the most references to race, yet most discussed race in terms of what Bryant's lawyer said and what impact it would have rather than discuss how race affects the case. One *Vail Trail* article (January 30, 2004) by Nickey Hernandez, "Dirty Dealing in the Kobe Case," angrily discussed Bryant's lawyer as "the hoop star's Frodo-sized legal thug, played the race card . . . from the bottom of the deck by needlessly, shamelessly, and vindictively suggesting (race) something to do with the alleged crime." See also the transcript from ABC *Good Morning America*, January 26, 2004; CBS *Saturday Early Show* (7:00 a.m. ET), January 24, 2004; *Fox News Big Story Weekend*, January 24, 2004; and *On the Record with Greta Van Susteren*, Fox News Network, January 23, 2004.

88. "Kobe Bryant Trial Update," *Good Morning America*, ABC News, January 26, 2004 (7:00 a.m. ET) show.

89. Quoted on MSNBC *The Abrams Report*, January 23, 2004. Furthermore, during a Fox news broadcast, Wendy Murphy, a former prosecutor, says Mackey's comments are false because it was not white women who falsely accused black men. *Fox News Big Story Weekend*, January 24, 2005. Also reporter Nicky Hernandez argues, "Team Kobe has already branded the accuser as a sexed up, suicidal . . . why not toss in a Klan membership to boot?" Nickey Hernandez, "Dirty Dealing in the Kobe Case," January 30, 2004, *Vail Trail*.

90. See Michael Staub, "The Whitest I: On Reading the Hill-Thomas Transcripts," chapter 4, for a discussion of the Thomas hearings and "how were the pro-Thomas forces able to misappropriate so successfully the history of lynching (and all its attendant meanings), so that nobody involved could correct . . . able to get away with being so blatantly racist toward Anita Hill and then succeed in styling themselves antiracist?" 51.

91. Jon Sarche (Associated Press), "Kobe D.A. Is 'Outgunned, Outclassed': Mackey, Haddon Have Put Focus on Accuser's Troubles," January 21, 2004. Accessed at www.msnbc.com/id/4010267. See BET *Nightly News*, January 22, 2004.

92. This exchange, and Dan Abrams's comments, were from the MSNBC *Abrams Report*, January 23, 2004. On this program, criminal defense attorney Karen Russell was one of the few voices on mainstream media that attempted briefly to say that Mackey was "not inventing a history of racial bias when it comes to rape accusations," citing the book *To Kill A Mockingbird* and the racist T-shirts, but she was surrounded by the other voices of Dan Abrams and Norm Early, the former Denver district attorney.

93. Steve Henson, "Bryant Case Still Moving Slowly," *Los Angeles Times*, June 22, 2004.

94. NBC *Today Show* (7:00 a.m. ET), June 22, 2004.

95. CBS *Early Show*, "Kobe Bryant's Rape Case Continues Today in Colorado," June 22, 2004.

96. Quoted on NBC *Today Show*, August 4, 2003.

97. Dahlia Lithwick, "The Shield That Failed," *New York Times*, August 8, 2004. See also BET *Nightly News*, August 18, 2003, which reported that "some are comparing the Kobe Bryant case with the O. J. Simpson case."

98. See Wilbert A. Tatum, "Invitation to a Legal Lynching," *Amsterdam News*, accessed at www.Amsterdamnews.org. *Amsterdam News* ran opinion and editorial pieces during the Bryant case expressing similar views.

99. See "Is It Open Season on Black Men?" *Ebony*, April 2004, which includes interviews with five prominent black "respected authorities" about the way prominent black men were being treated. See Elizabeth Alexander, "'Can you be BLACK and Look at This?': Reading the Rodney King Video(s)," in the Black Public Sphere Collective, ed., *Black Public Sphere* (Chicago: University of Chicago Press, 1995).

100. Another powerful example is the case of Marcus Dixon, an 18-year-old black male who was accused of raping a 15-year-old white classmate, charged as an adult, and found not guilty, yet imprisoned on the lesser charge of misdemeanor statutory rape and aggravated felony child molestation, which was eventually overturned. For full story see Andrew Jacobs, "Student Sex Case in Georgia Stirs Claims of Old South Justice," *New York Times*, January 22, 2004, A14; Marian Wright Edelman, "Old South Lingers in a Legal Lynching," *Los Angeles Times*, January 22, 2004, B17; Ellen Barry, "Race, Justice Go on Trial in Sex Case," *Los Angeles Times*, February 16, 2004, Part A, 11; Ellen Barry, "Georgia's Supreme Court Reverses 10-year Sentence," *Los Angeles Times*, May 4, 2004, Part A, 16; ABC *Nightline* "Nightline America in Black and White," (11:35 p.m. ET), January 21, 2004; "Child Molesting Conviction Overturned in Georgia Classmate Case," *New York Times*, May 4, 2004.

101. The local Durham, North Carolina, NBC station at WNCN-TV broadcast coverage, which was later found at www.msnbc.msn.com/id/12039143/.

102. Edie Magnus, "What Happened at Duke?" *Dateline*, June 24 transcript; Susannah Meadows, "Duke: New Questions about Credibility," *Newsweek*, May 8, 2006; Susannah Meadows, "Lacrosse Scandal: The Duke Accuser—New Credibility Questions," *Newsweek*, June 19, 2006; "Doubts About Duke," *Newsweek*, June 29, 2006; "Doubts Raised in Duke Case," *Newsday*.

103. See Susannah Meadows and Evan Thomas, "A Troubled Spring at Duke," *Newsweek*, April 10, 2006.

104. MSNBC, *The Situation*, hosted by Tucker Carlson, April 11, 2006. See Media Matters For America at www.Media matters.org for details on the show.

105. Quoted on ABC NEWS *Primetime* (10:00 p.m. ET), "Kobe Bryant Allegations Investigated," July 17, 2003.

106. Samiha Khanna, reporter for the *News & Observer* in Raleigh, interviewed her shortly after the allegations became known. After the Duke allegations surfaced, Rony Camille, the assistant editor of the campus newspaper at the school the accuser attended, North Carolina Central University, was interviewed about the campus reaction and the reply was, "The news media here in this area has been saying that it's just been an exotic dancer, and basically, as of now, now they're making the connection that the rape occurred and now that the student was an actual N.C. Central student . . . the *Raleigh News and Observer* was the only outlet that reported that the student was from Central." Quoted on the MSNBC news program *The Abrams Report*, March 30, 2006. (Transcript accessed at www.msnbc.msn.com/id/12080770.)

107. Another incident involving a Cleveland news anchor, Sharon Reed, who is black, stripped nude on camera during a broadcast about a nude photography exhibit that featured hundreds of nude people in a public place "at the request of two white men: Steve Doerr, the station's news director, and Bill Applegate, its general manager," yet somehow Reed was the one who came under criticism. See David Carr, "When a Talking Head Becomes a Talking Body," *New York Times*, November 25, 2004. Again, the black woman is blamed even though white men were involved, even the orchestrators. Even high-profile interracial "crimes" on television involving black women come at a high price to the reputation and credibility of the black woman more than the white man/men involved. See page 275 in Valerie Smith, "Split Affinities: The Case of Interracial Rape."

108. See page 275 in Valerie Smith, "Split Affinities: The Case of Interracial Rape."

109. See Associated Press, "Duke Suspects Had Privileged upbringings," April 26, 2006. Accessed at www.msnbc.msn.com/id/12373301.

110. See Associated Press, "Duke Suspects Had Privileged Upbringings," April 26, 2006. Accessed at www.msnbc.msn.com/id/12373301.

111. Quoted in *Newsday*, "Doubts Raised in Duke Case."

112. Former black Duke basketball players, like Elton Brand, now a NBA player with the Los Angeles Clippers, were also interviewed in articles with headlines like "Ex-Duke Stars Say They Didn't Feel Racism." As Brand argues, "There are a lot of multicultural people at Duke, and everybody felt that way, not just the athletes . . . my fiancee Shahara, also went to Duke and she had friends there of all different races. She loved it there, too, and she didn't have a problem with racism, so this seems out of character." See Associated Press, "Ex-Duke Stars Say They Didn't Feel Racism," April 17, 2006. Despite these reports in 2000, a Duke online publication written by Duke students published an article, "On Duke Campus, Interracial Dating Remains Rare," quoting a student who stated, "I don't think the climate necessarily promotes interracial dating just because it is such a self-segregating campus, due to the lack of interracial couples one sees on campus, people are uncomfortable about them." "On Duke Campus, Interracial Dating Remains Rare," *Chronicle* via U-Wire. Accessed at http://news.excite.com/news/uw/000209/university-314.

113. Associated Press, "Coach K Breaks Silence on Duke Lacrosse Case," Accessed at www.msnbc.msn.com/id/13446898.

114. Feagin and Vera, *White Racism*, 119–21. Similarly, in Stratford, Connecticut, where Tammy Imre pleaded guilty to sexually assaulting her daughter's 8-year-old playmate, the executive director of the Stratford Chamber of Commerce, Laura Hoydick, defended the community as "great people and great businesses," and a former neighbor of Imre even defends her, stating, "She was always polite. She was not a bad girl. . . . I am disgusted by the way the [media] is exploiting her. I have watched her grow up. She is not a bad person." Cited in Greg Shulas, "Stratford Forced to Cope with Recent Media Frenzy," *Connecticut Post*, November 12, 2004.

115. Anne Hull, "Lacrosse Players' Case a Trial for Parents," *Washington Post*, June 10, 2006. (Accessed at www.msnbc.com.)

116. Anne Hull, "Lacrosse Players' Case a Trial for Parents," *Washington Post*, June 10, 2006. (Accessed at www.msnbc.com.)

117. Anne Hull, "Lacrosse Players' Case a Trial for Parents," *Washington Post*, June 10, 2006. (Accessed at www.msnbc.com.)

118. See transcript "Sex Assault Scandal at Duke, The Abrams Report," MSNBC. Accessed at www.msnbc.msn.com/id/12065803. During this broadcast Dan Abrams makes the following statements/questions, "How can you be so certain at this point that the perpetrators were actually members of the Duke lacrosse team?" Abrams seems to want to clear the lacrosse team or Duke students rather than prove a rape did not occur, which pursuit he begins later.

119. See Associated Press, "Officials Try to Protect Durham's Image," April 26, 2006.

120. See Associated Press, "Duke Case Reopens Wounds for Black Women," April 17, 2006. Accessed at www.msnbc.msn.com/id/12305991.

121. See Associated Press, "Duke Case Reopens Wounds for Black Women.

122. Anne Hull, "Lacrosse Players' Case a Trial for Parents," *Washington Post*, June 10, 2006. (Can be accessed at www.msnbc.com.)

123. Quoted in "Lacrosse Players Describe Spat with Strippers," NBCSports.com news services, April 27, 2006.

124. Moreover, the case was coined the "Duke Lacrosse Controversy," deemphasizing the rape allegations and also emphasizing the backlash against the district attorney in "Anything but Nifong Drive Takes Shape," noting the large numbers of people who oppose Nifong's campaign for reelection.

125. See Aaron Beard, Associated Press, "Disbarred Duke Prosecutor's Future Dim," June 18, 2007; Susan Filan, "Nifong's Punishment Is Extreme, Appropriate," June 17, 2007, www.msnbc.com; and "Prosecutor in Duke Case Disbarred by Ethics Panel," *New York Times*, June 17, 2007.

126. See transcript form Rita Cosby, *Live and Direct*, on MSNBC (9 p.m. ET), March 31, 2006.

127. See page 272–73 in Valerie Smith, "Split Affinities: The Case of Interracial Rape."

128. Lipsitz 1998, 115, citing Lewis Gordon, "A Lynching Well Lost," *Black Scholar* 25, 4 (1995): 37.

129. Lipsitz 1998, 116–17. These cases, especially the criminal ones that involve interracial sex and celebrities, should highlight how someone not famous would fare, if celebrities enter the fight of their lives when accused of raping or murdering whites.

130. See Kobena Mercer, "Skin Head Sex Thing: Racial Difference and the Homoerotic Imaginary," *Competing Glances* 16 (Spring 1992): 12.

131. Smith, 275; See Valerie Smith, "Split Affinities: The Case of Interracial Rape," and Angela Davis, "Rape, Racism and the Myth of the Black Rapist," in *Women Race and Class* (New York: Random House, 1981), 172–201 for a discussion of how rape laws were primarily tools of white, upper-class men to protect their property, which included white women, especially since rape laws were rarely used to patrol elite white men's behavior but a tool white men used to police men of color's (men from lower classes) behavior and interactions with white women.

132. Joane Nagel, *Race, Ethnicity, and Sexuality: Intimate Intersections, Forbidden Frontiers* (New York: Oxford University Press, 2003), 28.

CHAPTER SIX

~

Multiracial Utopias: Youth, Sports, and Music

In contemporary media culture, there are intersecting realms in popular culture, particularly for the youth generations in music and sports on the radio, Internet, and television/film, which are often described as encouraging multiracialism. It is not uncommon in contemporary music videos or sports entertainment to see racially and ethnically diverse men and women gyrating together on the dance floor, yet the messages about interracial relationships may be less clear. Media reports often champion the younger generations enthralled with hip-hop music, YouTube, and MySpace as a multiracial utopia where different races and colors mesh. For example, in a 2003 *Time* article, "Color-Blind Love," the authors Tim Padgett and Frank Sikora argue,

> Young people, however, having grown up with the racially inclusive ethos of hip-hop and who are comfortable meeting potential mates via the racially neutral Internet, are even more color-blind than their elders when it comes to matters of the heart.[1]

Similarly in 1999, the *New York Times* ran a piece on "A TV Generation Is Seeing Beyond Color," which argued that young whites watch all-black comedies and are "casually crossing the racial divide."[2] Television show *ER* executive producer David Zabel, while discussing pairing interracial couples on his show, says that younger people do not notice racial difference and "they don't draw those lines. Watch MTV, and you'll see videos with all kind of people interacting."[3] Furthermore, popular culture geared toward youth, whether it be films or commercials, often merge music and sports,

159

such as the 2006 Disney film, *High School Musical,* which has a multiracial cast who deal with high school cliques for the picture-perfect conclusion that the most popular basketball player and the smartest student can come together to star in the school musical and unite the school. White suburban teens' consumption of hip-hop and rap has also been linked to the growing acceptance of interracial relationships. Moreover, these realms are often considered diverse, or even black-dominated, especially certain genres of music like rap and hip-hop and sports culture in basketball and football. Rap artists like 50 Cent and Jay-Z, despite the controversy over references to drugs, violence, and sex, are viewed as crossovers because they appeal to white and Asian audiences as well as Latino and black audiences. As Herman Gray argues, "Representations of black youth culture are major conduits through which the commodification of multiculturalism—sexuality, youth, race and gender—proceed."[4]

Therefore it is important to look critically at these places we see or hear about multiracialism and race mixing, such as sports, music, and other popular culture geared toward the younger generations and the association of these music and movies with black culture.[5] While youth cultures are diverse, hip-hop music does not represent all youth culture, and hip-hop music and culture is often erroneously used to represent black culture. It is important to consider the dominant role that music and sports play in the popular culture of the younger generations and the cultural messages about interracial relationships, particularly black-white relationships, that are given in popular culture geared toward the under-30 generation.[6] Through the chapters looking at the separate realms of television, film, and news media, there were certain types of stories about interracial liaisons, with very clear underlying messages. Yet does there exist any different representations, particularly in popular culture? Looking at these two overlapping areas in sports and music geared toward the younger generations, does it represent breaking boundaries and breaking down the taboos of interracial intimacy? First, I will explore two sports-related media incidents involving interracial pairings, including the 2004 Super Bowl halftime fiasco with Janet Jackson, and the responses to these incidents. Then, using an analysis of images and discourses from various media outlets such as MTV, BET, radio stations, and films/magazines that are part of the hip-hop culture, the role these mediums play in putting forth messages about interracial relationships and their acceptability will be explored. What are the common discourses surrounding crossing the color line in these contemporary venues, and do the messages change depending on who is producing it? Given that much of hip-hop culture is written and produced by African Americans and yet also controlled, regulated, and under white surveillance, what representations emerge and how do different audiences receive them in different social locations? In this context we will explore the different meanings and interpretations of interracial relationships among media directed at the younger generations. Are interracial relationships acceptable in these realms or is it only interracial sex, even just the illusion of interracial sex, and under what circumstances?

Crossing the Line in Sports

Since professional and college sports were desegregated and games have been televised, sports like basketball, football, baseball, and even more recently tennis and golf depict whites, blacks, Latinos, and Asians playing together. Media reports often argue that sports is a place where race doesn't matter, despite the still persistent inequality in minority access to coaching and ownership roles as well as the exploitation of minority athletes in college. Sports is highly racialized, with race-specific stereotypes of black masculinity and physical prowess on display. Yet in terms of interracial sex, it is widely argued that athletes, particularly black athletes, date interracially. Some of the high-profile cases and interracial events addressed last chapter involved black athletes like Jack Johnson, O. J. Simpson, and Kobe Bryant and their alleged white female victims. Yet further illustrating the contradictory attitudes toward interracial relationships, in September 2005, the media reported that the popular New York Yankees baseball player Derek Jeter received hate mail with articles like, "Hate Mailer Targets Jeter: Sicko Rants at Jeter," which reported that "a poison-pen racist being hunted for threatening dozens of prominent African-American men because of their interracial marriages,"[7] with the news reports discussing these hate letters as an extreme case, as if opposition to interracial unions no longer existed. Other black athletes such as Miami Dolphins defensive end Jason Taylor and tennis star James Blake's parents also received letters, which the FBI believes comes from the same white man, though the letter is signed "angry white woman."

In 2004, there were two sports-related media spectacles that occurred involving interracial pairings during the Super Bowl halftime show and a Monday Night Football spot that pushed the boundaries of color blindness and multiracialism and for debatable reasons sounded the alarms of indecency, morality, and family values. It is no coincidence that these two incidents that caused so much controversy involved the illusion of interracial sex. During the MTV-produced Super Bowl halftime show on CBS, Janet Jackson, who is black, and Justin Timberlake, who is white, performed together. While singing a song that promises "I'll have you naked by the end of this song," Timberlake ripped off Jackson's top covering, exposing her breast. This incident and the ensuing response bring to light the contradictions of color blindness and the limits of acceptability that still operate. In a color-blind world, we would see a superstar like Janet Jackson, a black woman, performing opposite Justin Timberlake, a white man. The sexually suggestive lyrics and sensual dancing were safely contained in the space of prime-time television and even within the safer space of American nationhood, since it was during the Super Bowl, a national past time. Their performance was designed to show how race does not matter because if it did then we wouldn't see a white man and black woman singing in the halftime show of one of the biggest events in American sports and media cultures. Yet by all accounts something went wrong, or as it was called, a "wardrobe malfunction," which sparked outrage and uproar over issues of family values, morality, and censorship. The Super Bowl incident was deemed a "new low for prime time television,"[8] and the FCC charged Viacom's MTV Networks with a $550,000 fine.[9] Michael Powell, the FCC chairman, described the Super Bowl performance: "To have that kind of thing just burst into your living room, you know, with no warning, no expectation, was—was really shocking."[10] Numerous references were made to MTV producing the halftime show, and as *Washington Post* columnist Sally Jenkins commented, "If the NFL is going to go into the entertainment business with MTV, this is the kind of thing that they can potentially expect and they knew that."[11]

A similar outrage followed a Monday Night Football commercial, particularly from FCC Chairman Michael Powell, which featured black Philadelphia Eagles receiver Terrell Owens and white *Desperate Housewives'* television star Nicolette Sheridan alone in a empty locker room, when a towel-clad Sheridan suggestively asks Owens to skip the game for her. He initially declines stating that the team needs him, but after she drops her towel showing her naked from the back waist up, he happily agrees, and she jumps into his arms. This Monday Night Football skit with Nicolette Sheridan/Terrell Owens was also deemed "inappropriate for family viewing"[12] and "at least one team owner thought it more egregious than Janet Jackson's baring her breast." Yet if sexually suggestive content was the problem, there was no outrage over the airing of a "Cialis advertisement that promised men 36 hours of relief from impotence, then warned that if they should experience an erection for four hours straight, they should seek 'immediate medical care.'"[13] Moreover, every televised football game shows scantily clad cheerleaders bouncing around with no complaints, which points to the multiracial, sexually suggestive, crossracial integration of these incidents being at the heart of the problem.[14] These two "incidents" highlighted how problematic the illusion of interracial sex can still be. The "public outrage" included a reported 50,000 complaints to the FCC by the Wednesday after the Monday night airing and complaints to Terrell Owens's Web site and agent's office.

After the two events, the responses of those involved differed. Following the Super Bowl, Janet Jackson backed out of the Grammys where she was scheduled to perform, but Justin Timberlake did attend. In these responses the blame is placed on Janet Jackson for her breast being exposed by Timberlake. On *Entertainment Tonight*, an unidentified woman says, "You got nasty with Ms. Jackson," and Timberlake responds, "Hey man, it's every man's dream."[15] While Janet Jackson apologized and took full responsibility in a videotaped statement that was released two days after the halftime show, Timberlake expressed embarrassment, "I was completely shocked and—and appalled and all. . . . I was under the impression that what was going to be revealed . . . was a red brassiere."[16] According to a CBS statement, Janet Jackson and Justin Timberlake were informed that they could still participate in the Grammys if they agreed "to apologize on the air" for the Super Bowl halftime show, which Timberlake accepted and apologized on air, while Jackson declined.[17] Jackson was interviewed in *Ebony* magazine ten days after the incident, and she called "The media onslaught . . .'unfair,' 'blown out of proportion,' and 'racist.'"[18] Timberlake never seemed to feel a media backlash and continues to make light of the situation, most recently as the host of the 2008 ESPN sports award program, where the image of him revealing her breast flashed on screen numerous times during his opening comments.

Yet at that time the media made an immediate connection between the two separate incidents.[19] The *New York Times* reported media personality Rush Limbaugh's response to the Sheridan-Owens encounter, which reminded him of the Kobe Bryant case:

> I was stunned, I literally could not believe what I had seen. At various places on the Net you can see the video of this, and she's buck naked, folks. I mean when they dropped the towel she's naked. . . . I mean there are some guys with their kids that sit down to watch Monday Night Football.[20]

While CBS was fined for the Super Bowl incident, ABC was not fined for the Monday Night Football spot, because "the scene was no racier than what's routinely seen on soap operas . . . although the scene apparently is intended to be titillating, it simply is not graphic or explicit enough to be indecent under our standard."[21] This further highlights how seeing a black man—particularly a defiant, strong, aggressive black man—seduced by an equally assertive, sexually confident, attractive blonde woman on prime-time television is too much for mainstream America to handle. A few reporters, such as Bernie Lincicome of the *Rocky Mountain News* and Grahame L. Jones

of the *Los Angeles Times*, noted the hypocrisy that NFL cheerleaders "are every bit as suggestive as naked actresses in locker rooms,"[22] yet these reporters
did not point out how the interracial pairing undoubtedly had some effect on
the reaction. The Indianapolis Colts Tony Dungy, who is African American,
spoke to the press about why he found the sketch racially offensive: "To
me, that's the first thing I thought of as an African American. I think it's
stereotypical in looking at the players, and on the heels of the Kobe Bryant
incident I think it's very insensitive."[23] While both Tony Dungy and Rush
Limbaugh compared it to the Kobe Bryant rape allegations, there is a difference between the white shock that can be read as disgust at a black man with
white woman and black opposition that can be read as fear of repercussions
from interracial allegations.[24]

The media referenced the racial aspect of the Monday Night Football
sketch in reference to Dungy's comments.[25] William Rhoden, a sports reporter for the *New York Times*, wrote about Dungy's comments and the racial
dynamic, but this is his analysis:

> I wasn't offended that it depicted a white woman seducing a black man. White
> women and black men have been jumping into one another's arms for cen-
> turies . . . what I found troubling was . . . a biased system that holds African
> Americans to different standards of behavior . . . judged more harshly for the
> same offenses and given less credit for the same accomplishments . . . a black
> woman (referring to Janet Jackson) has her clothes ripped off by a white man
> and she's demonized. A naked white woman jumps into a black man's arms,
> and he apologizes.[26]

Rhodes is one of the few media persons to recognize and report this contradiction, but even he seems to miss how the interracial aspect contributed to the
problems. Given the patterns of representation discussed throughout television, film, and media, it is not surprising that Justin Timberlake, as a white
man, would not be blamed and would be protected, while Janet Jackson is held
responsible and her credibility immediately questioned. Similarly, with the
Monday Night Football skit, Owens, as a black man, is blamed as the sexual aggressor, even though it is clearly Sheridan, the white woman, who propositions
him. Would it have mattered as much if a black woman jumped in Owens's
arms or if a white performer's top had been ripped off by Timberlake—would
there have been such certainty that it was staged? Yet Rhoden concludes,
"With all due respect to Dungy, children know better than their parents that
much of what they see and hear is an act. . . . Owens is narrowing the gap
between the 'Pimp My Ride' culture (a show on MTV) and the stodgy NFL."[27]
Much of the outrage over the Super Bowl halftime show where Timberlake

removed Jackson's top also featured other acts that the FCC found offensive, including Nelly, a black singer grabbing his crotch, and what was described by a senior NFL league official that MTV, "which has a narrow agenda to reach young viewers," was the problem.[28] Let's see if Rhodes's optimism for the younger generations and the MTV hip-hop nation is warranted.

A Multiracial Music Nation?

Widespread media accounts and experts present music and the younger generation as a multiracial world, breaking barriers and boundaries, from black music mogul Sean "Puffy" Combs partying with Donald Trump to Jay-Z producing music with white rock group Linkin Park to the success of white rapper Eminem and the crossover appeal of black singers and rappers. Yet this multiracial accord is tenuous at best, as numerous incidents show us. The Justin Timberlake/Janet Jackson Super Bowl halftime incident shows just how tenuous this interracial harmony and acceptance is. Given that this was a musical performance, radio stations across the country also debated the "wardrobe malfunction," yet there was a slightly different response among the self-defined urban radio stations and hip-hop music personalities. Justin Timberlake had previously experienced a level of acceptance among black hip-hop stations, not necessarily just for his music and dancing, which was definitely influenced by African American styles, but also his deference to African American greats. Radio personality Miss Info, on New York's hip-hop radio station Hot 97, commented that the radio audience "feel[s] like he's been accepted by a multicultural audience, and they want him to stand by his multicultural musical co-workers."[29] On the VH1 *Ego Trip's Race-O-Rama* documentary, Michael Eric Dyson remarks that Justin Timberlake "sold Janet out" because he still appeared at the Grammy awards and because of his comments about being appalled and implying that he was better than Jackson by stating, "I've had a good year. . . . I don't feel I need publicity like this."[30] As Wendy Williams, a popular black media personality who has a nationally syndicated radio show stated, the audience will "support Janet, but they'll look at Justin and say, 'Your ghetto pass has been revoked. You're no longer an honorary brother.'"[31] Not long after the Super Bowl incident, Timberlake backed out of cohosting a *Motown 45* tribute because there was a massive campaign by a coalition of African American organizations to remove him, stating,

> the selection of Timberlake as a co-host of this Motown special is a cultural insult to the black community. This special celebrating the success of the legendary label, should not be compromised in the pursuit of a crossover audience.[32]

These responses show how fragile the acceptability of interracial pairings are in hip-hop culture, which becomes more apparent when a wardrobe malfunction like this brings the tension to light.

Another recent controversy in the music scene occurred in 2003 over the white rapper Eminem's early recording of a song in which he talks degradingly about black women. The owners of a popular hip-hop magazine *The Source*, who were involved in a court battle with Eminem, released a ten-year-old amateur tape on which he made racist and degrading statements about black women. In the 1993 tape, Eminem rapped,

> Black girls only want you money. . . . Black girls and white girls just don't mix because black girls are dumb and white girls are good chicks. White girls are good. I like white girls . . . all over the world. White girls are fine and they blow my mind. And that's why I'm here now, telling you this rhyme 'cause black girls, I really don't like.[33]

On another track he rhymes, "All the girls I like to bone/have the big butts, not they don't/'Cause I don't like that nigger shit . . . black girls are bitches."[34] Eminem responded, "(this) was something I made out of anger, stupidity and frustration when I was a teenager. I'd just broken up with my girlfriend who was African-American, and I reacted like the angry, stupid kid I was. I hope people will take it for the foolishness that it was."[35] The magazine owner's attempts, which even led to legal battles to discredit Eminem as a racist who has co-opted hip-hop at the expense of black people, were met with mixed responses from hip-hop and black communities.[36] While the mainstream media barely registered the controversy in its coverage, music magazines, radio stations, and Internet blogs covered it extensively. Some argued that Eminem should be boycotted and his racist comments about black women should not be overlooked, such as former hip-hop mogul Suge Knight in the *XXL* hip-hop magazine and black scholar Michael Eric Dyson on NPR's *Tavis Smiley* show.[37] Yet for the most part this tape was largely ignored, or dismissed, as evidenced by Russell Simmons, the owner of the powerful Def Jam Records, and a top rapper Jay-Z's public comments supporting Eminem.[38] Eminem was not the target of music attacks by other artists common in this music genre, and he continued to record music.

While Eminem may not have been penalized for his early lyrics because of the support of prominent African American rap moguls such as Russell Simmons and because of his young age of fifteen when he made them, I argue that the overall message that he will not chase after black women is also an important factor. The racialized and gendered lyrics are key: for example, would it have been as accepted if Eminem had been rapping that he loves to use black women as sex objects or if he was degrading black men as "stupid" or weak? In some ways Eminem not wanting black women makes him more acceptable because of the taboo against interracial sex, and it shows the gendered contradiction where black men degrade black women but that is probably different than if Eminem did. Also, the overall acceptance of degrading women in general in songs may make it less offensive than if he had degraded black men.[39]

As these two incidents illustrate, the multiracialism of music and hip-hop is still racialized on many levels. Despite music videos that are often touted for their multiracial dance scenes, the limits of interracial acceptance are often debated on the top hip-hop stations, on popular Internet gossip sites, and even in the music lyrics of popular performers. Interracial relationships are routinely referenced on hip-hop stations, which are often referred to as urban or black stations. Wendy Williams, a popular black syndicated radio talk personality and television talk show host, refers to the danger of interracial sex, especially for certain celebrities. For example, Williams and her supporting radio staff were talking about Lindsay Lohan being spotted with a prominent black singer. Williams joked that Lohan "had it in her contract" that she wouldn't publicly be with a black man, since it "wouldn't be good" for her career, and it "wouldn't be good" for the black singer's music credibility and career either. She has also discussed her own uncomfortability and inability to be involved interracially because her perception that whites will use a racial slur at some point.[40] Other stations like Hot 97 in New York City and Power 106 in Los Angeles often joke about which music artists are involved interracially, or disparagingly discuss interracial hookups. While mainstream (white) entertainment blogs and Web sites avoid ever mentioning race even if showing interracial couples, popular Internet celebrity blogs and gossip sites that identify as hip-hop, urban, or black gossip sites regularly post pictures of celebrity interracial hookups or breakups under the heading of the "swirl,"[41] a slang term for interracial relationships, and often lament the occurrence of these unions.[42] These hip-hop radio stations and Internet sites clearly mark interracial unions and label them as problematic or humorous, while mainstream media, as we discussed in the last chapter, problematize interracial relationships too yet do it using color-blind language.

Despite the diversity of people involved in hip-hop as performers and consumers, the importance of race, especially in attraction and intimate relationships, is often referenced. Some of the most successful hip-hop performers who enjoy widespread success with white audiences as well as audiences of color, such as Grammy award–winners Kanye West, Alicia Keys, Ludacris, and Mary J. Blige, have explicitly written about opposition to interracial relationships. Many black hip-hop artists affirm their own preference for women of color and aversion to interracial dating, such as a popular song in 2005 by Ludacris which discusses the beautiful women around the world, yet ends by saying the best women are in Africa.[43] The importance of celebrating successful intraracial relationships is emphasized by other performers such as Alicia Keys, who has a white mother yet identifies as black, and released a song in 2005 about "Love," celebrating successful black couples.[44] Songs also point out the problems with those who do date interracially, such as singer Me'Shell Ndegeocello, who writes in her song, "Excuse Me, Does the White Woman Go Better with the Brooks Brothers Suit?" In the critically acclaimed billboard hit "Golddigger" by Kanye West and Oscar-winner Jamie Foxx, West sings about women who want men for their money, ending with a frame about a (black) woman sticking by a man as he works his way up at a fast food restaurant, but when he makes it "he'll leave your ass for a white girl." In his follow-up song "Touch the Sky," West continues the theme, casting his love interest as white actress Pamela Anderson and his former girlfriend played by a black woman, who confronts him with her black friend about being with a white woman (though the song lyrics do not address it).[45] The Grammy-winning, platinum-selling R & B singer Mary J. Blige, who has been recognized in many venues, has a song on her 2005 album entitled "Ain't Really Love," where she sings about being in a relationship where the man is never satisfied, "and then you came with a whole 'nother level of bullshit saying you wouldn't have to deal with this from a white chick." These songs contain the same messages about interracial relationships that black men who are successful often turn to white women, which can be distressing to black families and the black women who are left behind.

Similarly, on cable music channel VH1, a documentary, *Race-O-Rama*, explored issues of race and sex in music, featuring various radio and music personalities. One part of the documentary addresses interracial dating and shows a popular female rapper, MC Lyte, who describes it as "sewing" your "interracial oats." Similar to the ideas that surfaced in film comedies geared toward black audiences, the documentary pokes fun at the idea that black men too often chase after white women and that white women want a stereotypical black "thug."[46]

Reality series such as MTV's *The Real World* and VH1 celebrity *The Surreal Life* place a group of strangers together in a house for a specific period of time, often purposefully casting certain mixtures of individuals of different races, ethnicities, and sexual identities to accentuate the drama, which includes interracial liaisons. For example, in 2004 the VH1 celebrity reality show *The Surreal Life* featured a racially mixed group of former celebrities, including Flavor Flav, a black rapper from the controversial Public Enemy, and Brigitte Nielsen, a blond European woman who had been married to Sylvester Stallone. On the show, they appeared to begin a relationship, to the disgust and delight of viewers. Based on viewers' strong love/hate relationships with their relationship, VH1 introduced a subsequent show, *Strange Love*, which showed Flav and Brigitte exploring a relationship together and exploited the perceived absurdity of this relationship between a short, black, former militant rap icon and a tall, Nordic, washed-up actress. In one show, Flav brings Nielsen on stage at a Public Enemy concert, which is the first time a white woman was on stage with them, and he kisses her in front of the whole audience, to the dismay of Public Enemy and many concert attendees. Still, the opposition of black communities is highlighted.

The unacceptability of interracial relationships was also highlighted in a MTV-produced film, *Save the Last Dance*, about an interracial relationship. When Derek becomes involved with a white girl, his friends question him on why he hasn't been around as much and ask, "Are you tapping that white girl? . . . that's why you don't have no time for your boys no more . . . too busy snowflaking (a term for engaging with a white person), and if that's the case you best be watching your back, 'cause white women don't bring nothing but trouble," expressing their opposition to their friend being with a white woman. It is significant that black opposition is clearly portrayed on-screen and in song, even exaggerated for dramatic or comedic purposes, while white opposition is rarely seen or heard. This illustrates the powerful influence of white writers, producers, and promoters who maintain the idea that race does not matter by using a color-blind discourse and situating black communities as the source of opposition and racism.[47] Yet this movie appeals to a wide audience because it addresses opposition to interracial dating that many can relate to, yet it does not implicate whites in the opposition. It also appeals to those who date interracially because it shows an interracial couple and the movie ends with an individualistic message of color-blind love, not unlike the idea that any individual regardless of race has the same opportunities in society. Therefore, *Save the Last Dance* ends up as a picture-perfect example of the multiracial utopia the media points to, yet underlying the multiracial world put forth are all the old stereotypes of pregnant black teens, criminal young black men, and dangerous black neighborhoods, with one "exceptional" black young man who rises above his failing black family and community to excel in school and date a sweet, innocent white girl.

Many such as David Schwartz, chief curator of film at the American Museum of the Moving Image in New York, argues, "One thing I think is great about teen movies is issues of class and race are right there on the surface," such as recent teen movies like *Save the Last Dance*, *O* (a 2001 boarding-school remake of Shakespeare's *Othello*), *Cruel Intentions*, and *Romeo Must Die*.[48] Yet these representations still reproduce the idea of interracial relationships as problematic and dangerous. Furthermore, even in music and films geared toward younger generations, the idea of difference between racial groups, particularly blacks and whites, is highlighted. *Save the Last Dance* emphasizes the idea of difference when Derek's sister Chenille invites Sara to a hip-hop club and Chenille needs to make her over before she looks appropriate to go in the club. While Sara is a quiet, studious ballet dancer, Chenille and the other black girls are portrayed as loud, academically challenged club divas. In the film *Beauty Shop*, about a multiracial beauty shop in a predominantly black area, the white hairdresser is portrayed as naïve in relation to the women of color and is often ridiculed, particularly when she mentions black men. These ideas of difference are also played up with the black actress, musical performer, and media personality Queen Latifah, who often crosses boundaries between mainstream (white) popular culture, hip-hop culture, and black popular culture. In 1995, Gray described Queen Latifah as one of a number of rap artists who "cleverly use the media, especially music video, to transform and reposition images of black menace and threat into expressions of affirmation and defiance . . . without apology or regard for the public codes of civility or the culture of politeness with respect to race that so saturates public discourse."[49] Having briefly hosted a television talk show, Queen Latifah is now best known for her roles in a number of mainstream films, particularly for her supporting role in *Chicago* and her starring role in *Bringing Down the House*. This film plays on the comedy of racial difference and unacceptance with a stereotypical representation of Queen Latifah as a big, loud, finger-snapping, low-class black woman who is pursued by a short, white, wealthy lawyer. Multiracial casts may be common in films geared toward the under-25 MTV/BET generation like *Bring It On* and *Soul Plane*, yet this does not mean they don't reinforce the idea that there are significant racial differences and that interracial romantic pairings are still rare.

Still, the *notion* of multiracialism and consuming color as exotic is increasingly popular. As Amy Barnett, *Teen People*'s managing editor, says, "We're seeing more of a desire for the exotic, left-of-center beauty that transcends race or class . . . represents the new reality of America which includes considerable mixing."[50] Similarly, Elise Koseff, the vice president of a New York company that represents children for television, J. Mitchell Management, describes how racially ambiguous individuals are in demand, citing recent casting calls the agency has gotten, such as a call for a boy "Zach, 12 to 14, African-American. Zach's father is Caucasian" for a Nickelodeon show

Unfabulous.[51] Ivan Bart, the director of IMG Models, describes a model who represents a leading cosmetics brand as ideal because she is "a woman of color . . . but look at her and begin to play a guessing game: Is she Mexican, Spanish, Russian? The fact that you can't be sure is part of her seductiveness."[52] Many shows and films geared toward the tween crowd embrace the idea of multiracialism by featuring racially diverse casts, yet the romantic pairing occurs along racial lines with films such as Disney's *High School Musical* or *Camp Rock*, or TV shows such as Disney's *Hannah Montana* and *The Suite Life of Zack & Cody* or Nickelodeon's *Zoey 101* and *Drake & Josh*. Thus, there is a desire for the illusion of multiracialism without it actually happening.

Conclusion

The underlying beliefs about interracial relationships depicted in music, sports, and popular culture geared toward youth are often ambivalent and still emphasize stereotypes of difference and opposition, even while attempting to celebrate the meshing of different races and cultures. Multiracialism and interracial couples are more accepted when they remain outside of mainstream culture, which also points to why cultural realms that are identified as black- or minority-dominated may be better able to incorporate interracial couples. As Samuels wrote in 1991, but still has relevance, "Rap's appeal to whites rested in its evocation of an age old image of blackness: a foreign sexually charged and criminal underworld against which the norms of white society are defined, and by extension, through which they may be defied."[53] This increased visibility and engagement in interracial unions does not necessarily signal racial progress or a lasting relationship but possibly just a temporary trend or fad, similar to the 1920s era of the Harlem Renaissance and the white fascination with "slumming." As Gray argued in 1995 about the emergence of literal and suggestive sexual movements of black popular culture dance, which were viewed as particularly dangerous and disturbing to white society, "this disturbance is not so much about the place of the erotic and the sexual in black popular culture" but how black popular culture is tied to moral panics over AIDS, teen pregnancy,[54] and I would add, sexual deviance, which can include interracial sex, group sex, lesbian sex, and public exposure. Media reports may herald the multiracial and racially ambiguous individuals popping up in movies, videos, and sports culture, yet their existence does not symbolize racial harmony or acceptance. As the Super Bowl halftime "wardrobe malfunction" and other incidents discussed show, these representations are allowed in very specific ways as long as they are "safely contained," but any deviation can cause outrage and disruption.

For example, Janet Jackson and Justin Timberlake could be tolerated, even indulged, as part of a hip-hop Super Bowl halftime show, even by mainstream audiences, until the threat of interracial sex became too real when Jackson's breast was revealed by Timberlake. There seems to be a desire for the illusion of multiracialism without it actually happening. While there may be some variation in images and sounds, the underlying messages remain where inter-racial relationships are problematized even if for different reasons, whiteness is not challenged, and black opposition and prejudice is made visible while white racism is allowed to stay hidden. Even when there is change, the battle over representation remains, as we see how 2008 presidential candidate Barack Obama, who is widely supported by the younger generation, is first imagined in the media as questionably "not black enough" because of his white mother and biracial identity, yet within months as he became closer to securing the Democratic nomination for president, the question became is he "too black," which was also framed in questions about his citizenship in accusations about his (lack of) patriotism and his father's religion (Muslim). Will there be a new era of representations given the generation of youth growing up today, under President Barack Obama, and will the representa-tions get better or worse? In the last chapter I will explore just what better representations might look like.

Notes

1. Tim Padgett and Frank Sikora, "Color-Blind Love," *Time*, May 12, 2003; See also Grace Aduroja, "Teen Movies Embracing Interracial Couples," *Times-Picayune*, July 27, 2001.

2. Nancy Hass, "A TV Generation Is Seeing beyond Color," *New York Times*, February 22, 1998, Section 2.

3. As cited in Ann Oldenburg, "Love Is No Longer Color-Coded on TV," *USA Today*, December 20, 2005.

4. Gray 2005 [1995], xvi.

5. I do not include a discussion of films geared toward Latinos and Asians or mov-ies produced/written/directed by Latinos or Asians in this section because they are rare and do not necessarily discuss interracial relationships.

6. It is important to note that much of hip-hop culture is written and produced by African Americans, and yet also controlled, regulated, and under white surveillance. The same can be argued about professional sports, which is a multimedia enterprise and is often dominated by black players, particularly in basketball and football, but controlled by white team owners and advertising agencies that control their images.

7. See *Daily News* (New York), September 26, 2005, "Hate Mailer Targets Jeter."

8. See Fox, *The Big Story with John Gibson*, February 11, 2004.

9. See Jube Shiver, Jr., "FCC Punishes Viacom for Indecency," *Los Angeles Times*, November 24, 2004.

10. Quoted on CBS *Early Show*, headline "Janet Jackson Says Super Bowl Halftime Incident Was Planned after Final Rehearsals," (7:00 a.m. ET), February 3, 2004.

11. Quoted on CBS *Evening News with Dan Rather* (6:30 p.m. ET), February 3, 2004.

12. See Larry Stewart, "Antics Not Suitable for Younger, If Any, Viewers," *Los Angeles Times*, November 26, 2004; also Judy Battista, "ABC Puts NFL in Desperate Situation," *New York Times*, November 17, 2004; and Associated Press, "ABC Apologizes for Steamy MNF Intro," November 2, 2004, accessed at www.msnbc.com.

13. Alessandra Stanley, "A Flash of Flesh: CBS Again Is in Denial," *New York Times* February 3, 2004, where she highlights this contradiction but does not critique why the outrage was focused on Janet Jackson.

14. After the Monday Night Football clip aired, news reports cited that the "Federal Communication Commission announced (Wednesday) that it would examine a television promotion for the ABC drama *Desperate Housewives* after viewers complained about the spot's depiction of an apparently nude actress." Jube Shiver, "FCC to Examine ABC TV Spot," *Los Angeles Times*, November 18, 2004, Part C, 4.

15. See Transcript from CBS *Morning News*, February 4, 2004.

16. See Transcript from CBS *Morning News*, February 5, 2004.

17. See Alessandra Stanley, "Clothing On, Lips Buttoned," *New York Times*, February 9, 2004.

18. Quoted in Lynn Norment, "Janet Speaks," *Ebony*, April 2004.

19. See Sam Farmer, "ABC Apologizes for Steamy Scene," *Los Angeles Times*, November 17, 2004.

20. Frank Rich, "The Great Indecency Hoax," *New York Times*, November 28, 2004. See also Fox *Hannity and Colmes*, February 2, 2004, and February 4, 2004; and Fox *O'Reilly Factor*, February 2, 2004, for similar discussions of the disgust these white men felt over the Super Bowl Janet Jackson incident.

21. See Associated Press, "FCC Says Nothing Indecent about Sheridan: Regulators Won't Fine ABC for Racy 'Monday Night Football' Spot," www.msnbc.com, March 14, 2005.

22. See Grahame L. Jones, "ABC Must Have Been Really Desperate," *Los Angeles Times*, November 22, 2004.

23. William C. Rhoden, "In 'Monday Night' Fallout, a Deeper Racial Issue," *New York Times*, November 21, 2004.

24. In my work on societal views on black-white interracial couples, I argue that whites interviewed express opposition to interracial couples in color-blind language, but it is still based on racism and beliefs of inferiority. Blacks interviewed vocalized problems they had with interracial relationships, yet it is based on interracial symbols such as the devaluation of blackness, internalization of racism, and detrimental effects on black communities, but they still also knew and loved numerous family members who had married interracially and had multiracial family members. See

Navigating Interracial Borders: Black-White Couples and Their Social Worlds (Rutgers, 2005).

25. For example, on Fox *News Watch*, November 20, 2004, one of the guests, Cal Thomas, said, "Nobody has brought up the interracial thing . . ." and Eric Burns, the host, ends this possibility by replying, "Actually, Tony Dungy . . . brought up the racial aspect . . . so lots of objections." Also there was an article posted online on the sports network ESPN Web site by freelance journalist Aaron Kuriloff, "The Racial Undercurrent," (accessed February 3, 2005, at http://sports.espn.go.com/espn /print?id=1983393&type=story) wrote about the issue of interracial relations, but argued "America was not ready to see a white woman portrayed in assignation with a black man. . . ."

26. William C. Rhoden, "In 'Monday Night' Fallout, a Deeper Racial Issue," *New York Times*, November 21, 2004.

27. William C. Rhoden, "In 'Monday Night' Fallout, a Deeper Racial Issue."

28. See Bill Carter and Richard Sandomir, "Pro Football: Halftime-Show Fallout Includes FCC Inquiry," February 3, 2004. See also Alessandra Stanley, "A Flash of Flesh: CBS Again Is in Denial," *New York Times*, February 3, 2004, wrote "and one can understand the league's confusion. Does anyone who loves the CBS hit *Everybody Loves Raymond* enjoy watching the hip-hop singer Nelly repeatedly grab his crotch?"

29. Quoted from Rafer GuzmanTimberlakes LoyaltyNewsday, February 11, 2004.

30. Guzman, "Black Music Fans Question Timberlake's Loyalty."

31. Guzman, "Black Music Fans Question Timberlake's Loyalty."

32. Quoted in Lawrence Van Gelder, "The Arts/Cultural Desk," *New York Times*, February 26, 2004.

33. Lyrics quoted in Kelefa Sanneh, "Unguarded Lyrics Embarrass Eminem," *New York Times*, November 20, 2003. See also Glenn Gamboa, "Tape of Slurs Ramps Up Squabble between Eminem and *The Source*," *Milwaukee Journal Sentinel*, November 20, 2003.

34. Quoted in N'Gai Croal and Mark Starr, "Newsmakers," *Newsweek*, December 1, 2003.

35. Lola Ogunnaike, "Rivals Call Eminem Racist over Lyrics from the Past," *New York Times*, November 19, 2003.

36. Not surprisingly, these representations produce different effects and meanings for "differently situated publics."

37. See transcript for the "Michael Eric Dyson: Eminem's Racist Rap," *Tavis Smiley*, November 20, 2003, at www.npr.org, the 2005 October XXL magazine, and Gregory Kane, "Why Do Black Rappers Give Eminem a Free Pass for Dissing Black Women?" www.blackamericaweb.com, September 21, 2005.

38. This story was covered in articles such as Michael Brick, "Lyrical Judge Praises Eminem in Lyrics Fight," *New York Times*, June 10, 2004; Marian Liu, "Eminem Apparently Being Forgiven for Racial Slur," *Pittsburgh Post-Gazette*, November 28, 2003; Lola Ogunnaike, "Rivals Call Eminem Racist over Lyrics from the Past," *New York*

Times, November 19, 2003; Chris Pizzello, "Judge Rules for Eminem in Magazine Flap," *USA Today,* June 10, 2004; and NPR *Tavis Smiley* (9:00 a.m. ET on November 20, 2003); as well as in other publications and programs such as *BET Nightly News, Boston Herald; CBS Nightly News; Daily News; Denver Post; Houston Chronicle; Milwaukee Journal Sentinel; MTV News; Pittsburgh Post Gazette; VH1 News; Vibe Magazine; Washington Post,* and *XXL* magazine.

39. This debate over who can use what words was raised during the Isiah Thomas sexual harassment suit where Thomas asserted that because he was a black man it was different and less offensive if he called a black woman a "bitch" than if a white man did.

40. She made these comments on March 30, 2006, but she routinely discusses interracial relationships in-depth or even in a passing comment about the problems or ridiculousness of interracial unions.

41. "The swirl" was discussed in an interview by James Hill, a staff writer for Black Entertainment Television Web site, of the black actor Blair Underwood. For example, Hill asks Underwood about being cast opposite the white actress Heather Locklear in the TV series *LAX* and whether his character was "written Black" as well as questions about the differences "working on Black shows vs. ones pitched to a more diverse audience." Hill also specifically asks, "OK, in *Sex and the City* you got down with the swirl (meaning interracial relationship), and again, on *LAX* there is [a] past relationship between you and Heather Locklear. Were you ever concerned with backlash from the Black community when it comes to interracial dating?" Blair Underwood answers by saying, "My concern is that I'm allowed to play a variety of roles"; he quickly notes that on the show *LAX* he is married to a "beautiful African American woman . . . I suggested."

42. Bossip.com is described as "snarky gossip about African American celebrities," by a *Washington Post* article by Jill Hudson Neal, May 11, 2004 (*bossip* stands for black gossip). Another site, mediatakeout.com, calls itself an urban gossip site. Both of these sites are referenced on hip-hop radio shows such as the *Wendi Williams Show.* There is also a Latina gossip site, www.lossip.com, for Latina gossip.

43. The lyrics in one of rapper 50 Cent's songs, "Position of Power," also references interracial relationships, "I touched the Hollywood paper, go and shoot me some flicks, Have some supermodel bitches come and suck on my dick, My mom turn in her grave if I married a white chick but baby'll suck the chrome off the Chevy and shit." Lyrics accessed at www.lyricstop.com/albums/50Cent/positionofpower.html, January 2006.

44. This sentiment of celebrating successful black couples, or successful black athletes or celebrities who choose a black partner, is common on black Internet blogs. For example, on entertainment sites such as bossip.com and mediatakeout.com, readers post comments about this issue.

45. Kanye West also posts provocative posts on his own blog like "My Favorite White Girl," referring to the actress Scarlett Johansson.

46. Comedy bits give advice on how black men can "pick up white chicks," such as "let them dance better," and act like a "real ethnic thugs" because that is what white women like.

47. In my research with white and black communities on their views on interracial relationships for my book *Navigating Interracial Borders: Black-White Couples and Their Social Worlds* (Rutgers, 2005), a similar dynamic emerged where the white communities didn't want to talk about interracial dating, stated they had never thought about it, and only after prodding stated they "did not have a problem with it," yet clearly expressed that interracial marriage was something that didn't and hopefully wouldn't happen in their families or communities. On the flip side, black communities were very vocal about their views about interracial relationships and expressed that this was an issue they had thought about often, and many blacks expressed opposition. Yet I argued that while blacks expressed reasons they were opposed in general, in their everyday lives they knew and loved a number of interracial couples and biracial children. Whites claimed they were not opposed, yet they expressed racist views and didn't know any interracial couples and actively worked to keep their families from becoming interracial.

48. Other movies that "bet their popularity on teen-age appeal" (Jones 2002), such as *Swordfish, Mission: Impossible II*, and *Die Another Day*, also featured story lines that involve an interracial romance, which is addressed earlier in the book.

49. Gray 2005:157. See also Hebdige 1989.

50. Quoted in *New York Times*, December 28, 2003.

51. Quoted in *New York Times*, December 28, 2003.

52. Quoted in *New York Times*, December 28, 2003.

53. See page 25 in D. Samuels, "The Real Face of Rap," *New Republic* (November 11, 1991).

54. Gray 2005, 154–55.

~

Conclusion: Changing the Channel

The book started with miscegenation tales of violation, tragedy, and capture; amalgamation stories of sacrifice, salvation, loss, and redemption; and utopian fairy tales where love conquers all, yet the focus was to see whether "something new" existed in terms of representations. Traveling through the worlds of television, film, media coverage, Internet, and music, it is clear that certain stories about interracial sex and relationships are retold in a limited number of ways. If these stories were nothing more than entertainment, and the images had no significance in our everyday lives, then we wouldn't need to be concerned. Yet unfortunately, these images influence how individuals interact with one another in the larger society and reflect existing racial inequalities. Whites have been simultaneously appalled and intrigued, offended and attracted to racial Others sexually, while monitoring, disciplining, and indulging, and this hasn't changed. As Joane Nagel (2003) argues:

> Ethnosexual transactions and associations are endlessly fascinating to observers . . . the capacity of ethnicity to sexually attract and repel, in the success of sexuality as an ideology of superiority and inferiority, and in the power of sexuality as an instrument of racial formation—as a means of domination or resistance, as a badge of honor or shame (261).

Throughout the various media realms—television, film, news media, and the less clearly defined intersecting worlds of music, sports, and youth culture—representations of interracial sex and relationships follow certain patterns, and what emerges is a delicate dance between interracial sex sells and interracial sex alienates. The small number of representations as well as the particular types of depictions of interracial relationships, when they are shown, reveals the lingering opposition to interracial sexuality and marriage as well as the persistent racialized images of racial Others and the protection of whiteness. Interracial representations are symbolic struggles over meaning, not only in how interracial relationships are portrayed but also in how they are received, understood, and responded to in the larger society. In particular, interracial images are used to perpetuate negative stereotypes yet are simultaneously marketed as an example of how color-blind we have become and of the declining significance of race. Yet one may ask, Why are interracial relationships shown at all if they are still widely opposed by whites and other racial groups? The answer is twofold, as we have seen throughout the book, that showing interracial relationships is a necessary piece of the current rhetoric that asserts race no longer matters and the representations are only shown in ways that either deviantize these relationships, privilege whiteness, or support the contention that America is color-blind.

Framing the Images

One of the central questions of the book was to explore what "interracial couple" meant by looking at media and popular culture representations. Throughout the representations, the dominant theme or frame was that interracial unions are represented outside the norm or deviant. This view of interracial relationships as deviant has existed throughout America's history; therefore, it is not surprising that most media and popular culture still depict interracial sexual relations as outside the realm of acceptable behavior.

Overwhelmingly, representations of interracial relationships reinforce the idea that these unions are problematic. These unions, if presented at all, are part of marginal story lines rather than centered. Moreover, there are virtually no films that include a happily partnered interracial couple or interracial wedding within the context of a stable, middle-class world. Through these cultural images, interracial relationships between whites and nonwhites are most often constructed as deviant, undoubtedly because these unions are still unacceptable to large numbers of whites.

The deviant nature of interracial relationships is reinforced in various ways. They are invisible,[1] as evidenced in how rarely we see interracial couples on television or film, particularly men of color with white women. In the media, black and Latino victims are less likely to be acknowledged or believed, and as we saw in the differential coverage between the Central Park jogger and the Tawana Brawley case or the Kobe Bryant and Duke University lacrosse team rape allegations, the media tends to ignore or misrepresent women of color who allege they are victims of sexual assault by white men. Another way they are rendered deviant is by portraying the relationships as taboo, used in television and film to provide added comedy, mockery, tragedy, suspense, or a temporary distraction to the real plotline because the interracial relationship is outside the norm. In many films, the interracial relationship is the symbol of a downward spiral and deviant world, particularly if it involves a white woman with a man of color. Also deviant, interracial relationships are presented as a fantasy or fetish through a make-believe world, a dream sequence, a temporary crush, or a rendezvous in an exotic locale that allows the viewer to dabble in difference, living vicariously through the characters: this happens most in representations of women of color on television who only desire white men like on *Friends* and *ER*, or with film actresses like Halle Berry, Thandie Newton, and Jennifer Lopez, who are mostly paired opposite white men. Since those who produce the images are interested in making money, they will produce images that sell, which reveals the fine line between having diverse casts that may attract the maximum number of viewers because they appeal to all racial groups and losing viewers because of the diverse mix. Those who track how much money a film will gross, such as Robert Bucksbaum, president of the company Reel Source Inc., argue that "money is the driving force behind interracial couples in film,"[2] the relative lack of depictions may signal otherwise or, based on what images appear, depicting deviant interracial relationships is the moneymaker.

This book also sought to understand not only how interracial unions were represented but also what function these representations have. If interracial unions are continuously constructed as outside the norm, who creates the images and what purposes do they serve? This brings us from the first frame to the second frame: By constructing interracial relationships as a deviation from the norm, it is not only a means of privileging same-race unions, but also, more importantly, it is a way of perpetuating ideas about racial difference, white superiority, and racial stereotypes. Most stories involving an interracial union depict whites as progressive and good, like television's Dr. Carter on *ER* and Amy Gray on *Judging Amy*, or in films like *Bulworth*, *The Bodyguard*, *Fools Rush In*, *Monster's Ball*, and *Something New*, yet still the dangers of interracial intimacy are clear. Casting interracial relationships does not change the racial images that exist, but instead it works as "part of a broader program of hegemonic recuperation, a program that has at its main focus the reconstruction of white masculine power." For example, the relationship between a white man and woman of color is acceptable as long as the white man saves her and her world or

the woman comes to his world, either symbolically through a transformation, like Jennifer Lopez's character who goes from a maid to a business
executive, or geographically, by moving into his house or country. Yet if a
white woman is paired interracially, most often it occurs in a deviant setting, where it causes problems and/or is met with opposition, usually from
communities of color who are used to symbolically represent the potential
problems that interracial intimacy causes. Not showing, deviantizing, or
creating very unique exceptions of interracial relationships between whites
and persons of color serves to reinforce the dominance of whiteness, and
white masculinity, in particular. What emerges is how the gaze of the film
is white male, and these depictions of interracial sex are white male fantasies that construct white masculinity in certain ways while reinforcing
certain representations of people of color, and even white women. The interracial relationships we see and hear do not challenge racial boundaries,
but rather happen securely within the constructed borders, such as a black
woman in an all-white world or an interracial nonwhite relationship. By
showing images of deviance, the racial hierarchy is not challenged; rather,
it is arguably strengthened.

Particular stories about race are woven into interracial representations
that erase white racism, paint the white world color-blind, and construct
communities of color as the ones who make race a problem, which is the
third frame of the book. Not acknowledging race does not make racial stereotypes disappear, rather as part of contemporary racism, it allows racist
thought and behavior to flourish subtly while denying race matters. Therefore, representations of interracial couples are very important to the success
of contemporary racism because by showing interracial couples, particularly
without mentioning race, it can be pointed to as proof that race and color
no longer matter. Just as whites claim a black friend to ward off charges of
being racist, putting an interracial relationship in a TV show or film allows
the creators and the audience to claim color-blind sensibilities, as many of
the producers', directors', and actors' comments showed. Mainstream news
media, which is white-owned and controlled, uses similar tactics where
they emphasize celebratory stories of how interracial couples are transform-
ing the racial landscape yet ignore everyday occurrences of racism enacted
against interracial couples. Then when covering high-profile interracial
rape allegations, the mainstream white media accuse any persons who
argue that race matters in how the allegations will be handled as "playing
the race card."

Despite these media reports to the contrary, individuals of different races
are not randomly hooking up on screen; instead, characters, depending on

their race and gender, occupy very specific roles. Not only are racial messages clearly conveyed but also the boundaries of race, gender, and sexuality are marked. Race and gender issues are often tied together with gender trumping race in terms of the characters addressing sexist comments or behavior, but not recognizing or addressing racism or racist comments. Issues of gender are highlighted, often as a way to discount or minimize the importance of race, like during the O. J. Simpson trial and the pretrial proceedings for the Kobe Bryant rape allegations. In these cases protecting women's rights was positioned in opposition to acknowledging the racial implications when both were operating at the same time. In films such as *Guess Who*, the movie concludes by linking the male characters of the black father/white boyfriend by gender that allows them to overcome their perceived racial differences. Also on TV shows such as *ER*, gender bias is regularly confronted, while racial bias denied.

While there is no denying the different historical and contemporary realities surrounding Asians, Latinos, and African Americans, I argue that interracial representations share certain aspects, regardless of the racial combination. "The black-white binary is particularly powerful because it is so efficient and effective in exaggerating racial difference, in helping to establish order—a racial order,"[3] and other racial positions can be understood along the continuum. In interracial representations, rarely if ever does the white man look bad, while the white woman is most often portrayed negatively and reads like a public service announcement against engaging in an interracial relationship. For example, in films like *Spanglish*, the white husband resists the temptation of the exotic, nurturing, and sensual Mexican maid despite having a white wife who is not compassionate, works too much, and is bossy during sex. These images affirm "white male identity against the threat of emerging feminism by warning white women to return to the 'feminine sphere'—to their duties of wife and mother—if they wish to attract and keep a man."[4] Furthermore, these interracial representations reinforce patriarchal dominance and control over white women as well as women and men of color. There are particular ideologies associated with Asian women as submissive, desirable, exotic, sexual beings, while Asian men are denied a sexual presence even with Asian women, who are portrayed as more attracted to white men, or even black men. Latino men and women can be portrayed as hot, sexual, and of a lower status, or if paired opposite a white person then they are more likely to be portrayed as "race-less" and highly desirable. Black women are most often portrayed as sexual, untrustworthy, of a lower status, and only paired with white men if light-skinned, while black men are either dangerous, deviant, and sexually problematic, or more rarely, they are exceptions, like the tamed black man who is removed from his family and any black communities. These images can also be found on the Internet, where there are a large number of pornographic Web sites and dating services catering to these interracial fetishes featuring "Asian submissives," "black phat booties," and "hot Latinas" all engaging in sexual acts with white men.[5] These representations are a "safely voyeuristic" experience that allows the audience to view what they already believe and obviously want to see. Multiracialism and consuming color as exotic is increasingly popular, with a growing acceptability of showing racially ambiguous and/or multiracial individuals, with fluid identities. While certain light-skinned African American actresses such as Halle Berry can occasionally play raceless characters, it is much more common for this option to be available for Latinas/os, like Jennifer Lopez or Jimmy Smits, who can play Italian, Latina, Mexican, or unraced "non-ethnic" white.[6] This fluidity of Latino/a characters shows how interracial sex remains both frightening and fascinating, something white viewers want but only in safe, contained ways, such as a character that is less dangerous, like a Latina woman who can be both white appearing or authentically exotic. Interracial sex and unions are shown because they satisfy the desire of what Houston Baker refers to as the "cultural, commercial, and sexual cannibalism of the other-who-is-not-wholly-other."[7] When presented in these very particular ways, interracial sex and intimacy can be consumed without a problem and without changing everyday realities or behaviors. Even in media forms geared toward the younger generations enthralled with hip-hop music, YouTube, and MySpace, rather than a multiracial utopia where different races and colors mesh, ideas about difference and maintaining boundaries are overwhelming. Not unlike mainstream media that problematize interracial relationships yet do it using color-blind language, films geared toward youth, as well as hip-hop radio stations and Internet sites, clearly mark interracial unions and label them as problematic or humorous while advocating against these relationships. Still in contemporary popular culture and media, the fascination with interracial sexuality may be more acceptable than the reality.

Framing Realities

The book interrogated the images and discourses surrounding interracial sexuality through the lens of structural racism and critical perspectives on popular cultural images. Media and popular culture is still overwhelmingly controlled by whites, in particular a small group of white men, and the representations of interracial sex and couples created emerge out of their everyday realities, experiences, and fantasies: an integral part of racial ideology is "a substantive set of ideas and notions defending white power and privilege as meritorious and natural and accenting the alleged superiority of whites and the inferiority of those who are racially oppressed."[8] In our contemporary world, the issue of power can never be overemphasized in terms of who creates the images, determines the discourses that prevail, and ultimately constructs the framework we watch and live in. While there are no longer public lynchings or laws denying racial groups full rights, the representations discussed serve similar purposes. These stories about interracial sex that are told in communities, in the media, and in popular culture are an integral part of the contemporary racist framework because they rationalize and legitimize white oppression of blacks and other racial minorities. This is achieved through presenting interracial couples as deviant, privileging and promoting whiteness, and strategically using interracial relationships to simultaneously deny race matters while perpetuating racial inequalities.

In both popular culture and real life, interracial couples are embraced under very specific circumstances and otherwise merely tolerated. In recent studies on the experiences of interracial couples, they tell stories of "supportive" families who make racist comments or won't allow their own children to marry interracially. Furthermore, white communities report that they "do not have a problem with interracial relationships but . . ." followed by a laundry list of reasons why they or their family shouldn't, couldn't, and wouldn't marry outside their race, particularly in relation to African Americans. Qualitative studies also document how even interracial couples report racialized thinking about their partners or the racial groups they come from.[9] These confusing, "color-blind" sentiments expressed by respondents that seemingly embrace and reject interracial unions are echoed in the cultural representations covered in this book. Representations of interracial sex and relationships allow for whites to maintain the myth of color blindness because, as Patricia Hill Collins argues, to be color-blind we need to see color, or more accurately, color safely contained. These representations include racialized comments and symbolic images of difference while promoting the notion of color blindness by placing outright opposition and racial prejudice as existing with an extreme racist group or bigoted individual. What is most dangerous about contemporary images is that they pass as positive proof that racism no longer exists while still delivering only particular derogatory views of interracial sexuality, and more importantly, damaging stereotypes of African American, Latinas/os, and Asian Americans, which allow white communities' and other racial communities' coded, racialized thoughts and actions to go unchallenged. This widespread use of nonracial and coded language masks contemporary racism and prejudice to the point where the representations are actually used as proof that racism is no longer a problem.

The representations of interracial unions also mirror the different racial positions that groups occupy in society. The experiences of Latina/os vary greatly based on many factors such as ethnicity, skin color, and socioeconomic class status, similar to how Latina actresses like Jennifer Lopez's characters fluctuate. The traits and stories associated with the "Latina Lopez" as opposed to white Jennifer reveal how Latinas are represented in certain ways, but certain Latinas like Lopez have the ability to, at least temporarily, leave behind these representations. For Asian Americans, while still considered the model minority, Asian men and women are often relegated to service positions and mocked for their perceived language and cultural differences. The increasing number of marriages between white men and Asian women combined with the extremely low numbers of marriage between white women and Asian men can be understood at least partially through the different images. Illustrating the direct connection, one study of Asian-white couples found that these individuals often embrace the racialized stereotypes that dominate interracial representations, with Asian American men struggling with feeling inferior and being perceived as less masculine by Asian American women while white men with Asian women embrace the image of the Lotus Blossom: "Asian American women enforce Eurocentric gender ideology when they accept the objectification and feminization of Asian men and the parallel construction of white men as the most desirable sexual and marital partners."[10] For black Americans, on various societal indicators in terms of education, employment, health, income, and marriage, blacks as a group lag behind whites and other racial groups. Not surprisingly, rates of marriage between blacks and whites remain low, while racism against blacks remains strongest among all racial groups. Undoubtedly, the dominant images we see of dangerous black men and sexually available black women contribute to this antiblack racism that permeates all realms of society, such as education, work, health, and wealth. Furthermore, when blacks are accused or believed to have committed an "interracial crime," they will be (per)prosecuted harder, but their immediate community, and to an extent the entire black race, also comes under scrutiny. When black women are the victims of rape, particularly by whites, their story seems to be quickly doubted by both the criminal/legal system, and the media passes on this doubt. Yet for whites, accusations of a crime that involves interracial sex can actually serve as an excuse such as in the Yusef Hawkins murder or make it less likely the "crime" will be believed. By using the Kobe Bryant case (or O. J. trial) to argue whether or not race matters, it makes it easier for whites to affirm that race no longer matters, especially since the media pays little or no attention to the unknown black men who have been falsely accused or received stiffer penalties for crimes against white women—"the real racism that millions of people face every day is thus either too localized or generalized" and not the story that fits the white imagination.[11] At the same time, the media lets pass under their radar stories that do not fit these molds, like the countless black women who are victims of rape or the interracial couples who are harassed by a group of white men. Just as whites as a group sit atop the racial hierarchy, there emerges a pattern that when whites are accused—white young men in the Yusef Hawkins case, the white Italian community of Bensonhurst, the white community of Vail, Colorado, during the Kobe Bryant case, and the white lacrosse players, Duke University, and Durham—the media participates in the protection of whiteness either through the characterization of those accused or the validation of the white communities. Through the media coverage, the protection and privileging of whiteness is clear. The representations of whites as a group remain positive, particularly in relation to characters of color. The problem of race is squarely placed with people of color, and the idea that all groups can be equally prejudice is common without the acknowledgment of white racism.

These stories we hear and see are carefully constructed and serve specific purposes. Representations of interracial intimacy have less to do with how acceptable these unions are and more to do with whose interests are served. The media, like film and television, weave stories before the "story" is actually known, and how they decide to present the little bits of information they receive shows us the stories they assume to be true. These stories are based within a social structure that is organized on the idea of separate racial groups, with the accompanying ideology that there are distinct differences between the races: whites have produced this racial hierarchy and maintain it through continued separation, with a collective discourse against interracial unions being part of this. We see how the media approaches race as something that is played for a reason and manipulated for advantage, rarely acknowledging the extent to which race affects any interracial case. The reports are contradictory, where we hear that a white lawyer "playing the race card" carries more credibility, but we still hear from journalists that race does not matter and they "never think about race." The role of race is denied, yet people in Vail, Colorado, live in a area where there are virtually no black people, a popular sitcom like *Friends* can ignore the racial diversity of the city the show is set in, and we have darkened faces on magazine covers and Hangman T-shirts made of black athletes who have supposedly "transcended race." The fantasy of interracial relationships cannot be bogged down with the unpleasantness of racism, inequality, and discrimination, so it erases these structural and institutional realities that shape everyday social interaction.

Back to the Future

The last movie I watched was the 2008 summer blockbuster *Hancock*, billed as a "July blockbuster" featuring the box-office success Will Smith playing opposite the popular white actress Charlize Theron. While never marketed as having an interracial romance, there was some mention of the two being involved. As I watched the film wondering if this could be something new to end the book with, instead quite perfectly the film fit the three frames. The premise of *Hancock* is that he is a deviant superhero—drunk, unkempt, mean, and black. Furthermore, there is a white man Hancock saves, who then tries to help him change his image and just happens to be married to a white woman whom Hancock is drawn to. It turns out that she is also a superhero and they were once lovers but that they weren't meant to be together because their love would destroy them, which it almost does when they battle each other. While race is never discussed, these two do not belong together, which ultimately seems to be the underlying message of most interracial representations.[12]

Clearly, we need to start imagining different representations, which is no easy task. Even if those who produce the images wanted to create different representations, it would be difficult because if it dealt directly with racism it would probably not be popular or if they ignored race and cast characters of all different races in nonstereotypical roles, the audiences would still understand it through the racialized, gendered, and sexualized ideologies of society. It is also problematic to present images of interracial harmony without acknowledging the "well-institutionalized power and wealth hierarchy favoring whites, nor the centuries-old social reproduction processes of unjust enrichment and impoverishment that lie just beneath the surface of the recognized disharmonies."[13] So how do we define what "suitable representations" would look like? One way to begin would be to offer more diverse representations of all racial and ethnic groups throughout film and television. Rather than ignore racial dynamics, it could be embraced in more varied ways that illustrate the complexity, rather than reducing the casting of different races to side story lines, comic relief, or added suspense. For example, if a show like *Friends*, which was set in New York City, reflected the racial and ethnic diversity in its characters regularly, then the casting of an African American love interest that was simultaneously dating Ross and Joey would be less problematic. As this research has shown, it is not only a problem of what is shown but also what is not shown. Yet this is not simply a matter of representation, as it speaks to the very structure of our society and the limited ability to think outside the racial box.

Future research needs to explore the reception of these images, the meanings these images have in different communities, and how they are then used in racial communities' discourses, which we have seen can differ greatly. For example, how is an on-screen relationship between Halle Berry and Billy Bob Thornton in *Monster's Ball* received by black communities as opposed to white communities, or do audiences view Jennifer Lopez paired as the love interest of Ralph Fiennes in *Maid in Manhattan* as interracial, and what different meanings does the movie have in Puerto Rican communities as opposed to white and black communities?[14] For real change we have to not only understand what these images mean to different communities but also the creation and production of media and popular culture needs to reflect the diversity of these different communities that exist in society, which does not necessarily happen even when people of color create the images, as we saw with a film like *Something New*. While there are no easy answers, the first step is to recognize what representations exist and acknowledge the racist images and meanings they contain.

This research has not simply been an analysis of the images and discourses that are reproduced about interracial relationships but a critique of the underlying attitudes and practices that inform these representations. Interracial images do not appear out of nowhere, but rather they are carefully cultivated for very specific purposes. We need to challenge the stories that are told and recognize the patterns that exist. If we look at every film, song, TV show, or media story separately, it is easy to miss the larger significance and dismiss it as entertainment, or one isolated example. Pieced together, it is impossible to deny that race and color matter, in terms of representations and realties. Contemporary depictions of interracial couples do little more than reproduce ideas that interracial relationships and racial minorities are problematic, except in very "exceptional" instances. By repackaging old ideas in a new color-blind and multiracial packaging, whiteness is protected and privileged, while maintaining that racism is a thing of the past. When the high-profile media case ends and the movie screen fades to black and white, the images we are left with justify racial prejudices and inequalities. Maybe it's time to change the channel.

Notes

1. When whites are interviewed about interracial relationships, they often respond that they have never thought about it, do not know any interracial couples, and when interviewed in greater depth, express opposition to these unions in nonracialized

statements such as "I don't have a problem with it BUT . . ." citing lack of attraction, innate differences, negative outcomes such as problems for biracial children, and opposition from others in society. See Erica Chito Childs, *Navigating Interracial Borders: Black-White Couples and Their Social Worlds* (New Brunswick, NJ: Rutgers University Press, 2005); also Eduardo Bonilla-Silva, *Racism without Racists* (Lanham, MD: Rowman & Littlefield, 2003).

2. Grace Aduroja, "Teen Movies Embracing Interracial Couples," *Times-Picayune*, July 27, 2001.

3. Hunt 2005, 3.

4. See Espiritu 2000, 113.

5. J. Wood, a journalist, makes this argument about white Sony executives with the movie *Boyz 'n the Hood* in 1993. "John Singleton and the Impossible Greenback of the Assimilated Black Artist," *Esquire* (August): 65.

6. Some actresses like Cameron Diaz, whose father is Latino, is not referred to as Latina and always plays a white woman.

7. Page 158 in Houston A. Baker, Jr., "Spike Lee and the Commerce of Culture," in Manthia Diawara, ed., *Black American Cinema* (New York: Routledge, 1994), chapter 10.

8. Feagin 2006, 28.

9. See Chito Childs 2005, Dalmage 2000, and Nemoto (forthcoming)

10. See Nemoto forthcoming; Espiritu 2000, 115.

11. Lipsitz 1998, 116–17. These cases, especially the criminal ones that involve interracial sex and celebrities, should highlight how someone not famous would fare, if celebrities enter the fight of their lives when accused of raping or murdering whites.

12. In September 2008, another film, *Lakeview Terrac*, was released, which featured popular black actor Samuel Jackson as a LAPD police officer who torments the married white man and black woman that moves next to him, because he disapproves of interracial relationships. Again though the movie features a married interracial couple, it involves a white man, and the opposition of a black individual is the focus.

13. Feagin 2006, 5.

14. For example, we can see to some extent how different racial communities understand interracial sexuality and the dominant images that exist in the media coverage of the allegations that Kobe Bryant raped a young woman in Vail, Colorado, especially in terms of how is race discussed, ignored, and "played" differently on BET News as compared to NBC.

Filmography

Forester, M. (director), Addica, M., and Rokos, W. (writers). (2001). *Monster's Ball* [Motion Picture]. United States: Lee Daniels Entertainment and Lions Gate Films.

Sanaa, H. (director), Turner, K. (writer). (2006). *Something New* [Motion Picture]. United States: Gramercy Pictures and Homegrown Pictures.

Jackson, M. (director), and Kasdan, L. (writer). (1992). *The Bodyguard* [Motion Picture]. United States: Kasdan Pictures, Tig Productions and Warner Brothers Pictures.

Gabriel, M., and Goldberg, E. (directors), Binder, C., Grant, S., LaZebnik, P., et al. (writers). (1995). *Pocahontas* [Motion Picture]. United States: Walt Disney Feature Animation and Walt Disney Pictures.

Zwick, E. (director and writer), Logan, J., and Herskovitz, M. (writers). (2003). *The Last Samurai* [Motion Picture]. United States: Warner Brothers Pictures, The Bedford Falls Company, Cruise/Wagner Productions, and Radar Pictures.

Cimino, M. (director and writer), Daley, R., and Stone, O. (writers). (1985). *Year of the Dragon* [Motion Picture]. United States: De Laurentiis Entertainment Group and Metro-Goldwyn-Mayer.

Hicks, S. (director and writer), Guterson, D., and Bass, R. (writers). (1999). *Snow Falling on Cedars* [Motion Picture]. United States: The Kennedy/Marshall Company, Universal Pictures.

Brooks, J. (director and writer). (2004). *Spanglish* [Motion Picture]. United States: Columbia Pictures Corporation and Gracie Films.

Shankman, A. (director), and Filardi, J. (writer). (2003). *Bringing Down the House* [Motion Picture]. United States: Touchstone Pictures and Hyde Park Films.

Younger, B. (director and writer). (2000). *Boiler Room* [Motion Picture]. United States: New Line Cinema and Team Todd.

Usher, K. (director), Burden, B., and Cuthbert, N. (writers). (1999). *Mystery Men* [Motion Picture]. United States: Dark Horse Entertainment and Lawrence Gordon Productions.

Dobkin, D. (director), Faber, S., and Fisher, B. (writers). (2005). *Wedding Crashers* [Motion Picture]. United States: Avery Pix, New Line Cinema, and Tapestry Films.

Hess, J. (director and writer), and Hess, J. E. (writer). (2004). *Napoleon Dynamite* [Motion Picture]. United States: Access Films.

Shelton, R. (director and writer). (1992). *White Men Can't Jump* [Motion Picture]. United States: Twentieth Century-Fox Film Corporation.

Roach, J. (director), Myers, M., and McCullers, M. (writers). (2002). *Austin Powers in Goldmember* [Motion Picture]. United States: New Line Cinema, Gratitude International, Team Todd, and Moving Pictures.

Donner, R. (director), Black, S., Lemkin, J., Gough, A., and Millar, M. (writers). (1998). *Lethal Weapon 4* [Motion Picture]. United States: Donner/Schuler-Donner Productions, Silver Pictures, and Warner Brothers Pictures.

Shyer, C. (director and writer), Naughton, B., and Pope, E. (writers). (2004). *Alfie* [Motion Picture]. United States: Paramount Pictures and Patalex Productions.

Payne, A. (director and writer), Pickett, R., and Taylor, J. (writers). (2004). *Sideways* [Motion Picture]. United States: Fox Searchlight Pictures, Michael London Productions, and Sideways Productions Incorporated.

Ratner, B. (director), Zbyszewski, P., and Rosenberg, C. (writers). (2004). *After Sunset* [Motion Picture]. United States: New Line Cinema, Firm Films, and Rat Entertainment.

McGuigan, P. (director), and Smilovic, J. (writer). (2006). *Lucky Number Slevin* [Motion Picture]. United States: FilmEngine, Lucky Number Slevin Incorporated, Ascendent Pictures, Capitol Films, and VIP 4 Medienfonds.

Jordan, N. (director), and Rice, A. (writer). (1994). *Interview with the Vampire: The Vampire Chronicles* [Motion Picture]. United States: Geffen Pictures.

Twohy, D. (director and writer), Wheat, J., and Wheat, K. (writers). (2004). *The Chronicles of Riddick* [Motion Picture]. United States: Universal Pictures, Radar Pictures, One Race Pictures, and Primal Foe Productions.

Demme, J. (director and writer), Stone, P., Schmidt, S., and Bendinger, J. (writers). (2002). *The Truth about Charlie* [Motion Picture]. United States: Clinica Estetico, Mediastream Zweite Film GmbH & Co. Productions KG, and Universal Pictures.

Woo, J. (director), Geller, B., Moore, R., Braga, B., and Towne, R. (writers). (2000). *Mission: Impossible II* [Motion Picture]. United States: Cruise/Wagner Productions, Munich Film Partners & Company (MFP) MI2 Productions, and Paramount Pictures.

Tamahori, L. (director), Fleming, I., Purvis, N., and Wade, R. (writers). (2002). *Die Another Day* [Motion Picture]. United States: Eon Productions, Danjaq, Metro-Goldwyn-Mayer, and United Artists.

Griffith, D. (director and writer), Dixon Jr., T., and Woods, F. (Writers). (1915). *The Birth of a Nation* [Motion Picture]. United States: David W. Griffith Corp., and Epoch Producing Corporation.

Griffith, D. (director and writer), and Burke, T. (writer). (1919). *Broken Blossoms* [Motion Picture]. United States: David W. Griffith Corp. and Paramount Pictures.

Chan, G. (director and writer), Cheung, A., Davlin, B., Logan, B., and Wheeler, P. (writers). (2003). *The Medallion* [Motion Picture]. United States: Emperor Multimedia Group, Golden Port Productions Ltd., Living Films, and Screen Gems.

Donovan, K. (director), Hay, P., Manfredi, M., Wilson, M., and Leeson, M. (writers). (2002). *The Tuxedo* [Motion Picture]. United States: Blue Train Productions, DreamWorks SKG, Parkes/MacDonald Productions, and Vanguard Films.

Nahon, C. (director), Li, J., Besson, L., Logan, B., and Kamen, R. (writers). (2001). *Kiss of the Dragon* [Motion Picture]. United States: Europa Corp., Twentieth Century-Fox Film Corporation, Quality Growth International Ltd., Current Entertainment, Immortal Entertainment, and Canal+.

Bartkowiak, A. (director), Kapner, M., Bernt, E., and Jarrell, J. (writers). (2000). *Romeo Must Die* [Motion Picture]. United States: Silver Pictures, and Warner Brothers Pictures.

Pakula, A. (director and writer), and Grisham, J. (writer). (1993). *The Pelican Brief* [Motion Picture]. United States: Warner Brothers Pictures.

Fleder, G. (director), Patterson, J., and Klass, D. (writers). (1997). *Kiss the Girls* [Motion Picture]. United States: Paramount Picture and Rysher Entertainment.

Franklin, C. (director), Finder, J., Zeltser, Y., and Bickley, G. (writers). (2002). *High Crimes* [Motion Picture]. United States: Regency Enterprises, Epsilon Motion Pictures, New Regency Pictures, Manifest Film Co., and Monarch Pictures.

Sonnenfeld, B. (director), Cunningham, L., and Solomon, E. (writers). (1997). *Men in Black* [Motion Picture]. United States: Amblin Entertainment, Columbia Pictures Corporation, and MacDonald/Parkes Production.

Proyas, A. (director), Asimov, I., Vintar, J., and Goldsman, A. (writers). (2004). *I, Robot* [Motion Picture]. United States: Canlaws Productions, Davis Entertainment, Laurence Mark Productions, Mediastream Vierte Film GmbH & Co. Vermarktungs KG, Overbrook Entertainment, and Twentieth Century-Fox Film Corporation.

Van Sant, G. (director), and Rich, M. (writer). (2000). *Finding Forrester* [Motion Picture]. United States: Columbia Picture Corporation, Fountainbridge Films, and Laurence Mark Productions.

Tennant, A. (director), and Bisch, K. (writer). (2005). *Hitch* [Motion Picture]. United States: Columbia Pictures Corporation, and Overbrook Entertainment.

Fuqua, A. (director), and Ayer, D. (writer). (2001). *Training Day* [Motion Picture]. United States: Warner Brothers Pictures, Village Roadshow Pictures, NPV Entertainment, Outlaw Productions (I), and WV Films II LLC.

Franklin, C. (director), and Collard, D. (writer). (2003). *Out of Time* [Motion Picture]. United States: Metro-Goldwyn-Mayer, Original Film, and Monarch Pictures.

Nair, M. (director), and Taraporevala, S. (writer). (1991). *Mississippi Masala* [Motion Picture]. United States: Columbia Pictures Corporation, and Overbrook Entertainment.

Franklin, C. (director and writer), and Mosley, W. (writer). (1995). *Devil in a Blue Dress* [Motion Picture]. United States: Clinica Estetico, Mundy Lane Entertainment, and TriStar Pictures.

Soderbergh, S. (director), and Hough, C. (writer). (2002). *Full Frontal* [Motion Picture]. United States: Miramax Films, Monophonic Inc., Populist Pictures, Propaganda Films, and Section Eight.

Lucas, G. (director and writer). (1977). *Star Wars* [Motion Picture]. United States: Lucasfilm and Twentieth Century-Fox Film Corporation.

Zemeckis, R. (director), Wolf, G., Price, J., and Seaman, P. (writers). (1998). *Who Framed Roger Rabbit* [Motion Picture]. United States: Amblin Entertainment, Silver Screen Partners III, Touchstone Pictures, and Walt Disney Feature Animation (uncredited).

Bergson, B., Jenson, V., and Letterman, R. (directors), Wilson, M., Letterman, R., Aukerman, S., and Porter, B. (writers). (2004). *Shark Tale* [Motion Picture]. United States: DreamWorks Animation, Dream Works SKG, and Pacific Data Images.

Jackson, P. (director and writer), Walsh, F., Boyens, P., Cooper, M., and Wallace, E. (writers). (2005). *King Kong* [Motion Picture]. United States: Big Primate Pictures, Universal Pictures, WingNut Pictures, and MFPV Film.

Schumacher, J. (director), Goodman, G., Himmelstein, D., Richman, J., and Browning, M. (writers). (2002). *Bad Company* [Motion Picture]. United States: Touchstone Pictures, Jerry Bruckheimer Films, and Stillking Films.

Kumble, R. (director and writer), and de Laclos, C. (writer). (1999). *Cruel Intentions* [Motion Picture]. United States: Columbia Pictures Corporation, Cruel Productions LLC, Newmarket Capital Group, and Original Film.

Bright, M. (director and writer). (1996). *Freeway* [Motion Picture]. United States: August Entertainment, Davis-Films, Illusion Entertainment, The Kushner-Locke Company, and Muse Productions.

Tarantino, Q. (director and writer), and Avary, R. (writer). (1994). *Cruel Intentions* [Motion Picture]. United States: A Band Apart, Jersey Films, and Miramax Films.

Mulcahy, R. (director), Dekker, F., Meyjes, M., and de Souza, S. (writers). (1991). *Richochet* [Motion Picture]. United States: Cinema Plus, Home Box Office, and Silver Pictures.

Hardwicke, C. (director and writer), and Reed, N. (writer). (2003). *Thirteen* [Motion Picture]. United States: Michael London Productions, Working Title Films, Antidote Films (I), and Sound for Film Inc.

Soderbergh, S. (director), Moore, S., and Gaghan, S. (writers). (2000). *Traffic* [Motion Picture]. United States: Bedford Falls Productions, Compulsion Inc., Initial Entertainment Group, Splendid Medien AG, and USA Films.

Stockwell, J. (director), Hay, P., and Manfredi, M. (writers). (2001). *Crazy/Beautiful* [Motion Picture]. United States: At 17 Films Inc., and Touchstone Pictures.

De Palma, B. (director), Trail, A., Hecht, B., Hawks, H., and Stone, O. (writers). (1983). *Scarface* [Motion Picture]. United States: Universal Pictures.

Reyes, F. (director and writer). (2002). *Empire* [Motion Picture]. United States: Arenas Entertainment, Bigel/Mailer Films, and Universal Pictures.

Brewer, C. (director and writer). (2005). *Hustle and Flow* [Motion Picture]. United States: Crunk Pictures, Homegrown Pictures, MTV Films, and New Deal Productions.

Lee, S. (director and writer). (1990). *Mo' Better Blues* [Motion Picture]. United States: 40 Acres & A Mule Filmworks, and Universal Pictures.

Baird, S. (director), Huggins, R., and Pogue, J. (writers). (1998). *U.S. Marshals* [Motion Picture]. United States: Kopelson Entertainment, and Warner Brothers Pictures.

Davis, A. (director), Huggins, R., Twohy, D., and Stuart, J. (writers). (1993). *The Fugitive* [Motion Picture]. United States: Warner Brothers Pictures.

Lee, S. (director and writer). (1998). *He Got Game* [Motion Picture]. United States: 40 Acres & A Mule Filmworks, and Touchstone Pictures.

Hanson, C. (director), and Silver, S. (writer). (2002). *8 Mile* [Motion Picture]. United States: Imagine Entertainment, and Mikona Productions GmbH & Co. KG.

Figgis, M. (director and writer). (1997). *One Night Stand* [Motion Picture]. United States: New Line Cinema, and Red Mullet Productions.

Hytner, N. (director), McCauley, S., and Wasserstein, W. (writers). (1998). *The Object of My Affection* [Motion Picture]. United States: Twentieth Century-Fox Film Corporation.

Farrelly, B., Farrelly, P. (directors and writers), and Cerribe, M. (writer). (2000). *Me, Myself, & Irene* [Motion Picture]. United States: Conundrum Entertainment, and Twentieth Century-Fox Film Corporation.

Hughes, J. (director and writer). (1984). *Sixteen Candles* [Motion Picture]. United States: Channel Productions, and Universal Pictures.

Terrero, J. (director), Zenga, B., and Wilson, C. (writers). (2004). *Soul Plane* [Motion Picture]. United States: Metro-Goldwyn-Mayer, Turbo Productions, and Boz Productions.

Dylan, J. (director), and Abraham, D. (writer). (2001). *How High* [Motion Picture]. United States: Jersey Films, and Native Pictures Productions.

Wayans, K. (director and writer), Wayans, S., Wayans, M., McElfresh, A., Snowden, M., and Cook, X. (writers). (2004). *White Chicks* [Motion Picture]. United States: Gone North Productions Inc., Revolution Studios, and Warner Brothers Entertainment.

Barclay, P. (director), Wayans, S., Wayans, M., and Beauman, P. (writers). (1996). *Don't Be a Menace to South Central While Drinking Your Juice in the Hood* [Motion Picture]. United States: Island Pictures, and Ivory Way Productions.

MacDonald, P. (director), and Wayans, D. (writer). (1992). *Mo' Money* [Motion Picture]. United States: Columbia Pictures Corporation, and Wife 'n' Kids Inc.

Lee, M. (director), Ridley, J., and McCullers, M. (writers). (2002). *Undercover Brother* [Motion Picture]. United States: Imagine Entertainment, Universal Pictures, and Urban Media.

Lee, S. (director and writer). (2000). *Bamboozled* [Motion Picture]. United States: New Line Cinema, 40 Acres & A Mule Filmworks.

Singleton, J. (director), and Poirier, G. (writer). (1997). *Rosewood* [Motion Picture]. United States: New Deal Productions, Peter Entertainment, and Warner Brothers Pictures.

Haynes, T. (director and writer). (2002). *Far from Heaven* [Motion Picture]. United States: Clear Blue Sky Productions, John Wells Productions, Killer Films, Section Eight, TF1 International, USA Films, and Vulcan Productions.

Lee, S. (director and writer). (1991). *Jungle Fever* [Motion Picture]. United States: 40 Acres & A Mule Filmworks, and Universal Pictures.

Whitaker, F. (director), McMillan, T., and Bass, R. (writers). (1995). *Waiting to Exhale* [Motion Picture]. United States: Twentieth Century-Fox Film Corporation.

Curtis, R. (director and writer). (2003). *Love Actually* [Motion Picture]. United States: Universal Pictures, Working Title Films, and DNA Films.

Carter, T. (director), Adler, D., and Edwards, C. (writers). (2001). *Save the Last Dance* [Motion Picture]. United States: Cort/Madden Productions and MTV Films.

~

Bibliography

Alexander, Elizabeth. "'Can You Be BLACK and Look at This?': Reading the Rodney King Video(s)." In *The Black Public Sphere*, edited by the Black Public Sphere Collective. Chicago: University of Chicago Press, 1995.

Allinson, Ewan. "Music and the Politics of Race." *Cultural Studies* 8, 3 (October 1994): 438–56.

Amber, Jeannine. "A Course in Commitment." *Essence* 35, 5 (September 2004): 214.

Appiah, Osei. "Black and White Viewers' Perception and Recall of Occupational Characters on Television." *Journal of Communication* 52, 4 (2002): 776–93.

Baker, Jr., Houston A. "Spike Lee and the Commerce of Culture." In Manthia Diawara (ed.) *Black American Cinema*. New York: Routledge, 1994.

Baldwin, James. *The Price of the Ticket: Collected Nonfiction, 1948–1985*. New York: St. Martin's Press, 1985.

———. *Notes of a Native Son*. New York: Beacon Press, 1984 [1955].

Bell, Derrick. *Silent Covenants: Brown v. Board of Education and the Unfulfilled Hopes for Racial Reform*. New York: Oxford University Press, 2004.

———. "The Race Charged Relationship of Black Men and Black Women." In Maurice Berger, Brian Wallis, and Simon Watson (eds.) *Constructing Masculinity*. London: Routledge, 1995.

Bennett, Lerone. *Before the Mayflower: A History of Black America*. New York: Penguin Books, 1984 [1962].

Berg, Bruce L. *Qualitative Research Methods for the Social Sciences*. New York: Allyn & Bacon, 2003.

Berkhofer, Jr., Robert F. *The White Man's Indian: Images of the American Indian from Columbus to the Present*. New York: Alfred A. Knopf, 1978.

Berwanger, Eugene H. *The Frontier against Slavery: Western Anti-Negro Prejudice and the Slavery Extension Controversy.* Urbana: University of Illinois Press, 1967.

Billings, Andrew C. "Selective Representation of Gender, Ethnicity, and Nationality in American Television Coverage of the 2000 Summer Olympics." *International Review for the Sociology of Sport* 37, 3–4 (2002): 351–70.

Black, Gregory. *Hollywood Censored: Morality Codes, Catholics, and the Movies.* New York: Cambridge University Press, 1996.

Bogle, Donald. *Bright Boulevards, Bold Dreams: The Story of Black Hollywood.* New York: One World, Ballantine Books, 2005.

Bonilla-Silva, Eduardo. *Racism without Racists: Color-Blind Racism and the Persistence of Racial Inequality in the United States.* Lanham, MD: Rowman & Littlefield, 2003.

Bridges, George, and Rosalind Brunt. *Silver Linings: Some Strategies for the Eighties.* London: Lawrence and Wishart, 1981.

Brown, Matthew P. "Basketball, Rodney King, Simi Valley." Pp. 102–16 in Mike Hall (ed.) *Whiteness: A Critical Reader.* New York: New York University Press, 1997.

Butler, Judith. *Excitable Speech: A Politics of the Performative.* New York: Routledge, 1997.

Caldwell, Dan. "The Negroization of the Chinese Stereotype in California." *Southern California Quarterly* 53 (June 1971): 123–31.

Campbell, Christopher P. "A Myth of Assimilation: 'Enlightened' Racism and the News." Pp. 137–54 in Darnell M. Hunt (ed.) *Channeling Blackness: Studies on Television and Race in America.* Oxford: Oxford University Press, 2005.

Cardullo, Bert. "Law of the Jungle." *Hudson Review* 44 (1992): 639–47.

Carey, Gary. *Katharine Hepburn: A Biography.* New York: Pocket Books, 1975.

Carby, Hazel. "Encoding White Reseentment: Grand Canyon—A Narrative for Our Times." In Cameron McCarthy and Warren Crichlow (eds.) *Race, Identity and Representation in Education.* New York: Routledge, 1993.

Carlson, James M., and Rebecca Trichtinger. "Perspectives on Entertainment Television's Portrayal of a Racial Incident." *Communication Review* 4, 2 (2001): 253–78.

Chan, Kenneth. "The Construction of Black Male Identity in Black Action Films of the Nineties." *Cinema Journal* 37, 2 (Winter 1998): 35–48.

Chan, S. "The Exclusion of Chinese women." Pp. 94–146 in S. Chan (ed.) *Entry Denied: Exclusion and the Chinese Community in America, 1882–1943.* Philadelphia, PA: Temple University Press, 1991.

Chancer, Lynn. "O. J. Simpson and the Trial of the Century: Uncovering Paradoxes in Media Coverage." Pp. 78–103 in Gregg Barak (ed.) *Representing O. J.: Murder, Criminal Justice, and Mass Culture.* New York: Harrow and Heston Publishers, 1996.

———. *High-Profile Crimes: When Legal Cases Become Social Causes.* Chicago: University of Chicago Press, 2005.

Chin F., and J. P. Chan. "Racist Love." Pp. 65–79 in R. Kostelanetz (ed.) *Seeing Through Shuck.* New York: Ballantine, 1972.

Chiricos, Ted, and Sarah Eschholz. "The Racial and Ethnic Typification of Crime and the Criminal Typification of Race and Ethnicity in Local Television News." *Journal of Research in Crime and Delinquency* 39, 4 (2002): 400–420.

Chito Childs, Erica. *Navigating Interracial Borders: Black-White Couples and Their Social Worlds*. New Brunswick, NJ: Rutgers University Press, 2005.

———. "Can We Stand to Ignore the Perspectives of Black Women on Their Own Experiences?" *Du Bois Review* 3, 2 (2006): 471–79.

———. "Looking Behind the Stereotypes of the 'Angry Black Woman': An Exploration of Black Women's Responses to Interracial Relationships." *Gender & Society* 19, 4 (August 2005): 544–61.

Collier, Aldore. "Hottest TV Hunks." *Ebony* 59, 9 (2004): 172.

Collins, C. "Viewer Letter as Audience Research: The Case of Murphy Brown." *Journal of Broadcasting and Electronic Media* 41, 1 (1997): 109–31.

Collins, Patricia Hill. *Black Sexual Politics: African Americas, Gender and the New Racism*. New York: Routledge, 2004.

———. *Black Feminist Thought*. New York: Routledge, 2000.

Coltrane, Scott. "The Perpetuation of Subtle Prejudice: Race and Gender Imagery in 1990s Television Advertising." *Sex Roles* 42, 5–6 (2000): 363–89.

Coover, Gail E. "Television and Social Identity: Race Representation as 'White' Accommodation." *Journal of Broadcasting & Electronic Media* 45, 3 (2001): 413–31.

Cortés, Carlos E. "Who Is Maria? What Is Juan? Dilemmas of Analyzing the Chicano Image in U.S. Feature Films." In Chon A. Noreiga (ed.) *Chicanos and Film: Representation and Resistance*. Minneapolis: University of Minnesota Press, 1992.

Cottle, Simon. *Ethnic Minorities and the Media: Changing Cultural Boundaries*. Philadelphia, PA: Open University Press, 2000.

Crenshaw, Kimberle. "Whose Story Is It, Anyway?" Pp. 402–40 in Toni Morrison (ed.) "Feminist and Antiracist Appropriations of Anita Hill," in *Race-ing Justice, En-gendering Power*. New York: Pantheon, 1992.

Crenshaw, Kimberle, and Gary Peller, "Reel Time/ Real Justice." In Robert Gooding-Williams (ed.) *Reading Rodney King/ Reading Urban Uprising*. New York: Routledge, 1993.

Dalmage, Heather. *Tripping on the Color Line: Black-White Multiracial Families in a Racially Divided World*. New Brunswick, NJ: Rutgers University Press, 2000.

D'Emilio, John, and Estelle B. Freedman. *Intimate Matters: A History of Sexuality in America*. New York: Harper & Row, 1998.

DaCosta, Kimberly McClain. *Making Multiracials: State, Family and Market in the Redrawing of the Color Line*. Palo Alto, CA: Stanford University Press, 2007.

Datzman, Jeanine, and Carol Brooks Gardner. "'In My Mind, We Are All Humans': Notes on the Public Management of Black-White Interracial Romantic Relationships." *Marriage & Family Review* 30, 1–2 (2000): 5–24.

Davis, Angela. "Rape, Racism and the Myth of the Black Rapist." In *Women, Race, Class*. New York: Random House, 1981.

De Lauretis, Teresa. *Technologies of Gender: Essays on Theory, Film, and Fiction*. Bloomington: Indiana University Press, 1987.

Dearborn, Mary V. *Pocahontas's Daughters: Gender and Ethnicity in American Culture*. New York: Oxford University Press, 1986.

Delgado, Richard. *Critical Race Theory: The Cutting Edge*. Philadelphia, PA: Temple University Press, 1995.

Denzin, Norman K. *Reading Race: Hollywood and the Cinema of Racial Violence*. Thousand Oaks, CA: Sage Publications, 2002.

———. "White Men Can't Jump?: The Politics of Postmodern Emotionality." *Social Perspectives on Emotion* 3 (1995): 33–54.

———. *The Cinematic Society: The Voyuer's Gaze*. Thousand Oaks, CA: Sage Publications, 1995.

———. *Images of Postmodern Society: Social Theory and Contemporary Cinema*. Thousand Oaks, CA: Sage Publications, 1991.

Diawara, Manthia. "Black Spectatorship: Problems of Identification and Resistance." *Screen* 29, 4 (Autumn 1988): 66–79.

Dimitriadis, Greg. "Hip-Hop: From Live Performance to Mediated Narrative." *Popular Music* 15, 2 (1996): 179–94.

Dines, Gail. "King Kong and the White Woman: *Hustler* Magazine and the Demonization of Black Masculinity." Pp. 451–61 in Gail Dines and Jean M. Humez (eds.) *Gender, Race, and Class in Media: A Text-Reader*. Thousand Oaks, CA: Sage Publications, 2003.

Dixon, Travis L., and Daniel Linz. "Television News, Prejudicial Pretrial Publicity, and the Depiction of Race." *Journal of Broadcasting & Electronic Media* 46, 1 (2002): 112–36.

———. "Overrepresentation and Underrepresentation of African Americans and Latinos as Lawbreakers on Television News." *Journal of Communication* 50, 2 (2002): 131–54.

———. "Race and the Misrepresentation of Victimization on Local Television News." *Communication Research* 27, 5 (2000): 547–73.

Du Bois, W. E. B. *The Souls of Black Folks*. New York: Bantam. 1989 [1903].

Dyer Richard. *White: Essays on Race and Culture*. London: Routledge, 1998

Dyson, Michael Eric. *Race Rules: Navigating the Color Line*. Reading, MA: Addison-Wesley, 1997.

Ellison, Ralph. *Invisible Man*. New York: Random House, 1952.

Ellsworth, Scott. *Death in a Promised Land: The Tulsa Race Riot of 1921*. Baton Rouge: Louisiana State University Press, 1982.

Entman, Robert. "Modern Racism and the Images of Blacks in Local Television News." *Critical Studies in Mass Communication* 7, 4 (December 1990).

Entman, Robert, and Andrew Rojecki. *The Black Image in the White Mind: Media and Race in America*. Chicago: University of Chicago Press, 2000.

Espiritu, Yen. *Asian American Women and Men: Labor, Laws, and Love*. Walnut Creek, CA: AltaMira Press, 2000.

Essed, Philomena. *Understanding Everyday Racism*. Newbury Park, CA: Sage Publications, 1991.

Faery, Rebecca. *Cartographies of Desire: Captivity, Race, and Sex in the Shaping of an American Nation*. Norman: University of Oklahoma Press, 1999.

Feagin, Joe. *Systemic Racism: A Theory of Oppression*. New York: Routledge, 2006.

Feagin Joe, and Eileen O'Brien. *White Men on Race*. New York: Beacon Press, 2003.

Feagin, Joe, and Hernan Vera. *White Racism: The Basics*. New York: Routledge, 1993.

Ferguson, Marjorie, and Peter Golding. *Cultural Studies in Question*. Thousand Oaks, CA: Sage Publications, 1997.

Fiebert, Martin S., Holly Karamol, and Margo Kasdan. "Interracial Dating: Attitudes and Experience among American College Students in California." *Psychological Reports* 87 (2002): 1059–64.

Fink, Edward J., and Walter Gantz. "A Content Analysis of the Three Mass Communication Research Traditions: Social Science, Interpretive Studies and Critical Analysis." *Journalism and Mass Communication Quarterly* 73, 1 (1996):114–34.

Fiske, John. "Hearing Anita Hill (and Viewing Bill Cosby)." P. 121 in Darnell Hunt (ed.) *Channeling Blackness: Studies on Television and Race in America*. Oxford: Oxford University Press, 2005.

———. *Media Matters: Everyday Culture and Political Change*. Minneapolis: University of Minnesota Press, 1994.

Foeman, Anita, and Teresa Nance. "Building New Cultures, Reframing Old Images: Success Strategies of Interracial Couples." *Howard Journal of Communication* 13, 3 (2002): 237–49.

Foston, Nikitta A. "Campus Dilemma: Coping with the Acute Male Shortage." *Ebony* 59, 11 (2004): 128.

Foucault, Michel. *The History of Sexuality: An Introduction*. New York: Vintage Books, 1990.

Frankenberg, Ruth. *White Women, Race Matters: The Social Construction of Whiteness*. London: Routledge, 1993.

Freeman, Elizabeth. "'The We of Me': The *Member of the Wedding*'s Novel Alliances." Pp. 111–36 in Jose Munoz and Amanda Barrett (eds.) *Queer Acts: Women and Performance, A Journal of Feminist Theory* 8:2, 16. London: Routledge, Taylor & Francis, 1996.

Frye, Marilyn. *Willful Virgins: Essays in Feminism, 1976–1992*. Freedom, CA: Crossing Press, 1992.

Fu, Xuanning, Jessika Tora, and Heather Kendall. "Marital Happiness and Inter-Racial Marriage: A Study in a Multi-Ethnic Community in Hawaii." *Journal of Comparative Family Studies* 32, 1 (2001): 47–60.

Gaspar, David Barry, and Darlene Clark Hine. *More Than Chattel: Black Women in Slavery in the Americas*. Bloomington: Indiana University Press, 1996.

Gates, Henry. *The Signifying Monkey: A Theory of Afro-American Literary Criticism*. New York: Oxford University Press, 1988.

George, Douglas, and George Yancey. "Taking Stock of America's Attitudes on Cultural Diversity: An Analysis of Public Deliberation on Multiculturalism, Assimilation and Intermarriage." *Journal of Comparative Family Studies* 35, 1 (2004): 1–19.

Giddings, Paula. *When and Where I Enter: The Impact of Black Women on Race and Sex in America*. New York: Bantam Books, 1984.

Gilliam, Franklin D., Nicholas Valentino, and Matthew N. Beckmann. "Where You Live and What You Watch: The Impact of Racial Proximity and Local Television News on Attitudes about Race and Crime." *Political Research Quarterly* 55, 4 (2002): 755–80.

Giroux, Henry A. "Racial Politics and the Pedagogy of Whiteness." Pp. 294–315 in Mike Hill (ed.) *Whiteness: A Critical Reader*. New York: New York University Press, 1997.

Gitlin, Todd. *The Whole World Is Watching: Mass Media in the Making and Unmaking of the New Left*. Berkeley: University of California Press, 1980.

Goellnicht, Donald. "Tang Ao in America: Male Subject Positions in China Men." In *Reading the Literatures of Asian America*. Philadelphia, PA: Temple University Press, 1992.

Gooding-Williams, Robert. *Reading Rodney King/Reading Urban Uprising*. New York: Routledge, 1993.

Gordon, Lewis. "A Lynching Well Lost." *Black Scholar* 25, 4 (1995): 37.

Gray, Herman. *Watching Race: Television and the Struggle for Blackness*. Minneapolis: Univeristy of Minnesota Press, 2004 [1995].

Guerrero, Ed. "Spike Lee and the Fever in the Racial Jungle." P. 125 in Jim Collins (ed.) *Film Theory Goes to the Movies*. New York: Routledge, 1993.

———. "The Black Image in Protective Custody: Hollywood's Biracial Buddy Films of the Eighties." Pp. 237–46 in Manthia Diawara (ed.) *Black American Cinema*. New York: Routledge, 1993.

Gunning, Sandra. "Re-membering Blackness after Reconstruction: Race, Rape, and Political Desire in the Work of Thomas Dixon, Jr." Pp. 19–47 in Sandra Gunning (ed.) *Race, Rape, and Lynching: The Red Record of American Literature, 1890–1912*. New York: Oxford University Press, 1996.

Hale, Grace Elizabeth. *Making Whiteness: The Culture of Segregation in the South, 1890–1940*. New York: Pantheon. 1998.

Hall, Stuart. "Encoding and Decoding in the Television Discourse." P. 49 in Darnell Hunt (ed.) *Channeling Blackness: Studies on Television and Race in America*. Oxford: Oxford University Press, 2005.

———. "The Whites of Their Eyes: Racist Ideologies and the Media." Pp. 89–93 in George Bridges and Rosaline Brunt (eds.) *Silver Linings: Some Strategies for the Eighties*. London: Lawrence and Wishart Ltd., 1981.

———. "New Ethnicities." P. 445 in Ali Rattansi and James Donald (eds.) *Race, Culture and Difference*. Newberry Park, CA: Sage Publications (with the Open University), 1992.

———. "What Is This 'Black' in Black Popular Culture?" In *Black Popular Culture*, Gina Dent (ed.) Seattle: Bay Press, 1992.

Hall, Stuart, Charles Critcher, Tony Jefferson, John Clarke, and Brian Robert. *Policing the Crisis: Mugging, the State, and Law and Order*. London: Macmillan, 1978.

Haney López, Ian. *White by Law: The Legal Construction of Race*. New York: New York University Press, 1996.

Harris, Tina M., and Pamela J. Kalbfleisch. "Interracial Dating: The Implications of Race for Initiating a Romantic Relationship." *Howard Journal of Communications* 11 (2000): 49–64.

Harris, William A. "Cultural Engineering and the Films of Spike Lee." Pp. 3–23 in Venise T. Berry and Carmen L. Manning-Miller (eds.) *Mediated Messages and African-American Culture: Contemporary Issues.* Thousand Oaks, CA: Sage Publications, 1996.

Harrison, C. Keith, and Suzanne Malia Lawrence. "African American Student Athletes' Perceptions of Career Transition in Sport: A Qualitative and Visual Elicitation." *Race, Ethnicity and Education* 6, 4 (2003): 375–94.

Havens, Timothy. "'The Biggest Show in the World': Race and the Global Popularity of *The Cosby Show.*" *Media, Culture & Society* 22, 4 (2000): 371–91.

Hawthorne, Peter. "Smile, Beloved Country." *Time International* 163, 16 (2004): 34.

Hebdige, Dick. *Subculture: The Meaning of Style.* London: Routledge, 1989.

Henderson, Jennifer Jacobs, and Gerald J. Baldasty. "Race, Advertising, and Prime-Time Television." *Howard Journal of Communications* 14, 2 (2003): 97–112.

Hening, William W. *The Statutes at Large: Being a Collection of All the Laws of Virginia from the First Session of the Legislature in 1619*, Volume 2 (Richmond, VA: George Cochran, 1822), 260, 281.

Hernton, Calvin C. *Sex and Racism in America.* New York: Anchor Books, 1988.

Hibbler, Dan K., and Kimberly J. Shinew. "Interracial Couples' Experience of Leisure: A Social Network Approach." *Journal of Leisure Research* 34, 2 (2002): 135–56.

Higginbotham, Evelyn B. *Righteous Discontent: The Woman's Movement in the Black Baptist Church, 1880–1920.* Cambridge, MA: Harvard University Press, 1993.

Hill Collins, Patricia. *Black Sexual Politics: African Americans, Gender, and the New Racism.* New York: Routledge, 2004.

Hoberman, John. *Darwin's Athletes: How Sport Has Damaged Black America and Preserved the Myth of Race.* Boston: Houghton Mifflin, 1997.

Hodes, Martha. *Sex, Love, Race: Crossing Boundaries in North American History.* New York: New York University Press, 1999.

Hooks, bell. *Feminist Theory: From Margin to Center.* Boston: South End Press, 2000.

———. *Reel to Real: Race, Sex and Class at the Movies.* New York: Routledge, 1996.

———. *Black Looks: Race and Representation.* Boston: South End, 1992.

———. *Ain't I a Woman: Black Women and Feminism.* Boston: South End Press, 1981.

Hoppenstand, Gary. "Yellow Devil Doctors and Opium Dens: A Survey of the Yellow Peril Stereotypes in Mass Media Entertainment." Pp. 171–85 in Christopher D. Geist and Jack Nachbar (eds.) *The Popular Culture Reader*, 3rd ed. Bowling Green, OH: Bowling Green University Popular Press, 1983.

Horsman, Reginald. *Race and Manifest Destiny: Origins of American Racial Anglo-Saxonism.* Cambridge, MA: Harvard University Press, 1981.

Hsia, J. J. *Mass Communications Research Methods: A Step-by-Step Approach.* Hillsdale, NJ: Erlbaum Associates, 1988.

Hughes, Zondra. "Why Some Sisters Only Date Whites & 'Others.'" *Ebony* 58, 7 (2003): 55–57.

Hunt, Darnell. "2007 Hollywood Writers Report—Whose Stories Are We Telling?" Report commissioned by the Writer's Guild of America, West. Accessed at www .wga.org/uploadedFiles/who_we_are/HWR07_exec.pdf.

———. "Making Sense of Blackness on Television." P. 16 in Darnell Hunt (ed.) *Channeling Blackness: Studies on Television and Race in America.* Oxford: Oxford University Press, 2005.

Hutchinson, Earl Ofari. *Beyond O.J.: Race, Sex and Class Lessons for America.* Los Angeles: Middle Passage Press, 1996.

Ignatiev, Noel. *How the Irish Became White.* New York: Routledge, 1995.

Jefferson, Thomas. *Notes on the State of Virginia.* Richmond, VA: J. W. Randolph, 1853.

Jhally, Sut, and Justin Lewis. "White Responses: The Emergence of 'Enlightened' Racism." Pp. 74–88 in Darnell M. Hunt (ed.) *Channeling Blackness: Studies on Television and Race in America.* Oxford: Oxford University Press, 2005.

Jones, Jacquie. "The Construction of Black Sexuality." *Philadelphia Inquirer,* July 17, 2002.

Jordan, Winthrop. *White over Black: American Attitudes toward the Negro, 1550–1812.* Chapel Hill: University of North Carolina Press, 1968.

Julien, Isaac, and Kobena Mercer. "De Margin and De Centre." Originally appeared as the introduction to "The Last 'Special Issue' on Race?" *Screen* 29, 4 (1988): 2–10.

Kawaii, Yuko. "Stereotyping Asian Americans: The Dialectic of the Model Minority and the Yellow Peril." *Howard Journal of Communications* 16, 2 (2005): 109–30.

Kellner, Douglas. *Media Culture: Cultural Studies, Identity, and Politics between the Modern and Postmodern.* London: Routledge, 1995.

Kennedy, Randall. "Interracial Intimacy." *Atlantic Monthly* 290, 5 (December 2002): 103–8.

Killian, Kyle D. "Crossing Borders: Race, Gender, and Their Intersections in Inter-racial Couples." *Journal of Feminist Family Therapy* 13, 1 (2001): 1–31.

———. "Reconstituting Racial Histories and Identities: The Narratives of Interracial Couples." *Journal of Marital and Family Therapy* 27, 1 (2001): 27–42.

———. "Dominant and Marginalized Discourses in Interracial Couples' Narratives: Implications for Family Therapists." *Family Process* 41, 4 (2002): 603–18.

Kim, Claire Jean. "The Racial Triangulation of Asian Americans." *Politics and Society* 27, 1 (1999): 105–38.

King, C. Richard, and Charles Fruehling Springwood. "Body and Soul: Physicality, Disciplinarity, and the Overdetermination of Blackness." Pp. 185–206 in Darnell M. Hunt (ed.) *Channeling Blackness: Studies on Television and Race in America.* Oxford: Oxford University Press, 2005.

Knox, David, Marty E. Zusman, Carmen Buffington, and Gloria Hemphill. "Inter-racial Dating Attitudes among College Students." *College Student Journal* 34, 1 (2000): 69–71.

Korgen, K. O., J. Mahon, and G. Wang. "Diversity on College Campuses Today: The Growing Need to Foster Campus Environments Capable of Countering a Possible 'Tipping Effect.'" *College Student Journal* 37, 1 (2003): 16–26.

Lacayo, Richard. "For Better or for Worse? As More Gays Say 'I Do,' Bush Calls for a Constitutional Ban." *Time* 163, 10 (March 2004): 26.

Larson, Mary Strom. "Race and Interracial Relationships in Children's Television Commercials." *Howard Journal of Communications* 13, 3 (2002): 223–35.

———. "Gender, Race, and Aggression in Television Commercials that Feature Children." *Sex Roles* 48, 1–2 (2003): 67–75.

Lee-St. John, Jeninne. "Marketing 2004 Hot Spots." *Time* 164, 165, 26/1 (December 2004): 20.

Lewandowski, Donna A., and Linda A. Jackson. "Perceptions of Interracial Couples: Prejudice at the Dyadic Level." *Journal of Black Psychology* 27, 3 (2001): 288–303.

Li-Vollmer, Meredith. "Race Representation in Child-Targeted Television Commercials." *Mass Communication & Society* 5, 2 (2002): 207–28.

Lincoln, C. Eric. *Race, Religion and the Continuing American Dilemma.* New York: Hill and Wang, 1999.

Ling, A. *Between Worlds: Women Writers of Chinese Ancestry.* New York: Pergamon, 1990.

Lipsitz, George. *The Possessive Investment in Whiteness: How White People Profit from Identity Politics.* Philadelphia, PA: Temple University Press, 1998.

Litwack, Leon. *North of Slavery: The Negro in the Free States, 1790–1860.* Chicago: University of Chicago Press, 1961.

Luibheid, Eithne. *Entry Denied: Controlling Sexuality at the Border.* Minneapolis: University of Minnesota Press, 2002.

Lyman, Stanford. *A Sociology of the Absurd.* Dix Hills, NY: General Hall, 1997.

———. "Marriage and the Family among Chinese Immigrants to America, 1850–1960." *Phylon* 19 (1968): 321–30.

M'Carty, William. *National Songs, Ballads, and Other Patriotic Poetry.* Philadelphia, PA: William M'Carty, 1846.

Marchetti, Gina. *Romance and the "Yellow Peril": Race, Sex, and Discursive Strategies in Hollywood Fiction.* Berkeley: University of California Press, 1993.

Markovitz, Jonathan. *Legacies of Lynching: Racial Violence and Memory.* Minneapolis: University of Minnesota Press, 2004.

McCarthy, D., R. L. Jones, and P. Potrac. "Constructing Images and Interpreting Realities." *International Review for the Sociology of Sport* 38, 2 (2003): 217–38.

McClintock, Anne. *Imperial Leather: Race, Gender, and Sexuality in the Colonial Contest.* New York: Routledge, 1995.

McFadden, John. "Intercultural Marriage and Family: Beyond the Racial Divide." *Family Journal: Counseling and Therapy for Couples and Families* 9, 1 (2001): 39–42.

McFadden, John, and James L. Moore III. "Intercultural Marriage and Intimacy: Beyond the Continental Divide." *International Journal for the Advancement of Counseling* 23, 4 (2001): 261–68.

Mercer, Kobena. "Skin Head Sex Thing: Racial Difference and the Homoerotic Imaginary." *Competing Glances* 16 (1992): 17.

———. *Welcome to the Jungle: New Positions in Black Cultural Studies*. London: Routledge, 1994.

Miller Toby, and Alec W. McHoul. *Popular Culture and Everyday Life*. Thousand Oaks, CA: Sage Publications, 1998.

Moore, Robert M. III. "An Exploratory Study of Interracial Dating on a Small College Campus." *Sociological Viewpoints* 16 (2002): 46–64.

Morrison Toni. *Race-ing Justice, En-gendering Power*. New York: Pantheon, 1992.

Mouffe, Chantal. "Hegemony and the Integral State in Gramsci: Towards a New Concept of Politics." Pp. 167–87 in George Bridges and Rosalind Brunt (eds.) *Silver Linings: Some Strategies for the Eighties*. London: Lawrence and Wishart Ltd., 1987.

Moran, Rachel. *Interracial Intimacy: The Regulation of Race and Romance*. Chicago: University of Chicago Press, 2001.

Mumford Kevin. *Interzones: Black/White Sex Districts in Chicago and New York in the Early Twentieth Century*. New York: Columbia University Press, 1997.

NAACP Diveristy Report. "Out of Focus, Out of Sync, Take 3," 2003.

Nagel, Joane. *Race, Ethnicity, and Sexuality: Intimate Intersections, Forbidden Frontiers*. New York: Oxford University Press, 2003.

Nakayama, Thomas. "Show/Down Time: 'Race,' Gender, Sexuality, and Popular Culture." *Critical Studies in Mass Communication* 11, 2 (1994): 162–79.

Namias, June. *White Captives: Gender and Ethnicity on the American Frontier*. Chapel Hill: University of North Carolina Press, 1993.

Negra, Diane. "Ethnic Food Fetishism, Whiteness, and Nostalgia in Recent Film and Television." *Velvet Light Trap* 50 (2002): 62–76.

Negy, Charles, and Douglas K. Snyder. "Relationship Satisfaction of Mexican American and Non-Hispanic White American Interethnic Couples: Issues of Acculturation and Clinical Intervention." *Journal of Marital and Family Therapy* 26, 3 (2002): 293–304.

Nemoto, Kumiko. *Racing Romance: Love, Power, and Desire among Asian American/ White Couples*. New Brunswick, NJ: Rutgers University Press, 2009.

Novack, Kate. "And the Bride Wore Lavender." *Time* 163, 19 (May 10, 2004): A1.

O'Connor, Lisa A., Jeanne Brooks-Gunn, and Julia Graber. "Black and White Girls' Racial Preferences in Media and Peer Choices and the Role of Socialization for Black Girls." *Journal of Family Psychology* 14, 3 (2000): 510–21.

Omi, Michael, and Howard Winant. *Racial Formation in the United States: From the 1960s to the 1990s*. New York: Routledge, 1994.

Ortiz, Christopher. "The Forbidden Kiss: Raúl Ferrera-Balanquet and Enrique Novelo Cascante's Merida Proscrita." Pp. 244–59 in Chon A. Noriega and Ana M. Lopez (eds.) *Ethnic Eye: Latino Media Arts*. Minneapolis: University of Minnesota Press, 1990.

Osumi, Megumi Dick. "Asians and California's Anti-Miscegenation Laws." Pp. 2, 6 in Nobuya Tsuchida (ed.) *Asian and Pacific American Experiences: Women's Per-*

spectives. Minneapolis: University of Minnesota, Asian/Pacific American Learning Resource Center, 1982.

Perry, Alex. "A Force of Nature." *Time International* 164, 11 (2004): 48.

Plane, Ann Marie. *Colonial Intimacies: Indian Marriage in Early New England*. Ithaca, NY: Cornell University Press, 2000.

Press, Andrea. *Women Watching Television*. Philadelphia: University of Pennsylvania Press, 1991.

Randall, Alice. "Act Two." *Essence* 35, 4 (2002): 124.

Raymond, Diane. "Popular Culture and Queer Representation: A Critical Perspective." In Gail Dines and Jean M. Humez (eds.) *Gender, Race, and Class in Media: A Text-Reader*. Thousand Oaks, CA: Sage, 2003.

Reed, L. 2002. "White Girl 'Gone Off with the Blacks.'" *Hecate* 28, 1 (2002): 2–22.

Ríos-Bustamante, Antonio. "Latino Participation in the Hollywood Film Industry, 1911–1945." In Chon A. Noriega (ed.) *Chicanos and Film: Essays on Chicano Representation and Resistance*. New York: Garland, 1992.

Rivero, Yeidy M. "Erasing Blackness: The Media Construction of 'Race' in *Mi Familia*, the First Puerto Rican Situation Comedy with a Black Family." *Media, Culture & Society* 24, 4 (2002): 481–97.

Robinson, Cedric J., and Luz Maria Cabral. "The Mulatta on Film: From Hollywood to the Mexican Revolution." *Race & Class* 45, 2 (2003): 1–20.

Rocchio, Vincent. *Reel Racism: Confronting Hollywood's Construction of Afro-American Culture*. Boulder, CO: Westview Press, 2002.

Rodriguez, Clara. *Heroes, Lovers, and Others: The Story of Latinos in Hollywood*. Washington, DC: Smithsonian, 2004.

Roediger David. *Towards the Abolition of Whiteness: Essays on Race, Politics, and Working Class History*. London: Verso, 1994.

———. *The Wages of Whiteness: Race and the Making of the American Working Class*. London: Verso, 1991.

Romano, Renee. *Race Mixing: Black-White Marriage in Postwar America*. Cambridge, MA: Harvard University Press, 2002.

Root, Maria P. P. *Loves' Revolution: Interracial Marriage*. Philadelphia, PA: Temple University Press, 2001.

Romer, D., K. H. Jamieson, and N. J. De Coteau. "The Treatment of Persons of Color in Local Television News: Ethnic Blame Discourse or Realistic Group Conflict?" *Communication Research* 25 (1998): 268–305.

Russell, Katheryn K. *The Color of Crime: Racial Hoaxes, White Fear, Black Protectionism, Police Harassment, and other Macroaggressions*. New York: New York University Press, 1997.

Russell, Margaret. "Race and the Dominant Gaze: Narratives of Law and Inequality in Popular Film." Pp. 56–63 in Richard Delgado (ed.) *Critical Race Theory: The Cutting Edge*. Philadelphia, PA: Temple University Press, 1995.

Said, Edward. 1979. *Orientalism*. New York: Vintage Books, 1979.

Sears, D. O. "Symbolic Racism." Pp. 53–845 in P. A. Katz and D. A. Taylor (eds.), *Eliminating Racism*. New York: Plenum, 1988.

Shevory, Thomas. *Notorious H.I.V: The Media Spectacle of Nushawn Williams*. Minneapolis: University of Minnesota Press, 2004.

Smith, Earl, and Angela Hattery. "Hey Stud: Race, Sex and Sports," *Sexuality Culture* 10, 2 (2006): 3–32.

Smith, Valerie. "Split Affinities: The Case of Interracial Rape." Pp. 272–73 in Anne C. Hermann and Abigail J. Stewart (eds.) *Theorizing Feminism: Parallel Trends in the Humanities and Social Sciences*. Boulder, CO: Westview Press, 1994.

———. *Not Just Race, Not Just Gender: Black Feminist Readings*. New York: Routledge, 1998.

———. *Representing Blackness: Issues in Film and Video*. New Brunswick, NJ: Rutgers University Press, 1997.

Snead, James. *White Screens/Black Images: Hollywood from the Dark Side*. New York: Routledge, 1994.

Squire, Corinne. "Who's White? Television Talk Shows and Representations of Whiteness." In M. Fine, L. Weis, L. C. Powell, and L. Mun Wong (eds.) *Off-white: Readings on Race, Power, and Society*. New York: Routledge, 1997.

Staiger, Janet. *Blockbuster TV: Must-See Sitcoms in the Network Era*. New York: New York University Press, 2000.

Stroman, Carolyn A., and Kenneth E. Jones. "The Analysis of Television Content." P. 275 in Joy Keiko Asamen and Gordon L. Berry (eds.) *Research Paradigms, Television, and Social Behaviour*. London: Sage Publications, 1998.

Sweeney, Gael. "The Trashing of White Trash: Natural Born Killers and the Appropriation of the White Trash Aesthetic." *Quarterly Review of Film & Video* 18, 2 (2001): 143–55.

Tajima, R. "Lotus Blossoms Don't Bleed: Images of Asian Women." Pp. 308–17 in *Making Waves: An Anthology of Writings by and about Asian American Women*. Boston: Beacon, 1989.

Takaki, Ronald. *A Different Mirror: A History of Multicultural America*. Boston: Little, Brown and Company, 1993.

Tasker, Yvonne. *Spectacular Bodies: Gender, Genre, and the Action Cinema*. New York: Routledge, 1993.

Taylor, Charles. "Black and White and Taboo All Over." Salon Arts and Entertainment online, accessed at http://archive.salon.com/ent/feature/2000/02/14/interracial_movies/index.html (February 14, 2000).

Taylor, Clyde. "The Re-Birth of the Aesthetic in Cinema." Pp. 15–37 in Daniel Bernardi (ed.) *The Birth of Whiteness: Race and the Emergence of U.S. Cinema*. New Brunswick, NJ: Rutgers University Press, 1996.

Thiesmeyer, Lynn. "The West's 'Comfort Women' and the Discourses of Seduction." Pp. 69–92 in Shirley G. Lim, Larry E. Smith, and Wimal Dissanayake (eds.) *Transnational Asia Pacific: Gender, Culture, and the Public Sphere*. Urbana: University of Illinois Press, 1999.

Thornbrough, Emma Lou. *The Negro in Indiana: A Study of a Minority.* Indianapolis: Indiana Historical Bureau, 1957.

Tocqueville, Alexis de. *Democracy in America.* Vol . 1: 373. New York: Vintage, 1990 [originally published in 1835].

Trailer Park in Contemporay Daytime Television Talk Shows," *Narrative Inquiry* 12, 1 (2002): 155–72.

Tuchman, Gaye. "Objectivity as Strategic Ritual: An Examination of Newsmen's Notion of Objectivity." *American Journal of Sociology* 77 (1972): 660–79.

———. "Making News by Doing Work: Routinizing the Unexpected." *American Journal of Sociology* 79 (1973): 110–31.

Tzeng, Jessie M. "Ethnically Heterogamous Marriages: The Case of Asian Canadians." *Journal of Comparative Family Studies* 31, 3 (2000): 321–37.

Vera, Hernán, and Andrew M. Gordon. *Screen Saviors: Hollywood Fictions of Whiteness.* Lanham, MD: Rowman & Littlefield, 2003.

Wang, A. "Maxine Hong Kingston's Reclaiming of America: The Birthright of the Chinese American Male." *South Dakota Review* 26 (1988): 18–29.

Ware, V. *Beyond the Pale: White Women, Racism and History.* London: Verso, 1992.

Weber, Max. "Membership of a Race." *Max Weber Selections in Translation,* W. G. Runciman (ed.) Cambridge, UK: Cambridge University Press, [1922] 1977.

Weigman, Robyn. "Black Bodies/American Commodities: Gender, Race, and the Bourgeois Ideal in Contemporary Film." Pp. 308–28 in Lester D. Friedman (ed.), *Unspeakable Images: Ethnicity and the American Cinema.* Urbana: University of Illinois Press, 1991.

Wells, Ida B. *On Lynchings: Southern Horrors, a Red Record, Mob Rule in New Orleans.* New York: Arno, 1969.

West, Cornel. *Race Matters.* Boston: Beacon, 1993.

———. "The New Cultural Politics of Difference." In *The Postmodern Turn: New Perspectives on Social Theory,* Steven Seidman (ed.) Cambridge, UK: Cambridge University Press, 1994.

White, Patricia. *Uninvited: Classical Hollywood Cinema and Lesbian Representability.* Bloomington: Indiana University Press, 1999.

Wilensky, Joe. "Relationships." *Human Ecology* 30, 1 (2002): 16–18.

Williams, Linda. *Playing the Race Card: Melodramas of Black and White from Uncle Tom to O. J. Simpson.* Princeton, NJ: Princeton University Press, 2001.

Williams, Patricia. *Seeing a Color-Blind Future: The Paradox of Race.* New York: Noonday, 1998.

——— "Alchemical Notes: Reconstructing Ideals from Deconstructed Rights." Pp. 84–94 in Richard Delgado (ed.) *Critical Race Theory.* Philadelphia, PA: Temple University Press, 1995.

———. *The Alchemy of Race and Rights.* Cambridge, MA: Harvard University Press, 1991.

Wing Adrien Katherine, and Sylke Merchan. "Rape, Ethnicity and Culture: Spirit Injury from Bosnia to Black America." Pp. 516–28 in Richard Delgado (ed.) *Critical Race Theory.* Philadelphia, PA: Temple University Press, 1995.

Yancey, George. "Who Interracially Dates: An Examination of the Characteristics of Those Who Have Interracially Dated." *Journal of Comparative Family Studies* 33, 2 (2002): 179–90.

Zavarzadeh, Mas'ud. *Seeing Films Politically*. Albany: State University of New York Press, 1991.

Newspaper and News Media Sources

ABC News Transcripts, 18 September 2004; *Good Morning America*, 7:00 a.m.; [online]; LexisNexis Academic Universe.

ABC News Transcripts, 3 February 2004; *Good Morning America*, 7:00 a.m.; [online]; LexisNexis Academic Universe.

ABC News Transcripts, 26 January 2004; *Good Morning America*, 7:00 a.m.; [online]; LexisNexis Academic Universe.

ABC News Transcripts, 21 January 2004; *Nightline*, 11:35 p.m.; [online]; LexisNexis Academic Universe.

ABC News Transcripts, 20 October 2003; *World News Tonight with Peter Jennings*, 6:30 p.m.; [online]; LexisNexis Academic Universe.

ABC News Transcripts, 6 August 2003; *World News Tonight with Peter Jennings*, 6:30 p.m.; [online]; LexisNexis Academic Universe.

ABC News Transcripts, 17 July 2003; *Primetime Thursday*, 10:00 p.m.; [online]; LexisNexis Academic Universe.

"ABC vs. FCC: Commercial Sparks Controversy," *ABC News Transcripts*, 17 November 2004; *Good Morning America*, 7:00 a.m.; [online]; LexisNexis Academic Universe.

Abrams, Dan. "Possible Effects of Kobe Bryant's Accuser Filing a Civil Lawsuit Before the Beginning of the Criminal Trial," *NBC News Transcripts*, 11 August 2004; *Today Show*, 7:00 a.m.; [online]; LexisNexis Academic Universe.

Abrams, Dan. "Attorneys of Kobe Bryant's Accuser Discuss State of the Criminal Case against Bryant," *NBC News Transcripts*, 5 August 2004; *Today Show*, 7:00 a.m.; [online]; LexisNexis Academic Universe.

Abrams, Dan. "Prosecutors in Kobe Bryant Case Say Case Will Go to Trial Amid Questions Whether Accuser Will Proceed with Criminal Case," *NBC News Transcripts*, 5 August 2004; *Today Show*, 7:00 a.m.; [online]; LexisNexis Academic Universe.

Abrams, Dan. "Latest Developments in Kobe Bryant Case and Why Bryant's Accuser Received Nearly $20,000 in Victim's Compensation," *NBC News Transcripts*, 30 July 2004; *Today Show*, 7:00 a.m.; [online]; LexisNexis Academic Universe.

Abrams, Dan. "Sexual Activity of Victim to be Allowed in Court in Kobe Bryant Case," *NBC News Transcripts*, 24 July 2004; *Saturday Today Show*, 7:00 a.m.; [online]; LexisNexis Academic Universe.

Abrams, Dan. "Update on Scott Peterson, Kobe Bryant, and Martha Stewart Cases," *NBC News Transcripts*, 15 July 2004; *Today Show*, 7:00 a.m.; [online]; LexisNexis Academic Universe.

Abrams, Dan. "Preliminary Hearing in Kobe Bryant Sexual Assault Case," *NBC News Transcripts*, 15 October 2003; *NBC Nightly News*, 6:30 p.m.; [online]; LexisNexis Academic Universe.

Abrams, Dan. "Heated Preliminary Hearing in Kobe Bryant Sexual Assault Case," *NBC News Transcripts*, 12 October 2003; *NBC Nightly News*, 6:30 p.m.; [online]; LexisNexis Academic Universe.

Abrams, Dan. "Kobe Bryant in Court for Alleged Sexual Assault," *NBC News Transcripts*, 9 October 2003; *NBC Nightly News*, 6:30 p.m.; [online]; LexisNexis Academic Universe.

Abrams, Dan. "Kobe Bryant Appears in Court Hearing," *NBC News Transcripts*, 6 August 2003; *NBC Nightly News*, 6:30 p.m.; [online]; LexisNexis Academic Universe.

Abrams, Dan, Jennifer London, James Hattori, Mark Potter, and Don Teague. MS-NBC *News Transcripts*, 23 January 2004; *The Abrams Report*, 6:00 p.m.; [online]; LexisNexis Academic Universe.

"Accounts of the Kobe Bryant Rape from One of the Accuser's Friends," *CBS News Transcipts*, 4 October 2003; *48 Hours Investigates*, 8:00 p.m.; [online]; LexisNexis Academic Universe.

"Accuser in the Kobe Bryant Rape Case Files a Civil Suit in Federal Court against the NBA Star," *CBS News Transcripts* 10 August 2004; *CBS Evening News*, 6:30 p.m.; [online]; LexisNexis Academic Universe.

"Actor Diggs Terrorized." *New York Post*. (December 5, 2004); "Actors Targets of Racist Threats." *Houston Chronicle* (December 72004): A2[online] LexisNexis Academic Universe.

Adande, J. A. "He Loves a Charade, Not a Parade," *Los Angeles Times* (July 17, 2004): p. D4. [online] LexisNexis Academic Universe.

"Admissible Evidence, New Ruling in Kobe Bryant Case," *ABC News Transcripts*, 24 July 2004; *World News Tonight*, Saturday, 6:30 p.m.; [online]; LexisNexis Academic Universe.

Aduroja, Grace. "Teen Movies Embracing Interracial Couples," *Times-Picayune* (July 27, 2001): p. 5.

Altschuler, Glenn C. "The Big Choose." *New York Times* (April 9, 2000): p. 4A.

"A Rival Breast." *New York Times* (February 29, 2004); p. 2 [online] LexisNexis Academic Universe.

Asman, David and Carol McKinley. "Kobe Bryant Case Rules on Accuser's Sexual History," *FOX News Transcripts* (April 26, 2004); *The Big Story with John Gibson*, 5:50 p.m.; [online]; LexisNexis Academic Universe.

Asman, David and Molly Henneberg. *FOX News Transcripts* (March 24, 2004); *The Big Story with John Gibson*, 5:00 p.m.; [online]; LexisNexis Academic Universe.

Associated Press. "Interracial Wedding Barred from Church," *San Diego Union-Tribune* (July 11, 2000); p. A-6; [online]; LexisNexis Academic Universe.

Associated Press. "Interracial Dating? Get a Note from Mom," *San Diego Union-Tribune* (March 8, 2000); p. A-15; [online]; LexisNexis Academic Universe.

Avila, Jim. "In Kobe Bryant's Rape Trial Case, Lawyers May Smear Reputation of Victim Like Many Other High-Profile Cases," *NBC News Transcripts* (October 14, 2003); *NBC Nightly News*, 6:30 p.m.; [online]; LexisNexis Academic Universe.

Atlanta Journal and Constitution (October 4, 1998): p. 02b; [online]; LexisNexis Academic Universe.

Atlanta Journal and Constitution (December 11, 1998): 13S [online] LexisNexis Academic Universe.

Atlanta Journal and Constitution (September 26, 2000): p. 11A; [online]; LexisNexis Academic Universe.

Avila, Jim. "Basketball Star Kobe Bryant's Tarnished Career," *NBC News Transcripts* (October 9, 2003); *NBC Nightly News*, 6:30 p.m.; [online]; LexisNexis Academic Universe.

Avila, Jim. "Basketball Star Kobe Bryant Officially Charged with Sexual Assault," *NBC News Transcripts* (July 18, 2003); *NBC Nightly News*, 6:30 p.m.; [online]; LexisNexis Academic Universe.

Avila, Jim. "Kobe Bryant Admits to Adultery but Claims Innocence of Rape Allegations," *NBC News Transcripts* (July 19, 2003); *NBC Nightly News*, 6:30 p.m.; [online]; LexisNexis Academic Universe.

Baldauf, Scott. "After a Teen's Death, a Small Mississippi Town Confronts One of Racism's Oldest Taboos." *Christian Science Monitor* (July 3, 2000); p. 1 [online] LexisNexis Academic Universe.

Barry, Ellen. "Georgia's Supreme Court Reverses 10-Year Sentence." *Los Angeles Times* (May 4, 2004) [online] LexisNexis Academic Universe.

———. "Race, Justice Go on Trial in Sex Case." *Los Angeles Times* (February 16, 2004) [online] LexisNexis Academic Universe.

Battista, Judy. "ABC Puts NFL in 'Desperate' Situation." *New York Times* (November 17, 2004) [online] LexisNexis Academic Universe.

Bedell, Geraldine. "Relationships: Britain Has One of the Fastest-Growing Mixed-Race Populations—But Many People Are Still Hostile towards Interracial Couples. We Asked Some of Them How Their Lives Have Been Affected." *Observer* (April 6 , 2003) [online] LexisNexis Academic Universe.

"Behaving Badly," *ABC News Transcripts*, 30 July 2003; *World News Tonight with Peter Jennings*, 6:30 p.m.; [online]; LexisNexis Academic Universe.

BET Nightly News Transcripts (July 2003–December 2004); [online]; LexisNexis Academic Universe.

"Biracial Couples Find Acceptance." *Houston Chronicle* (July 8, 2001); p. 12 [online] LexisNexis Academic Universe.

Blackstone, John. "Kobe Bryant Makes First Appearance in Court on Sexual Assault Charges in Eagle, Colorado," *CBS News Transcripts* (August 6, 2003); *CBS Evening News*, 6:30 p.m.; [online]; LexisNexis Academic Universe.

Bolton, Shyretha. "In the End, Justice System Worked for Marcus Dixon." *Athens Banner-Herald* (May 11, 2004); [online]; OnlineAthens.

Bowen, Jerry. "Fallout Continues from the CBS NFL Halftime Show that Left Janet Jackson Overexposed," *CBS News Transcripts*, 3 February 2004; *CBS Evening News*, 6:30 p.m.; [online]; LexisNexis Academic Universe.

Bowers, Cynthia, "Some Media Outlets Choosing to Release the Name of Kobe Bryant's Accuser," *CBS News Transcripts* (July 24, 2003); *CBS Evening News*, 6:30 p.m; [online]; LexisNexis Academic Universe.

Braxton, Greg. "Interracial Romances Blossom in Prime Time." *Gazette* (March 25, 2000) [online] LexisNexis Academic Universe.

Bresnahan, Mike. "Bryant Not Working with a Secret Agent." *Los Angeles Times* (July 14, 2004): p. 1 [online] LexisNexis Academic Universe.

Bresnahan, Mike. "Ball Back in His Court." *Los Angeles Times* (September 2, 2004): p. 1D) [online] LexisNexis Academic Universe.

Brick, Michael. "Lyrical Judge Praises Eminem in Lyrics Fight." *New York Times* (June 10, 2004): p. 1E [online] LexisNexis Academic Universe.

"Bring Back Sousa." *New York Times* (February 4, 2004): p. 24A [online] LexisNexis Academic Universe.

Brokaw, Tom. "Prosecutors in Kobe Bryant Rape Case Ask Judge to Drop Charges against Bryant," *NBC News Transcripts*, 1 September 2004; *NBC Nightly News*, 6:30 p.m.; [online]; LexisNexis Academic Universe.

Broussard, Chris. "Bryant Denies He's Leaving the Lakers." *New York Times*, February 14, 2004, p. 1; [online] LexisNexis Academic Universe.

Brown, Campbell. "Two Current High-Profile Court Cases Explored in Depth," *NBC News Transcripts* (January 24, 2004); *Saturday Today Show*, 7:00 a.m. [online]; LexisNexis Academic Universe.

Brown, G. "Ticket Source." *Denver Post* (October 31, 2003); pp. FF-10; [online] LexisNexis Academic Universe.

Brown, Marian Gail. "Why Did She Do It?" *Connecticut Post* (November 14, 2004) [online] LexisNexis Academic Universe.

Brown, Tim. "Bryant Is Off Olympic Team." *Los Angeles Times* (May 1, 2004): p. 8 [online] LexisNexis Academic Universe.

———. "Bryant Might Miss Olympics." *Los Angeles Times* (April 29, 2004): p. D10 [online] LexisNexis Academic Universe.

———. "Bryant to Stay with Retooled Lakers." *Los Angeles Times* (July 16, 2004): p. A1 [online] LexisNexis Academic Universe.

Browne, J. Zamgba. "Janet Jackson Stirs Up Controversy at Annual Gala of 100 Black Men." *Amsterdam News* (November 17, 2004) [online] LexisNexis Academic Universe.

Brownfield, Paul. "Unforgiven, Unapologetic." *Los Angeles Times* (January 17, 2005): p. 20E [online] LexisNexis Academic Universe.

"The Bryant Case." *Los Angeles Times* (September 2, 2004): p. 1D [online] LexisNexis Academic Universe.

Brzezinski, Mika. "Marcus Dixon's Conviction on Charges of Forcible Rape Is Called Miscarriage of Justice by Some Critics, Including Members of the Jury

That Convicted Him," *CBS News Transcripts*, 20 January 2004; *CBS Morning News*, 6:30 a.m.; [online]; LexisNexis Academic Universe.

———. "Marcus Dixon's Conviction on Charges of Forcible Rape Is Called Miscarriage of Justice by Some Critics, Including Members of the Jury That Convicted Him," *CBS News Transcripts* 20, January 2004; *The Early Show*, 7:00 a.m.; [online]; LexisNexis Academic Universe.

———. "Marcus Dixon's Conviction on Charges of Forcible Rape Is Called Miscarriage of Justice By Some Critics, Including Members of the Jury That Convicted Him," *CBS News Transcripts*, 19 January 2004; *CBS Evening News*, 6:30 p.m.; [online]; LexisNexis Academic Universe.

Burns, Eric. "Coverage of ABC Ad," *FOX News Transcripts*, 20 November 2004; *FOX News Watch*, 6:40 p.m.; [online]; LexisNexis Academic Universe.

Carr, David. "When a TV Talking Head Becomes a Talking Body." *New York Times* (November 25, 2004): p. 1E [online] LexisNexis Academic Universe.

Carr, Jay. "Spike Lee Takes the Fever's Measure." *Los Angeles Times* (January 15, 2005): p. 1 [online] LexisNexis Academic Universe.

Carr, Rebecca. "The Impeachment Hearings: Georgia Lawmaker Denies Courting Racists." *Boston Globe* (June 2, 1991): p. B5 [online] LexisNexis Academic Universe.

Carter, Bill, and Richard Sandomir. "Halftime-Show Fallout Includes F.C.C. Inquiry." *New York Times* (February 3, 2004): p. 1D [online] LexisNexis Academic Universe.

Cheakalos, Christina. "Did Judge Take Her Sons Because of 'Last Taboo'? Interracial Couple Loses in Mississippi Courts." *Atlanta Journal and Constitution* (April 25, 1993): p. 1A [online] LexisNexis Academic Universe.

Coleman, Sandy. "Diversity Takes the Cake: Ethnic, Multiracial, and Same-Sex Couples Want the Cake Topper to Reflect Who They Are and What They Look Like." *Los Angeles Times* (November 19, 2004): p. 2D [online] LexisNexis Academic Universe.

———. "Census Insights: The Changing Face of the Region." *Los Angeles Times* (September 2, 2004): p. 1A [online] LexisNexis Academic Universe.

Croal, N'Gai, and Mark Starr. "Newsmakers." *Los Angeles Times* (September 2, 2004): p. 1D [online] LexisNexis Academic Universe.

"Dating and Racism at Bob Jones." *New York Times* (December 6, 2002): p. 35 [online] LexisNexis Academic Universe.

"Dead Wrong." *Washington Post* (July 8, 2001): p. C02 [online] LexisNexis Academic Universe.

Deggans, Eric. "Can New Comedies Deliver for NBC?" *Los Angeles Times* (September 2, 2004): p. 1A [online] LexisNexis Academic Universe.

Dillman, Lisa. "At Least He Gets the Gravity of Situation." *Los Angeles Times* (September 2, 2004): p. 31A [online] LexisNexis Academic Universe.

DiOrio, Carl. "Report: White Males Still Dominate Writing Ranks," *Hollywood Reporter*, May 9, 2007. Accessed at www.hollywoodreporter.com.

Dolan, Maura. "Signs in Bryant Statement Point to Deal in Works." *Los Angeles Times* (November 22, 2004): p. 2D [online] LexisNexis Academic Universe.

"Don't Equate Gay, Interracial Marriage." *USA Today*, February 2, 2004.

DiOrio, Carl. "Report: White Males Still Dominate Writing Ranks." *Hollywood Reporter*, May 9, 2007.

Dreisinger, Baz. "Can This Hookup Survive?" *New York Times* (January 9, 2005): p. 1 [online] LexisNexis Academic Universe.

DuBrow, Rick. "South Central: The Right Time, the Right Stuff," *Los Angeles Times*, Calendar section, January 11, 1994; p. F1.

Ebbert, Stephanie. "Lynch Role in Racial Case Questioned, Represented Whites Accused of Violence." *Boston Globe* (April 15, 2001): p. B1 [online] LexisNexis Academic Universe.

Elber, Lynn. "Latinos Rare on the Air." *Los Angeles Times*, December 12, 2003.

Elliott, Stuart. "With a Back-to-Basics Message, the NFL Plays It Safe, and Marketers Are Responding." *New York Times* (September 8, 2004): p. 7C [online] LexisNexis Academic Universe.

Fabrikant, Geraldine. "CBS Fined over Super Bowl Halftime Incident." *New York Times* (September 23, 2004): p. 1C [online] LexisNexis Academic Universe.

———. "Market Place: In a Vexingly Competitive Media Environment, a Big Stakeholder Mutes His Enthusiasm for Viacom." *New York Times* (February 4, 2004): p. 4C [online] LexisNexis Academic Universe.

Farmer, Sam. "ABC Apologizes for Steamy Scene." *Los Angeles Times* (November 17, 2004): p. 1D [online] LexisNexis Academic Universe.

Fears, Darryl, and Claudia Deane. "Biracial Couples Report Tolerance: Survey Finds Most Are Accepted by Families." *Washington Post* (July 5, 2001): p. A01 [online] LexisNexis Academic Universe.

Fine, Mary Jane. "Love Is Color Blind: NYC's Biracial Couples Understand the True Meaning of Diversity." *Daily News* (September 24, 2000): p. 2 [online] LexisNexis Academic Universe.

"Free Speech." *Los Angeles Times* (July 31, 2004): p. E17 [online] LexisNexis Academic Universe.

Friedman, Thomas L. "The Home Team." *New York Times* (February 8, 2004): p. 15 [online] LexisNexis Academic Universe.

Fussell, James A. "Legal Hurdles of Segregation Are Gone, But Social Barriers Remain." *Kansas City Star* (May 17, 2004) [online] LexisNexis Academic Universe.

Gamboa, Glenn. "Tape of Slurs Ramps Up Squabble between Eminem and *The Source*." *Milwaukee Journal Sentinel* (November 20, 2003): p. 03E [online] LexisNexis Academic Universe.

Gendar, Alison. "Analyzing a Psycho: Profilers Track Racist Letter-Writer." *Daily News* (January 4, 2005): p. 12 [online] LexisNexis Academic Universe.

———. "More Race Hate Letters." *Daily News* (January 3, 2005): p. 3 [online] LexisNexis Academic Universe.

George, Tara. "Panic Over HIV Spree Say at Least 11 Infected By Bronx Man." *Daily News*, October 27, 1997.

Gonzalez, Roberto. "Five Men Charged in Attack on Interracial Couple." *Hartford Courant* (July 8, 2004): p. B3 [online] LexisNexis Academic Universe.

Good, Regan. "The Way We Live Now." *New York Times* (February 9, 2003): p. 19 [online] LexisNexis Academic Universe.

Gordon, Rachel. "Feds Sue S.F. Public Housing Authority, Interracial Couple Had Complained of Harassment for Years." *San Francisco Chronicle* (September 19, 2002): p. A1 [online] LexisNexis Academic Universe.

Gorman, Anna. "Bryant Trial Date Is Set; Fight Looms on Transcripts." *Los Angeles Times* (June 26, 2004): p. 1 [online] LexisNexis Academic Universe.

Gorov, Lynda. "Prospective Jurors in Simpson Case Get Lengthy Quiz." *Boston Globe* (October 1, 1994): p. 1 [online] LexisNexis Academic Universe.

Graham, Jennifer. "S.C. College: A Study in Calm Campaign Furor Is Kept at Bay Inside Quiet Halls of Bob Jones." *The Boston Globe* (March 6, 2000): p. A3 [online] LexisNexis Academic Universe.

Graham, Renee. "Eminem's Old Words Aren't Hip-Hop's Biggest Problem." *Boston Globe* (December 23, 2003): p. E1 [online] LexisNexis Academic Universe.

Greene, Bob. "Games People Want to Play." *New York Times* (November 22, 2004): p. 7A [online] LexisNexis Academic Universe.

Greenwood, Michael. "High Priest of Hate Spreads His Gospel on the Internet." *Pittsburgh Post-Gazette* (September 3, 2000): p. A-11 [online] LexisNexis Academic Universe.

Gregory, Ursula. "Interracial Dating Greeted with Acceptance, Acrimony." *Milwaukee Journal Sentinel* (April 24, 2000): p. 04E [online] LexisNexis Academic Universe.

"Guards Surround Broadway Star after Mailed Racist Threats." *Times Union* (Albany, NY) (December 7, 2004): p. A2 [online] LexisNexis Academic Universe.

Hall, Trish. "In Alphabet City, a Co-op Gives a Couple an 'A.'" *New York Times* (September 17, 2000): p. 2 [online] LexisNexis Academic Universe.

Hammond, Margo. "Mixing the Colors of Love." *St. Petersburg Times* (May 14, 2000): p. 1D [online] LexisNexis Academic Universe.

Harris, Lyle V. "Attitudes on Race." *Atlanta Journal and Constitution* (June 20, 1999): p. 1H [online] LexisNexis Academic Universe.

Hart, Ariel. "Child Molesting Conviction Overturned in Georgia Classmate Case." *New York Times* (May 4, 2004): p. 20 [online] LexisNexis Academic Universe.

Hartigan, Patti. "A Safe Place to Sound Off about Race." *Boston Globe* (September 17, 1999): p. C1 [online] LexisNexis Academic Universe.

Healy, Patrick. "Burning Cross Left at Home of Interracial Couple on L.I." *New York Times* (November 22, 2004): p. 7B [online] LexisNexis Academic Universe.

Heffernan, Virginia. "Flouting Convention to Embrace Eccentricity." *New York Times* (January 8, 2005): p. 7B [online] LexisNexis Academic Universe.

Hensen, Steve. "Bryant's Accuser Now Considers Civil Suit." *Los Angeles Times* (August 5, 2004): p. D1 [online] LexisNexis Academic Universe.

———. "Supreme Court Appeal Dropped." *Los Angeles Times* (August 4, 2004): p. D3 [online] LexisNexis Academic Universe.

———. "Court Releases Details." *Los Angeles Times* (August 3, 2004): p. D1 [online] LexisNexis Academic Universe.

———. "Judge Apologizes for Court's Errors." *Los Angeles Times* (July 31, 2004): p. D1 [online] LexisNexis Academic Universe.

———. "Witness Twist in Bryant Case." *Los Angeles Times* (July 30, 2004): p. D1 [online] LexisNexis Academic Universe.

———. "Bryant Case Has New Error." *Los Angeles Times* (July 29, 2004): p. D1 [online] LexisNexis Academic Universe.

———. "Judge Seeks Edits of Transcripts." *Los Angeles Times* (July 28, 2004): p. D3 [online] LexisNexis Academic Universe.

———. "Justice Stays Media Case." *Los Angeles Times* (July 27, 2004): p. D6 [online] LexisNexis Academic Universe.

———. "Ruling Doesn't Deter Prosecutors." *Los Angles Times* (July 27, 2004): p. D1 [online] LexisNexis Academic Universe.

———. "Some Details of Bryant Accuser's Sex Life Allowed." *Los Angeles Times* (July 24, 2004): p. A1 [online] LexisNexis Academic Universe.

———. "Pathologists Won't Testify in Bryant Case." *Los Angeles Times* (July 23, 2004): p. D9 [online] LexisNexis Academic Universe.

———. "Media Appeal to U.S. Justices on Transcripts." *Los Angeles Times* (July 22, 2004): p. D8 [online] LexisNexis Academic Universe.

———. "Bryant's Accuser Wavered on Case." *Los Angeles Times* (July 20, 2004): p. D7 [online] LexisNexis Academic Universe.

———. "Plea Deal Is Seen as Unlikely." *Los Angeles Times* (July 19, 2004): p. D5 [online] LexisNexis Academic Universe.

———. "Bryant's Statements Admissible." *Los Angeles Times* (July 15, 2004): p. D1 [online] LexisNexis Academic Universe.

———. "Rape-Shield Issue Resolved." *Los Angeles Times* (June 23, 2004): p. 9 [online] LexisNexis Academic Universe.

———. "Bryant Case Still Moving Slowly." *Los Angeles Times* (June 22, 2004): p. 7 [online] LexisNexis Academic Universe.

———. "Bryant Hearings Resume." *Los Angeles Times* (June 21, 2004): p. 4 [online] LexisNexis Academic Universe.

———. "Prosecutors Decide against DNA Retesting." *Los Angeles Times* (June 19, 2004): p. 11 [online] LexisNexis Academic Universe.

———. "Judge Allows Both Sides to View Text Messages." *Los Angeles Times* (June 18, 2004): p. 7 [online] LexisNexis Academic Universe.

———. "Both Sides Seeking Sanctions." *Los Angeles Times* (June 16, 2004): p. 7 [online] LexisNexis Academic Universe.

———. "Judge Rejects Bryant Motion." *Los Angeles Times* (June 11, 2004): p. 7 [online] LexisNexis Academic Universe.

———. "Defense Criticizes Detectives." *Los Angeles Times* (June 10, 2004): p. 9 [online] LexisNexis Academic Universe.

———. "Judge Halts DNA Testing." *Los Angeles Times* (June 5, 2004): p. 6 [online] LexisNexis Academic Universe.

———. "DNA Retesting Is Contentious in Bryant Case." *Los Angeles Times* (June 4, 2004): p. 10 [online] LexisNexis Academic Universe.

———. "Bryant Accuser's Name OK for Trial." *Los Angeles Times* (June 2, 2004): p. 6 [online] LexisNexis Academic Universe.

———. "Still No Trial Date for Bryant." *Los Angeles Times* (May 28, 2004): p. 1 [online] LexisNexis Academic Universe.

———. "Prosecutors Seek New DNA Tests." *Los Angeles Times* (May 27, 2004): p. 1 [online] LexisNexis Academic Universe.

———. "Bryant Gives Plea of Not Guilty." *Los Angeles Times* (May 12, 2004): p. 1 [online] LexisNexis Academic Universe.

———. "Bryant Accuser Attends Hearing." *Los Angeles Times* (May 11, 2004): p. 5 [online] LexisNexis Academic Universe.

———. "Bryant Hearing Starts Today." *Los Angeles Times* (May 10, 2004): p. 11 [online] LexisNexis Academic Universe.

———. "Prosecution Rejects Expert." *Los Angeles Times* (May 8, 2004): p. 8 [online] LexisNexis Academic Universe.

———. "Defense Seeks a Ban on Terms." *Los Angeles Times* (May 5, 2004): p. 5 [online] LexisNexis Academic Universe.

———. "Cameras Are Expected to Record Bryant's Plea." *Los Angeles Times* (May 1, 2004): p. 8 [online] LexisNexis Academic Universe.

———. "Trial Is Likely in Late Summer." *Los Angeles Times* (April 29, 2004): p. 1 [online] LexisNexis Academic Universe.

———. "Hearing Should Conclude Today." *Los Angeles Times* (April 28, 2004): p. D5 [online] LexisNexis Academic Universe.

———. "Wheels of Justice Turn Slowly in Bryant Case." *Los Angeles Times* (April 27, 2004): p. D4 [online] LexisNexis Academic Universe.

———. "Bryant Is Back in Court Today." *Los Angeles Times* (April 26, 2004): p. D11 [online] LexisNexis Academic Universe.

———. "Bryant Lawyers Denied Records." *Los Angeles Times* (April 22, 2004): p. D1 [online] LexisNexis Academic Universe.

———. "Bryant Prosecutors Fire Back." *Los Angeles Times* (April 10, 2004): p. D9 [online] LexisNexis Academic Universe.

———. "Bryant Wants Trial Date Set." *Los Angeles Times* (April 7, 2004): p. D6 [online] LexisNexis Academic Universe.

———. "Prosecutors Ask for Plea." *Los Angeles Times* (April 3, 2004): p. D9 [online] LexisNexis Academic Universe.

———. "Hearing Postponed." *Los Angeles Times* (March 30, 2004): p. D4 [online] LexisNexis Academic Universe.

———. "Bryant Accuser's Mother Pleads for Quicker Process." *Los Angeles Times* (March 26, 2004): p. A1 [online] LexisNexis Academic Universe.

———. "Bryant's Accuser Testifies at Hearing." *Los Angeles Times* (March 25, 2004): p. D1 [online] LexisNexis Academic Universe.

———. "Hearings in Bryant Case Not Taking Usual Turns." *Los Angeles Times* (March 24, 2004): p. D1 [online] LexisNexis Academic Universe.

———. "Evidence Battle Heats Up." *Los Angeles Times* (March 17, 2004): p. D8 [online] LexisNexis Academic Universe.

———. "Bryant Defense Team Seeks Evidence from Prosecution." *Los Angeles Times* (March 16, 2004): p. D8 [online] LexisNexis Academic Universe.

———. "Bryant's Accuser Required to Testify." *Los Angeles Times* (March 12, 2004): p. D3 [online] LexisNexis Academic Universe.

———. "Bryant Defense Goes on Offense." *Los Angeles Times* (March 2, 2004): p. D1 [online] LexisNexis Academic Universe.

———. "Accuser in Bryant Case to Testify Tuesday." *Los Angeles Times* (February 28, 2004): p. D5 [online] LexisNexis Academic Universe.

———. "Bryant Lawyers Subpoena Bellhop, Argue Shield Law." *Los Angeles Times* (February 11, 2004): p. D6 [online] LexisNexis Academic Universe.

———. "Hearing on Records Will Go Into March." *Los Angeles Times* (February 6, 2004): p. D6 [online] LexisNexis Academic Universe.

———. "Defense Pushes on Procedures." *Los Angeles Times* (February 4, 2004): p. D1 [online] LexisNexis Academic Universe.

———. "Judge to Rule on Two Matters." *Los Angeles Times* (February 2, 2004): p. D5 [online] LexisNexis Academic Universe.

———. "Bryant Wins a Legal Battle." *Los Angeles Times* (January 30, 2004): p. D4 [online] LexisNexis Academic Universe.

———. "No Major Security Changes for Bryant." *Los Angeles Times* (January 23, 2004): p. D1 [online] LexisNexis Academic Universe.

———. "Timetable Worries Bryant's Lawyers." *Los Angeles Times* (January 16, 2004): p. 10 [online] LexisNexis Academic Universe.

———. "Bryant Lawyers Say Accuser Had 'Scheme.'" *Los Angeles Times* (January 14, 2004): p. D6 [online] LexisNexis Academic Universe.

———. "Court Filings Seek Closure." *Los Angeles Times* (January 13, 2004): p. D4 [online] LexisNexis Academic Universe.

———. "Bryant Motions Made." *Los Angeles Times* (January 6, 2004): p. 10 [online] LexisNexis Academic Universe.

———. "Bryant Prosecution Team Grows." *Los Angeles Times* (November 19, 2003): p. D5 [online] LexisNexis Academic Universe.

Henson, Steven, and Henry Weinstein. "Court Bars Disclosure by Media." *Los Angeles Times* (July 20, 2004): p. D1 [online] LexisNexis Academic Universe.

Henson, Steven, and Lance Pugmire. "Prosecution Drops in Kobe Bryant Rape Case." *Los Angeles Times* (September 2, 2004): p. 1A [online] LexisNexis Academic Universe.

Hines, Steve. "One Rule Too Many at My Alma Mater." *New York Times* (March 4, 2000): p. A15 [online] LexisNexis Academic Universe.

Hirschberg, Lynn, "Warren Beatty Is Trying to Say Something," *New York Times Magazine* (May 10, 1998): pp. 20–38.

Holmes, Steven A. "The Confusion over Who We Are." *New York Times* (June 3, 2001): p. [online] LexisNexis Academic Universe.

"Interracial Marriages." *Washington Post* (July 8, 2001): p. C02 [online] LexisNexis Academic Universe.

Ives, Nat. "Online Columnist Quits, Citing Excessive Editing." *New York Times* (September 20, 2004): p. 9C [online] LexisNexis Academic Universe.

Jackson, Derrick Z. "So Who Really Gets the Juice?" *Boston Globe* 29 (July 29, 1994): p. 19 [online] LexisNexis Academic Universe.

"Jackson Revealed." *New York Times* (February 2, 2004): p. 1D [online] LexisNexis Academic Universe.

Jacobs, Andrew. "Student Sex Case in Georgia Stirs Claims of Old South Justice." *New York Times* (January 22, 2004): p. 14 [online] LexisNexis Academic Universe.

Janofsky, Michael. "Review of TV Decency Law Looks beyond Bare Breast." *New York Times* (February 12, 2004): p. 32A [online] LexisNexis Academic Universe.

Jensen, Elizabeth, and Greg Braxton. "Celebs Jam Docket for Court TV." *Los Angeles Times* (January 19, 2004): p. E1 [online] LexisNexis Academic Universe.

Johnson, Kirk. "Before Rape Arrest, Bryant Expressed Fear to Police," *New York Times* (October 9, 2004): p. 16A [online] LexisNexis Academic Universe.

———. "Bryant Records," *New York Times* (September 22, 2004): p. 18A [online] LexisNexis Academic Universe.

———. "Colorado Election Keeps Bryant Debate Bubbling." *New York Times* (September 21, 2004): p. 18A [online] LexisNexis Academic Universe.

———. "Case Dismissed." *New York Times* (September 5, 2004): p. 2 [online] LexisNexis Academic Universe.

———. "The Bryant Trial: Anatomy of a Case That Fell Apart." *New York Times* (September 3, 2004): p. 14A [online] LexisNexis Academic Universe.

———. "As Accuser Balks, Prosecutors Drop Bryant Rape Case." *New York Times* (September 2, 2004): p. 1A [online] LexisNexis Academic Universe.

———. "Bryant Judge Apologizes for Disclosure on Accuser." *New York Times* (July 31, 2004): p. 9 [online] LexisNexis Academic Universe.

———. "Information Leaks Prompt Questions in Kobe Bryant Case." *New York Times* (July 30, 2004): p. 15 [online] LexisNexis Academic Universe.

———. "Name of Bryant Case Accuser Is Again Mistakenly Released." *New York Times* (July 29, 2004): p. 16 [online] LexisNexis Academic Universe.

———. "Burden in Bryant Case Rises for Judge and Accuser." *New York Times* (July 26, 2004): p. 11 [online] LexisNexis Academic Universe.

———. "Judge Limiting Sex-Life Shield at Bryant Trial." *Los Angeles Times* (July 24, 2004): p. 1 [online] LexisNexis Academic Universe.

———. "Ban on Printing Information on Kobe Bryant Accuser Is Upheld." *New York Times* (July 20, 2004): p. 12 [online] LexisNexis Academic Universe.

———. "Rape Shield Law Will Be Accepted in Bryant Case, Judge Says." *New York Times* (June 11, 2004): p. 16 [online] LexisNexis Academic Universe.

———. "Kobe Bryant Enters Plea of Not Guilty." *New York Times* (May 12, 2004): p. 17 [online] LexisNexis Academic Universe.

———. "Besieged, Accuser and Family Urge Quick Bryant Trial." *New York Times* (March 26, 2004): p. 1 [online] LexisNexis Academic Universe.

———. "At Hearing, Defense for Bryant Tries to Show That Evidence Was Not Collected Freely." *New York Times* (February 4, 2004): p. 17 [online] LexisNexis Academic Universe.

———. "Focus of Pretrial Hearings Shifts to Player's Statements." *New York Times* (February 3, 2004): p. 12 [online] LexisNexis Academic Universe.

Jones, Grahame L. "ABC Must Have Been Really Desperate." *Los Angeles Times* (November 22, 2004): p. 2D [online] LexisNexis Academic Universe.

Kelly, David. "In Eagle, End of Case Brings Mixed Feelings." *Los Angeles Times* (September 2, 2004): p. 31A [online] LexisNexis Academic Universe.

"Kobe Bryant Trial Will Begin Aug. 27, Court Officials Say." *New York Times* (June 26, 2004): p. 8 [online] LexisNexis Academic Universe.

Kolker, Claudia. "Exhuming a City's Shame: 78 Years Later. Tulsa Reexamines a Deadly Race Riot." *Providence Journal* (November 28, 1999).

Kristof, Nicholas D. "Love and Race." *New York Times* (December 6, 2002): p. 35 [online] LexisNexis Academic Universe.

Lewis, Neil A. "A Judge, a Renomination, and the Cross-Burning Case That Won't End." *New York Times* (May 28, 2003): p. 16A [online] LexisNexis Academic Universe.

Liptak, Adam. "Privacy Rights, Fair Trials, Celebrities and the Press." *New York Times* (July 23, 2004): p. 20 [online] LexisNexis Academic Universe.

———. "Bryant Is Ordered to Stand Trial in Rape Case." *New York Times* (October 21, 2003): p. 16 [online] LexisNexis Academic Universe.

———. "Judge Warns against Naming the Accuser of Kobe Bryant." *New York Times* (July 30, 2003): p. 13 [online] LexisNexis Academic Universe.

Lithwick, Dahlia. "The Shield That Failed." *New York Times* (August 8, 2004): p. 11 [online] LexisNexis Academic Universe.

Liu, Marian. "Eminem Apparently Being Forgiven for Racial Slur." *Pittsburgh Post-Gazette* (November 28, 2003): p. 27 [online] LexisNexis Academic Universe.

"'Love Story,' White Blindness." *New York Times* (September 26, 1999): p. 4 [online] LexisNexis Academic Universe.

Lowery, Stephanie. "New Faces in Dating Race Matters Less for Many Teens." *Milwaukee Journal Sentinel* (April 22, 2002): p. A-11 [online] LexisNexis Academic Universe.

Lubet, Steven. "Appeals Court Nominee Carries Cross for Bigots." *Atlanta Journal-Constitution* (March 1, 2002): p. 20A [online] LexisNexis Academic Universe.

MacGregor, Jeff. "TV, the Movies' Abused (and Abusive) Stepchild." *New York Times* (October 8, 2000): pp. A-11, 34.

Maddox, Alton H. "Critical Thinking Takes a Hike in the Bryant Case." *Amsterdam News* (August 26, 2004)

Madigan, Nick, and Mindy Sink. "End of Kobe Bryant Case Brings Out Strong Sentiments." *New York Times* (September 3, 2004): p. 14A [online] LexisNexis Academic Universe.

"Magazine in Contempt for Publishing Eminem Lyrics." *St. Petersburg Times* (June 11, 2004): p. 2B [online] LexisNexis Academic Universe.

Mahoney, Dennis M. "Pastor Shuts Door on Interracial Couple." *Columbus Dispatch* (July 8, 2000): p. 1A [online] LexisNexis Academic Universe.

Mansbach, Adam. "In the Shadow of *White Girl*," *Boston Globe* (April 28, 2002): p. E5 [online] LexisNexis Academic Universe.

Markels, Alex. "Detective Details Accuser's Case against Bryant." *New York Times* (October 10, 2003): p. 1 [online] LexisNexis Academic Universe.

Martel, Ned. "A Champion Who Wasn't Shy about Enjoying His Title." *New York Times* (January 17, 2005): p. 13E [online] LexisNexis Academic Universe.

Mathabane, Gail. "Gays Face Same Battle Interracial Couples Fought." *USA Today* (Januuary 26, 2004): p. 13A [online] LexisNexis Academic Universe.

Mathabane, Mark. "Interracial Myths Still Nag Couples." *USA Today* (April 2, 2001): p. 15A [online] LexisNexis Academic Universe.

Mayko, Michael P. "'She Ruined My Boy.'" *Connecticut Post* (November 7, 2004) [online] LexisNexis Academic Universe.

"Melting Pot, Mixing Bowl Acceptance Is Accelerating, Changing the Face of America." *Pittsburgh Post-Gazette* (December 22, 2002): p. W-3 [online] Lexis-Nexis Academic Universe.

"Mental Rubbernecks." *New York Times* (February 29, 2004): p. 2 [online] Lexis-Nexis Academic Universe.

"Menzel, Diggs Receive Hate Mail over Marriage." *Chattanooga Times Free Press* (TN) (December 8, 2004): p. A2 [online] LexisNexis Academic Universe.

"Menzel's 'Wicked' Goes on Despite Racist Threats." *Commercial Appeal* (Memphis, TN) (December 8, 2004): p. M2 [online] LexisNexis Academic Universe.

Messing, Philip, Michael Riedel, and Hasani Gittens. "Racist Threats Hit Acting Couple." *New York Post* (December 5, 2004): p. 7.

Miller, Martin. "A Boxer's Last Battle Royal: A Film and Pardon Effort Fight for Jack Johnson." *Los Angeles Times* (January 15, 2005): p. 1 [online] LexisNexis Academic Universe.

Mitchell, Jerry. "Killen Arrest Challenges Nation's Views of Mississippi." *Clarion-Ledger* (January 11, 2005).

"Names and Faces." *Washington Post* (December 29, 2003): p. 03 [online] LexisNexis Academic Universe.

"Newsmakers." *Houston Chronicle* (November 19, 2003): p. 2A [online] LexisNexis Academic Universe.

"NFL Plans Tamer Halftime Show." *New York Times* (August 4, 2004): p. 6D [online] LexisNexis Academic Universe.

Nickel, Lori. "Color Lines Blur at MU." *Milwaukee Journal Sentinel* (February 22, 2002): p. 06C [online] LexisNexis Academic Universe.

Niebuhr, Gustav. "The 2000 Campaign: The Religion Issue; Interracial Dating Ban to End." *New York Times* (March 4, 2000) [online] LexisNexis Academic Universe.

"No Fun and Games for Bryant in Court." *Los Angeles Times* (March 27, 2004): p. D3 [online] LexisNexis Academic Universe.

Ogunnaike, Lola. "Rivals Call Eminem Racist over Lyrics from the Past." *New York Times* (November 19, 2003): p. 3B [online] LexisNexis Academic Universe.

"Old Recording Used in Old Feud." *The Houston Chronicle* (November 23, 2003): p. 2A [online] LexisNexis Academic Universe.

Palmer, Kimberly Shearer. "Movie Reflects Interracial Issues." *USA Today* (January 22, 2001): p. 15A [online] LexisNexis Academic Universe.

Parascandola, Rocco, and Deborah S. Morris. "Hate Crimes Investigation, Letters Threaten Actors." *Newsday* (December 5, 2004): p. A08

Parvaz, D. "Paul Allen and His Beauty May Be Serious." *Seattle Post-Intelligencer* (December 7, 2004): p. E2 [online] LexisNexis Academic Universe.

Plaschke, Bill. "Ball Back in His Court; Bryant Is Now Free to Decide His Fate." *Los Angeles Times* (September 2, 2004): p. 1D [online] LexisNexis Academic Universe.

Poitras, Colin. "Woman Pleads Not Guilty to Assault." *Hartford Courant* (December 1, 2004): p. B7 [online] LexisNexis Academic Universe.

"Pop Notes." *Washington Post* (December 24, 2004): p. C05 [online] LexisNexis Academic Universe.

Pugmire, Lance, and David Wharton. "Case Showed Cracks Early, Experts Say; Mistakes and Legal Rulings Eroded the Prosecution Effort from the Start, Analysts Add." *Los Angeles Times* (September 2, 2004): p. 0A [online] LexisNexis Academic Universe.

Rankin, Bill. "The Cross-Burning Trial: AJC Review Shows Fairness, Not Bias, at Root of Ruling." *Atlanta Journal-Constitution* (March 9, 2003): p. 1E [online] LexisNexis Academic Universe.

"Rape and Rights." *Los Angeles Times* (August 1, 2004): p. M4 [online] LexisNexis Academic Universe.

Rhoden, William C. "In 'Monday Night' Fallout, a Deeper Racial Issue." *New York Times* (November 21, 2004): p. 11 [online] LexisNexis Academic Universe.

Rich, Frank. "The Great Indecency Hoax," *New York Times* (November 28, 2004): p. 1 [online] LexisNexis Academic Universe.

———. "My Hero, Janet Jackson," *New York Times* (February 15, 2004): p. 1 [online] LexisNexis Academic Universe.

Riddle, Lyn. "Interracial Couple Continues, Book Details Hatred toward Couples." *The Atlanta Journal and Constitution* (October 4, 1998): p. 02b [online] LexisNexis Academic Universe.

——. "South Carolina May End Ban on Mixed Marriages." *The Atlanta Journal and Constitution* (April 18, 1998): p. 06A [online] LexisNexis Academic Universe.

Rimer, Sara. "Convicted in Youth, Inmates Accept Fate and Look Ahead." *New York Times* (July 30, 2001): p. 3 [online] LexisNexis Academic Universe.

Ringel, Eleanor. "'Mississippi Masala.'" *New York Times* (July 30, 2001): p. 13 [online] LexisNexis Academic Universe.

Roberts, Selena. "Mistakes and Miscues Prove Too Much for Byant's Accuser." *New York Times* (September 2, 2004): p. 1D [online] LexisNexis Academic Universe.

Robertson, Tatsha. "Changing Face of the Racial Divide, Mixed Marriages Alter Longtime Boundaries." *Boston Globe* (January 2, 2000): p. B1 [online] LexisNexis Academic Universe.

Rock, Rich. "*The Source* Mag Fined for Publishing Eminem Lyrics." *Wire/Daily Hip-Hop News* (June 10, 2004) [online] www.sohh.com.

Rodman, Sarah. "Teen Eminem's Racist Track May Fuel Latest Rap Beef." *Boston Herald* (November 19, 2003): p. 056 [online] LexisNexis Academic Universe.

Romney, Lee. "Judge Hears Debate on Gay Unions." *Los Angeles Times* (December 24, 2004): p. 1B [online] LexisNexis Academic Universe.

Rush, George, and Joanna Molloy. "Rap Moguls Spar over Shady Sincerity." *Daily News* (November 26, 2003): p. 22 [online] LexisNexis Academic Universe.

——. "Rap Gets Eminem on Anti-Black List." *Daily News* (November 19, 2003): p. 26 [online] LexisNexis Academic Universe.

Sagario, Dawn. "Interracial Couples Becoming More Common: The 'Halle Berry' Syndrome." *Seattle Times* (December 29, 2002): p. L2 [online] LexisNexis Academic Universe.

Saint Clair, Justin. "Unreality Television: Million Watch as TV Reinforces Negative Racial Stereotypes." *Seattle Times* (April 11, 2004): p. D4 [online] LexisNexis Academic Universe.

Sandomir, Richard. "10-Second Delay for Show." *New York Times* (September 7, 2004): p. 5D [online] LexisNexis Academic Universe.

——. "Forgiving 'Unforgivable Blackness.'" *New York Times* (January 18, 2005): p. 3D [online] LexisNexis Academic Universe.

——. "It Did Not Remain Dull for Too Long." *New York Times* (February 2, 2004): p. 4D [online] LexisNexis Academic Universe.

Sanneh, Kelefa. "Two Lessons at the School for Scandal." *New York Times* (March 28, 2004): p. 1 [online] LexisNexis Academic Universe.

——. "Television." *New York Times* (February 8, 2004): p. 2 [online] LexisNexis Academic Universe.

——. "During Halftime Show, a Display Tailored for Video Review." *New York Times* (February 2, 2004): p. 4D [online] LexisNexis Academic Universe.

——. "Unguarded Lyrics Embarrass Eminem." *New York Times* (November 20, 2003): p. 1E [online] LexisNexis Academic Universe.

Savage, David G., and Maura Dolan. "Bryant Case Latest to Show Tighter Rein on the Media." *Los Angeles Times* (August 1, 2004): p. A24 [online] LexisNexis Academic Universe.

Sawicki, Stephen. "Filming the Family." *New York Times* (June 13, 2004): p. 4 [online] LexisNexis Academic Universe.

Schleiff, Henry. "The Case for TV." *New York Times* (September 3, 2003): p. 19 [online] LexisNexis Academic Universe.

Schmitt, Eric. "West Is Face of Changing Lifestyles." *Denver Post* (March 30, 2003): p. A-29 [online] LexisNexis Academic Universe.

———. "For 7 Million People in Census, One Race Category Isn't Enough." *New York Times* (March 13, 2001): p. 1A [online] LexisNexis Academic Universe.

Scott, A. O. "The Season of Humane, Nuanced On-Screen Sex." *New York Times* (December 12, 2004): p. 30 [online] LexisNexis Academic Universe.

Sederstrom, Jotham. "Show Goes on for 'Wicked.'" *New York Post* (December 6, 2004): p. 7 [online] LexisNexis Academic Universe.

"Shame on Us." *Los Angeles Times* (January 14, 2005): p. 10 [online] LexisNexis Academic Universe.

Sheppard, Judy. "Alabama Voters May Bury Interracial Marriage Ban, It Hasn't Had Legal Force for Decades." *Atlanta Journal and Constitution* (September 26, 2000): p. 11A [online] LexisNexis Academic Universe.

Shiver, Jube, Jr. "FCC Punishes Viacom for Indecency." *Los Angeles Times* (November 24, 2004): p. 1A [online] LexisNexis Academic Universe.

———. "FCC to Examine ABC TV Spot." *Los Angeles Times* (November 18, 2004): p. 4C [online] LexisNexis Academic Universe.

Shmith, Michael. "Defiant Lovers Shed Light on the Colour of Love." *Age* (February 27, 2002): p. 6 [online] LexisNexis Academic Universe.

Shulas, Greg. "Stratford Forced to Cope with Recent Media Frenzy." *Connecticut Post* (November 12, 2004) [online] LexisNexis Academic Universe.

Siegel, Ed. "On Film, Stage, and TV, Love Is Becoming Colorblind." *Boston Globe* (June 25, 2000): p. N6 [online] LexisNexis Academic Universe.

Sink, Mindy. "Kobe Bryant Says He Too Wants an Early Trial in His Rape Case." *New York Times* (April 7, 2004): p. 13 [online] LexisNexis Academic Universe.

Smith, Jeffrey. "Judge's Fate Could Turn on 1994 Case Pickering Fought to Reduce Sentence for Cross-Burning." *Washington Post* (May 27, 2003): p. A01 [online] LexisNexis Academic Universe.

Smith, Lynn. "Poll: TV Content Troubles Parents." *Los Angeles Times* (September 24, 2004): p. 2E [online] LexisNexis Academic Universe.

———. "NFL Picks New Halftime Team." *Los Angeles Times* (August 11, 2004): p. 3E [online] LexisNexis Academic Universe.

Springer, Steve. "Now Bryant Takes Even Greater Role." *Los Angeles Times* (July 17, 2004): p. D1 [online] LexisNexis Academic Universe.

Stanley, Alessandra. "Clothing On, Lips Buttoned," *New York Times* (February 9, 2004): p. 1E [online] LexisNexis Academic Universe.

———. "L'Affaire Bodice: Why We Are Shocked, Shocked." *New York Times* (February 8, 2004): p. 16 [online] LexisNexis Academic Universe.

———. "A Flash of Flesh: CBS Again Is in Denial." *New York Times* (February 3, 2004): p. 1E [online] LexisNexis Academic Universe.

Stein, Joel. "The New Quiz Show Scandal—Reality Television." *Los Angeles Times* (December 5, 2004): p. 1 [online] LexisNexis Academic Universe.

Steinberg, Jacques. "Bryant Case Is New Quandry for Press as Accuser Is Told to Put Name on Suit." *New York Times* (October 11, 2004): p. 9C [online] LexisNexis Academic Universe.

Stewart, Larry. "They Ought to Consider Sanity Clause." *Los Angeles Times* (January 2, 2004): p. D2 [online] LexisNexis Academic Universe.

——— "Antics Not Suitable for Younger, if Any, Viewers." *Los Angeles Times* (November 26, 2004): p. 3D [online] LexisNexis Academic Universe.

Sykes, Bonnie. "Letting Love Rule: Interracial Dating.". *New York Amsterdam News* (December 6, 2001).

Tatum, Wilbert A. "A 'C' Cup for Your Pleasure, Sir." *Amsterdam News* (February 12, 2004).

Taylor, Linda Guydon. "Survey Finds Interracial Relationships Well Accepted." *Pittsburgh Post-Gazette* (Decmeber 22, 2002): p. W-3 [online] LexisNexis Academic Universe.

Tepfer, Daniel, "Accused of Sex with Boy, Woman Draws a Crowd," *Connecticut Post* (December 1, 2004) [online] LexisNexis Academic Universe.

———. "Lawyer: Imre's Story on Boy Sex Not Told." *Connecticut Post* (November 17, 2004) [online] LexisNexis Academic Universe.

———. "Bizarre Case of Boy-Woman Sex Moves Forward." *Connecticut Post* (November 11, 2004) [online] LexisNexis Academic Universe.

———. "Woman Blames Boy, 8." *Connecticut Post* (November 9, 2004) [online] LexisNexis Academic Universe.

———. "Woman Accused of Sex with Boy." *Connecticut Post* (November 6, 2004) [online] LexisNexis Academic Universe.

Texeira, Erin. "Multiracial Scenes Now Common in TV Ads." February 15, 2005. Accessed at www.msnbc.msn.com/id/6975669.

"The Racial Subtext." *New York Times* (December 5, 2004): p. 4 [online] LexisNexis Academic Universe.

"Through the Years." *Milwaukee Journal Sentinel* (April 22, 2002): p. 04E [online] LexisNexis Academic Universe.

Vecsey, George. "Spotlight Should Have Been on the Game, Not the Show." *New York Times* (February 3, 2004): p. 5D [online] LexisNexis Academic Universe.

"Violence, Lust, Halftime." *New York Times* (February 5, 2004): p. 30A [online] LexisNexis Academic Universe.

White, Joe. "John Singleton and the Impossible Greenback of the Assimilated Black Artist." *Esquire* (August, 1991): p. 65.

"Why I Won't Go Out with a White Man." *Guardian* (February 21, 2000): p. 6 [online] LexisNexis Academic Universe.

"'Wicked' Star, Actor, Husband Threatened." *Providence Journal (RI)* (December 7, 2004): p. G-01 [online] LexisNexis Academic Universe.

"Wild Will Smith on the 'Race Thing,'" *Providence Journal Bulletin*, July 3, 1999.

Williams, David O. "Bryant's Accuser Won't Have to Testify." *New York Times* (October 3, 2003): p. 5 [online] LexisNexis Academic Universe.

Winters, Rebecca. "Stereo Playah." *Time* 164, no. 18 (2004): 105.

Wise, Mike. "Mulling Shaky Future, Bryant Joins Lakers. "*New York Times* (October 5, 2003): p. 12 [online] LexisNexis Academic Universe.

Wise, Mike, and Alex Markels. "Bryant Case Puts a County in the Spotlight." *New York Times* (July 20, 2003): p. 4 [online] LexisNexis Academic Universe.

"Woman Charged with Abusing 8-Year-Old Boy." *Los Angeles Times* (November 9, 2004): p. 12A LexisNexis Academic Universe.

Zernike, Kate. "What Privacy? Everything Else but the Name." *New York Times* (August 3, 2003): p. 4 [online] LexisNexis Academic Universe.

———. "The Wifely Art of Standing By." *New York Times* (October 19, 2003).

Zhao, Yilu. "A Place to Blend Together." *New York Times* (September 7, 2003); p. 14WC [online] LexisNexis Academic Universe.

Zucchino, David. "With Unearthing of Infamous Jail, Richmond Confronts Its Slave Past." *Los Angeles Times*, December 18, 2008.

Zuckerman, Julia. "Panelists Say Pressures on Interracial Couples Come from Many Sources." University Wire (November 4, 2002) [online] LexisNexis Academic Universe.

Index

~

About the Author

Erica Chito Childs is an associate professor of sociology at Hunter College/ City University of New York. She has published extensively on the areas of race, gender, sexualities, and families in *Gender & Society*, the *Du Bois Review*, *Race & Society*, as well as other journals and edited volumes. Her first book *Navigating Interracial Borders: Black-White Couples and Their Social Worlds* (2005) looked at the experiences of black-white interracial families and societal attitudes toward these unions. She is currently working on an ethnographic study of the experiences of black and Latino children in kindergarten, and a separate study of the racial and gendered dynamics of caregivers and their employers.